Aldous Huxley's
Quest for Values

Patriotism is not enough. But neither is anything else. Science is not enough, religion is not enough, art is not enough, politics and economics are not enough, nor is love, nor is duty, nor is action however disinterested, nor, however sublime, is contemplation. Nothing short of everything will really do.

—ALDOUS HUXLEY, *Island*

Aldous Huxley's
Quest for Values

Milton Birnbaum

THE UNIVERSITY
OF TENNESSEE PRESS

Library of Congress Catalog Card Number 71–142146 International Standard Book Number 0–87049–127–X Copyright © 1971 by The University of Tennessee Press, Knoxville. All rights reserved. Manufactured in the United States of America. First edition.

Chapters VII and X of this book are based on the following publications: "Aldous Huxley" in *Politics of Twentieth-Century Novelists*, ed. George A. Panichas. Copyright © 1971 by the University of Maryland. Reprinted by permission of Hawthorn Books, Inc., New York.

"Aldous Huxley's Quest for Values: A Study in Religious Syncretism" in *Mansions of the Spirit: Essays in Literature and Religion*, ed. George A. Panichas. Copyright © 1967 by the University of Maryland. Reprinted by permission of Hawthorn Books, Inc., New York.

To Ruth   "The heart of her husband doth safely trust in her."

and Ellen   "Many daughters have done valiantly,
But thou excellest them all."

In the lead article in the *New York Times Magazine* for August 18, 1968, James A. Michener wrote of two prospective college drop-outs who came to consult him on a problem: they had decided not only to drop college, but also to leave home and to head for Haight-Ashbury to find what they hoped would be a more meaningful life. As the "attractive" young boy and girl confided in him, their alienation from adult society became quite apparent. They said, "We no longer find the values you lived by to have any significance. We're sure you know they're phony, too, and that's why we wanted to talk with you."

As I look back over the last few decades and try to figure out what first attracted me and thousands of other college students to Aldous Huxley in the 1920's and early 1930's, I suppose it was the feeling that Huxley also no longer found the values of his society of any significance. In debunking the traditional sources of value he was, in a sense, acting as our surrogate. Curiously enough, however, as I grew older and shifted my philosophical position, I found that Huxley also kept shifting the direction of his quest: debunking was replaced by a Lawrentian endorsement of the life-worshiping idea; this, in turn, yielded to a longing for inner meaning; sense gratification yielded to a search for spiritual substance. This spiritual quest in turn was intensified by his desire to expand the threshold of consciousness by experimenting with hallucinogenic drugs. And always there was the Donnean belief that insularity leads to isolation and that therefore it is preferable to involve oneself not only in self-fulfillment, but in attempts at societal amelioration.

My interest in Huxley has been both professional and personal. If I am allowed to have more than one alter ego, I would certainly include Huxley as one of my other selves. In addition to his entertaining facility as a writer and his seemingly encyclopedic mind, it was his preoccupation with a moral quest that made me maintain my interest in him; paradoxically, his moral quest led him to attack puritanism, but then Huxley's awareness of the paradoxes in the human condition only enhanced the fascination he has always held for me.

In this book I shall attempt to analyze critically the search for values that has characterized all of Aldous Huxley's works. The discussion will be by subject matter rather than by separate analysis of the individual works. Major consideration will be devoted to Huxley's novels, his books of essays, and those portions of his biographies, letters, and poetry which bear directly on his search for values. His collections of short stories (some of which, incidentally, like "Young Archimedes" and "The Gioconda Smile" contain some of his best, most sustained emotional artistry), his many adaptations of both his own works and those of others for the stage and screen[1] are essentially reworkings of ideas found in his other writings; consequently, they have been omitted from my discussion.

In *Ends and Means*, Huxley asked: "Does the world as a whole possess the value and meaning that we constantly attribute to certain parts of it (such as human beings and their works); and, if so, what is the nature of that value and meaning?"[2] In the process of answering this question, Huxley searched the traditional sources of value—art, education, government, love, nature, philosophy, religion, and science—and gave us his answers, found scattered throughout his works. Similarly, he analyzed certain types of people—the introverted individual, the hedonist, and the man of action, types to whom he sometimes attaches Dr. William Sheldon's designations of "cerebrotonic," "viscerotonic," and "somatotonic."

The subsequent chapters in the book will discuss Huxley's reactions to these traditional sources of value and types of people.

It is my belief that such a study will not only help in a better understanding of the significance of Aldous Huxley, but will, in some measure, illuminate the period from about 1920 to the present. As B. Ifor Evans has observed of Huxley:

> His novels and criticism are a mirror in which the age could perceive itself with its shifting hopes and disillusionments, the changes from the harsh gaiety of the twenties to the solemn acceptance of the thirties that tragedy is approaching. More than any other writer of that time he had an instructed appreciation of the other arts, of painting and particularly of music . . . . Further, he, more than any of his contemporaries, had the equipment to construct some bridge between science and the arts in an age when those two great aspects of human activity were so unhappily divided.[3]

Acknowledgments

I would like to extend my appreciation and acknowledgment to Harper & Row Publishers, Inc., Chatto & Windus, Ltd., and Mrs. Laura A. Huxley for permission to quote three of Huxley's poems ("Books and Thoughts," "The Life Theoretic," and "Two Realities") —found in *The Collected Poetry of Aldous Huxley* (1971)—and to quote illustrative passages of unusual length from the following books by Aldous Huxley: *After Many a Summer Dies the Swan, Grey Eminence, Music at Night and Other Essays, The Perennial Philosophy, Point Counter Point,* and *Time Must Have a Stop.*

Grateful acknowledgment is made for permission to reprint, in modified form, "Aldous Huxley's Quest for Values: A Study in Religious Syncretism" from *Mansions of the Spirit: Essays in Literature and Religion,* ed. George A. Panichas (New York: Hawthorn Books, Inc., 1967, Copyright © 1967 by the University of Maryland), and "Aldous Huxley" from *Politics of Twentieth-Century Novelists,* ed. George A. Panichas (New York: Hawthorn Books, Inc., Copyright © 1971 by the University of Maryland). My thanks, too, are extended to the following: *Texas Studies in Literature and Language* and the University of Texas Press for permission to reprint much of "Aldous Huxley's Animadversions upon Sexual Love" (Vol. 8, No. 2, Summer 1966); *The Personalist: An International Review of Philosophy* for permission to include "Aldous Huxley's Conception of the Nature of Reality" (Vol. 47, No. 3, July 1966); *The Hibbert Journal* for permission to reprint "Aldous Huxley's treatment of nature" (Vol. 64, No. 255, Midsummer 1966); *The Journal of Popular Culture* for permission to reprint "Aldous Huxley: An Aristocrat's Comments on Popular Culture" (Vol. II, No. 1, Summer 1968); the International Society for General Semantics for permission to include "Aldous Huxley's Views on Language" (*ETC.: A Review of General Semantics*, Vol. XXVI, No. 1, March 1969); and *Xavier University Studies* for permission to reprint "Aldous Huxley's Views on Education" (Vol. 6, No. 2, May 1967). All of these articles have been revised slightly for inclusion as chapters or parts of chapters in this book.

I am heavily indebted to many people who have advised me over the many years my book was being rewritten for publication after its submission as a doctoral dissertation (New York University, 1955). Professor Bruce W. McCullough (Emeritus Professor of English at New York University), whose patient and helpful guidance made problems connected with my work seem solvable, and my colleagues at American International College (Professor Evelyn Jackson, Librarian; Professor Francis M. Kelly, Jr., and Professor Frederick A. Palmer) were kind at moments when kindness was most needed. My sincere thanks also go to American International College's Emeritus President John F. Hines, Jr., President Harry J. Courniotes, and Dean John F. Mitchell (whose approval of a half year's sabbatical and a Summer Study Grant enabled me to devote more time to completing my book than otherwise would have been possible); to Mr. Arthur C. Kulp, Circulation Librarian at Cornell University, for allowing me to use the university's library facilities; to Mr. Benjamin Silbermann (of H. R. Huntting Co.), congenial lover and seller of books, who never turned me down whenever I asked for a book; and to Professor George A. Panichas, of the University of Maryland, whose friendship, help, and encouragement through the years have been far more meaningful than I could possibly express.

Aldous Huxley's
Quest for Values

That Aldous Huxley has been a force in the literature of the twentieth century few will deny. During his lifetime he published over forty books, his period of creativity continuing almost to the day of his death in 1963. Although known chiefly for his novels, he also wrote poetry, essays ranging from art criticism to the effects of the hallucinogenic drugs, travel books, introductions to other people's books, biographies, and adaptations for both the stage and screen. He has been translated into Spanish (*Contrapunto*, from *Point Counter Point*), Greek (*Meta ta Pyrotèchnemata*, from "After the Fireworks"), and French (*Richard Greenow: grande nouvelle inédite*, from "The Farcical History of Richard Greenow"), to cite but three examples. One finds references to him not only in the usual critical books on the British novel in the twentieth century (for example, B. Ifor Evans, *English Literature between the Wars*; Millett, Manly and Rickert's *Contemporary British Literature*; David Daiches, *The Novel and the Modern World*; H. V. Routh, *English Literature and Ideas in the Twentieth Century*), but also in books dealing with philosophy, religion, and the social history of our times (for example, C. E. M. Joad's *The Recovery of Belief* and *Return to Philosophy*; Morris R. Cohen's *The Faith of a Liberal*; Robert Graves and Alan Hodge's *The Long Week End*; F. S. C. Northrop, *The Meeting of East and West*).

Whether Aldous Huxley has been a force for good or evil, whether he is an artist more noted for his contributions to the novel of ideas or for the ideas themselves, whether he is chiefly a romantic or a neoclassicist—on these questions, critics have not agreed. He has been called a frustrated romantic by one critic;[1] he has been attacked because he has joined Freud, Jung, Adler, and Lawrence "to sow distrust of reason, and to represent it as a mere tool of the unconscious."[2] His view of life has been characterized as "essential sterility,"[3] and his embracing of mysticism has been called "the rationalist's substitute for suicide."[4] But Huxley has had his defenders, too. His description of the modern world has been hailed as "far more honest and decent than the early Victorian age depicted in Bulwer Lytton's *Pelham*."[5] Similarly, "despite the temptations which beset a successful author," he never "seriously compromised with his intellectual integrity."[6]

Even his most ardent admirers, however, will not claim for Huxley a seminal role in the shaping of twentieth-century literature. He was no James Joyce or D. H. Lawrence creating new paths for artists to follow. In his nonfiction he was no Nietzsche forging revolutionary ideas to unsettle smug consciences. He was not so much a pioneer as a reflector, not so much an earthquake as a seismograph. This is not to imply that Huxley was barren in creative imagination; certainly his *Brave New World* would belie such an inference, but even that book reminds us of other fictional utopias.

Wherein then lies the value in giving serious consideration to Huxley? Precisely in his being able to articulate the intellectual and moral conflicts being fought in the collective soul of the twentieth century. D. H. Lawrence would express his reactions viscerally but failed to look through a microscope, as Huxley reminds us. James Joyce could disentangle himself from the nets in which he felt caught, but he did not seem aware of the oases to be found in Eastern meditative systems. E. M. Forster knew of passages to other cultures but preferred to regard art as self-sufficient rather than as catalytic. Virginia Woolf knew the agony of private torment but did not realize the healing that can emerge from societal involvement. It was Huxley of all these twentieth-century English writers who best reflected and coordinated the divisions of the modern world; he best expressed its *Weltanschauung* in its most

universal sense. Thomas Henry Huxley, Aldous Huxley's grandfather, was called "Darwin's bulldog" because he so tenaciously
clung to and advocated Darwin's theories; similarly, Aldous Huxley may become best known for being both an observer of and a
contributor to the shifting values of our world.

That Huxley's works have always demonstrated a search for
values can be shown by an analysis of his works from the very beginning. The novels published in the 1920's (*Crome Yellow, Antic
Hay, Those Barren Leaves,* and *Point Counter Point*) were all concerned with showing how some of the traditional sources of value
—religion, love, family life—were absent from the postwar generation. Most readers thought these books to be cynically entertaining
and did not see their essentially moral undercurrent. What Mary
Thriplow, the self-conscious author in *Those Barren Leaves,* says
about her books could be applied to what Huxley thought about
the public and critical reaction to his own books:

> They like my books because they're smart and unexpected and rather
> paradoxical and cynical and elegantly brutal. They don't see how
> serious it all is. They don't see the tragedy and the tenderness under-
> neath. You see . . . I'm trying to do something new—a chemical com-
> pound of all the categories. Lightness and tragedy and loveliness and
> wit and fantasy and realism and irony and sentiment, all combined.
> People seem to find it merely amusing, that's all.[7]

Huxley's preoccupation with values was not confined to the
novels. In *Jesting Pilate* (1926), a book of observations made on his
travels throughout the world, Huxley is also concerned with values:

> Our sense of values is intuitive. There is no proving the real existence
> of values in any way that will satisfy the logical intellect. Our stan-
> dards can be demolished by argumentation; but we are none the less
> right to cling to them. Not blindly, of course, not uncritically . . . .
> Understanding diversity and allowing for it, he [the traveler] will
> tolerate, but not without limit. He will distinguish between harmless
> perversions and those which tend actually to deny or stultify the
> fundamental values. Towards the first he will be tolerant. There can
> be no compromise with the second.[8]

Similarly, when Huxley discusses the arts, he is not so much concerned with the aesthetic as with the moral implications. When he
is talking about Christopher Wren, the English architect, he says

that the quality that distinguished Wren's work is "rather moral than aesthetic . . . . For Wren was a great gentleman; one who valued dignity and restraint and who, respecting himself, respected also humanity . . . ."[9] When he is talking about Marcel Proust, Huxley bewails the fact that Proust was a "scientific voluptuary of the emotions" and says that there is "a strange moral poverty about his book."[10] Most of the essays in *Proper Studies* (1927), *Do What You Will* (1929), and *Music at Night* (1931) emphasize the values —or their disappearance—in our civilization. In *Texts and Pretexts* (1933) he says, "There are values which persist, because there is a physiology which persists and, along with a physiology, a mental structure."[11] *Point Counter Point* (1928), considered by most critics his finest novel, describes the problem of the disintegrated personality of our times, a personality not living in accordance with the philosophy of the instinctive life which Huxley, under the influence of D. H. Lawrence, was then advocating. In the 1930's, in *Ends and Means*, Huxley made a very significantly teleological statement:

> What sort of world is this, in which men aspire to good and yet so frequently achieve evil? What is the sense and point of the whole affair? What is man's place in it and how are his ideals, his systems of values, related to the universe at large? . . . To the "practical man" they [these questions] may seem irrelevant. But in fact they are not. It is in the light of our beliefs about the ultimate nature of reality that we formulate our conceptions of right and wrong; and it is in the light of our conceptions of right and wrong that we frame our conduct, not only in the relations of private life, but also in the sphere of politics and economics. So far from being irrelevant, our metaphysical beliefs are the finally determining factor in all our actions. That is why it has seemed to me necessary to round off my cookery book of practical recipes with a discussion of first principles. (P. 11)

Even when Huxley is discussing whether or not the British government should buy the Codex Sinaiticus, he considers whether the contemplated purchase will serve the interests of the "Good, True, Beautiful"; the reason he gives for his concern is that the government's business is "to encourage all manifestations of the Good, the True and the Beautiful."[12]

One can see the same concern with values in Huxley's other novels and nonfiction works. He attacks the growing preoccupation with hedonism, materialism, technology, and false intellectualism in *Brave New World* (1932), *Eyeless in Gaza* (1936), *After Many a Summer Dies the Swan* (1939), *Time Must Have a Stop* (1944), and *Ape and Essence* (1948). He considers alternatives to materialism: mysticism (*The Perennial Philosophy*, 1946), an intelligent application of science (*Science, Liberty and Peace*, 1947), and a fusion of mysticism and science (*Island*, 1962). Occasionally, as in *The Doors of Perception* (1954) and *Heaven and Hell* (1956), he endorses the use of hallucinogenic drugs as a means of heightening one's spiritual and aesthetic awareness. *Brave New World Revisited* (1948) considers "the subject of freedom and its enemies." Even in books that are purportedly biographical, there is evident concern with moral directions; when he writes about the life of Father Joseph, adviser to Cardinal Richelieu, he deplores the evil mingling of spiritual and material values—saying, in effect, that Caesar and God cannot be served simultaneously. Similarly, in *The Devils of Loudun* (1952), he impregnates the biography of a seventeenth-century monk with meaning for this century. The life of Maine de Biran, the eighteenth-century French philosopher, occupies about half of *Themes and Variations*, but here again, as with the other subjects found in this 1950 volume, Huxley's observations are tinged with moral implications.

There are several advantages to considering Huxley's novels and nonfiction works by subject matter rather than as separate entities. To begin with, in a letter to Jean E. Hare, he admits that he "is not congenitally a novelist and therefore is compelled to resort to devices which the born novelist would never think of using."[13] In a famous passage from the notebook of Philip Quarles (who, as Huxley's sister-in-law Lady Juliette Baillot tells us, bears resemblance to his own character[14]), Huxley reveals what one of these "devices" is:

> All you need is a sufficiency of characters and parallel, contrapuntal plots. While Jones is murdering a wife, Smith is wheeling the perambulator in the park. You alternate the themes. More interesting, the modulations and variations are also more difficult. A novelist modu-

lates by repudiating situations and characters. He shows several people falling in love, or dying, or praying in different ways—dissimilars
solving the same problems. Or, *vice versa,* similar people confronted
with dissimilar problems. In this way you can modulate through all
the aspects of your theme, you can write variations in any number of
different moods. Another way: The novelist can assume the god-like
creative privilege and simply elect to consider the events of the story
in their various aspects—emotional, scientific, economic, religious,
metaphysical, etc. He will modulate from one to the other—as, from
the aesthetic to the physico-chemical aspects of things, from the religious to the physiological or financial. But perhaps this is too a
tyrannical imposition of the author's will.[15]

Huxley, in other words, prefers to consider his characters as states
of being rather than what E. M. Forster would call "round characters." It is no wonder then that his characters can be classified under
so many "humors." First, there is the intellectual who has developed his mentality but pathetically neglected the emotional and
physical sides of life—people like Philip Quarles (*Point Counter
Point*), Denis Stone (*Crome Yellow*), Bernard Marx (*Brave New
World*), Shearwater (*Antic Hay*), Anthony Beavis (*Eyeless in
Gaza*). Then there is the sardonic cynic—people like Spandrell
(*Point Counter Point*) and Mark Staithes (*Eyeless in Gaza*). There
is the promiscuous female—characters like Mary Thriplow (*Those
Barren Leaves*), Mrs. Viveash (*Antic Hay*), Lucy Tantamount
(*Point Counter Point*), Lenina Crowne (*Brave New World*), and
Virginia Maunciple (*After Many a Summer Dies the Swan*). The
mystic began to appear in the novels of the 1930's—characters like
Mr. Propter (*After Many a Summer Dies the Swan*), Dr. Miller
(*Eyeless in Gaza*), and Bruno Rontini (*Time Must Have a Stop*).
Other characters of humors could be listed to make the point that
most of Huxley's characters are used to illustrate the values (or
more often, the lack of values) of certain ways of life. How specifically these characters symbolize the values or lack of values in
our civilization will be discussed in Chapter Four of this book.

Besides Huxley's own admission that he is not a "congenital novelist" and that he prefers to think of his characters as modulations
of various themes, there is unanimous critical opinion to corrob-

orate the belief that Huxley's significance lies in the ideas he expounds rather than in the creation of structurally sound, or otherwise memorable, novels.[16]

The same fluidity of form found in his novels characterizes his nonfiction as well. With the essayist's freedom that he well loves, he quite often strays from his avowed purpose to comment on a wide range of subjects. In the midst of describing his journey through India, he can readily start discoursing on the reasons for the low state of the arts. While talking about a seventeenth-century monk, he will deviate from his subject to give an excellent analysis of the dangers inherent in the ambiguity of words. As he frequently says himself, he uses the professed subject of the essay as a starting point to talk about himself or about something else that happens to be on his wide-ranging mind at the moment. Like Francis Bacon before him, Huxley has taken all knowledge to be his province; however, unlike Bacon, Huxley seldom categorizes his knowledge, and even when he does, he refuses to abide by his self-imposed limitations of subject matter. It is the reader's task to reconstruct order from these divagations. Huxley himself has indicated in *After Many a Summer Dies the Swan* his intention of doing something in the nature of this encyclopedic categorizing of his opinions. Mr. Propter (the mystic in the novel) says:

> I've sometimes thought of writing a little treatise, like a cook-book. "One Hundred Ways of Mocking God," I'd call it. And I'd take a hundred examples from history and contemporary life, illustrating what happens when people undertake to do things without paying regard to the nature of reality. And the book would be divided into sections, such as "Mocking God in Agriculture," "Mocking God in Politics," "Mocking God in Education," "Mocking God in Philosophy," "Mocking God in Economics." It would be an interesting little book. But a little depressing.[17]

Perhaps analyzing Huxley according to topics rather than according to his individual works may seem somewhat artificial, but, as Huxley says, "it is impossible to think clearly about reality unless we make use of some classificatory system" (*End and Means*, p. 267). Besides the advantage of making sense of what at times seems a chaotic mass of unrelated comments in Huxley's novels and nonfiction works, analysis by subject matter will have the additional asset of enabling the reader to see the continuous development of Huxley's beliefs on each subject. It will be seen that Huxley's diagnosis of the world's ills has been fairly consistent; his prognosis has not been quite so consistent.

Even a cursory glance at the different historical and literary epochs of England reveals how the arts, education, government, love and marriage, science, and religion influenced people's thinking and conduct. Different eras, of course, place their own emphasis on the areas of experience they find most meaningful, but reflective individuals have generally placed their faith in the traditional sources of value. The *Ars longa, vita brevis* philosophy of the ancients has been handed down to later generations. Austin Dobson, in "Ars Victrix," states a belief held by writers from Horace to E. M. Forster:

> All passes. Art alone
>   Enduring stays to us.
> The Bust outlasts the throne,—
>   The Coin, Tiberius.

Similarly, people have looked to education for supplying direction to their lives. The Spartans emphasized a rigorous discipline; the Elizabethans provided courtesy books as a guide to proper conduct; other Britishers put their faith in "the public-school" system, a faith not shared by E. M. Forster and Samuel Butler. Similarly, a belief in the right kind of government has also served as a source of value to writers in different periods of history. To John Milton, a government of the aristocracy of the best minds and characters would result in a better world; to the young Wordsworth and the more radical of the Romantic poets, a belief in the efficacy of the French Revolution led to visions of an earthly utopia. Some of the English poets of the 1930's like Stephen Spender, W. H. Auden, and C. Day-Lewis turned temporarily to a communistic type of government to relieve their dissatisfaction with the capitalistic system.

It is almost axiomatic that love has served as a source of value to all generations; the argument has been over the question of what kind of love and relationship between the sexes is the best. No one, however, will dispute the validity of Chaucer's statement, expressed in Book One of *Troilus and Criseyde*, that "For evere it was, and evere it shal byfalle, / That Love is he that alle thing may bynde." Similarly, men have looked to Nature for solace and guidance for thousands of years; expressions of this faith in Nature have ranged from the Psalmist's "The heavens declare the glory of God, and the firmament sheweth his handywork" to Wordsworth's "Nature never did betray / The heart that loved her. . . ." This belief in Nature is reflected also in such modern writers as D. H. Lawrence (who in the character of Birkin expresses how wonderful it would be to contemplate "a world empty of people, just uninterrupted grass, and a hare sitting up")[18] and E. M. Forster (who ends *The Longest Journey* by having Stephen take his little daughter to sleep in the fields so that she can learn the lessons that Nature has to teach). Similarly, a belief in science, which has so dominated the thoughts of nineteenth- and twentieth-century writers, can be traced back many centuries as a source of value. From the pseudo-scientific alchemist, who placed his faith in the philosopher's stone or the elixir of life, to Francis Bacon, who searched for a New Atlantis, many men have turned to science, objective or ersatz, to give them a source of at least materialistic satisfaction.

Faith in the arts, education, love, government, Nature, and science fades into comparative insignificance, however, when placed alongside religion as a source of value. Until fairly recently, it has been religion that has always dominated man's thoughts and action, be it the anthropomorphism of primitive societies, the polytheism of the ancient Greeks, the monotheism of Western cultures, or even the denial of the value of religion expressed by E. M. Forster: "I do not believe in belief . . . . My lawgivers are Erasmus and Montaigne, not Moses and St. Paul."[19]

The areas of experience Huxley has examined in his books have always served as the traditional sources of value. The question remains, however, why Huxley, like many other writers of this century, sought to erode these foundations. Probing the influences that helped mold Huxley into the kind of writer he became may reveal at least part of the answer.

In an essay on Maine de Biran in *Themes and Variations*, Huxley notes, "it may be that certain environments are favorable to the development of creative gifts, while others are unfavorable. But meanwhile we must remember that every individual has his or her genes . . . ."[1] A knowledge of his heredity and environment may help us understand the reasons for the shifting direction of Huxley's quest for values.

The chief facts of Huxley's life may be found in the works of Alexander Henderson, Charles J. Rolo, Jocelyn Brooke, and Harold H. Watts. The ten-page chronology included in Grover Smith's edition of the *Letters of Aldous Huxley* is factually very useful; Ronald W. Clark's *The Huxleys* is a definitive study of the entire Huxley family and *This Timeless Moment: A Personal View of Aldous Huxley*, by his widow, Laura Archera Huxley, is a highly intimate account of the personal relationship between them. The biographic and personal facts, however, are only part of the world of Huxley. The emotional, intellectual, and spiritual growth can be best grasped by autobiographical comments in Huxley's works, despite Huxley's remark that "with regard to myself, I can tolerate only reticence."[2]

Aldous Huxley was born on July 23, 1894, the year before his famous paternal grandfather, Thomas Henry Huxley, died. Much has been written about this brilliant nineteenth-century biologist and defender of Darwin's theory of evolution, but the evaluation given by Sir Julian Huxley, his distinguished grandson, provides an insight into the influence that Thomas Henry probably exercised upon the intellectual development of his family:

> T. H. Huxley was indeed remarkable, a rebel Victorian, pro-Darwin and anti-clerical, who coined the word agnostic to describe his own religious position, as one not prepared to accept orthodox or indeed any dogmatic views on the origin and destiny of man in the absence of scientific evidence. He preferred to remain a free-thinker in Hume's sense, refusing to accept the existence of an all-powerful and omniscient God, religious miracles or personal immortality until they were properly validated. He rejected the term atheist for the same reason: the non-existence of God could not be scientifically proved.[3]

It is important to note, however, that T. H. Huxley's espousal of pro-Darwin and anticlerical positions did not lead to a rejection of Victorian proprieties. Sir Julian comments that T. H. Huxley "was also, in the true sense of the word, a puritan," who did not allow his wife to go with him to visit George Eliot because she "was 'living in sin' with a man who was not her legal husband."[4]

Aldous was the third son of Dr. Leonard Huxley and Julia Arnold. His father, although not quite the outstanding intellectual that his grandfather was, nevertheless made significant contributions as a scholar (especially in Greek), teacher, biographer, and editor of the progressive *Cornhill Magazine*. He edited *The Letters of Elizabeth Barrett Browning, The Letters of Jane Welsh Carlyle, The Life and Letters of Sir Joseph Hooker*, and *The Life and Letters of Thomas Henry Huxley*. The rational turn of mind which Dr. Leonard Huxley inherited from his father and which he passed on to his own sons can be seen in this excerpt from the appreciation he wrote to commemorate the centenary of Darwin's birth:

> Unreason in every form is the enemy of scientific method, and the victory of science which we associate with the name of Darwin means the gradual banishment of unnumbered bogeys and fanciful superstitions, offspring of strong sensibilities and false reasoning. With these, also, go many fancies and myths and fairy tales, which

survived to form a beautiful if misty background to everyday thought.
Is it then true, as the lovers of the day before yesterday deplore, that
the march of evolutionary science has robbed the world of its illusions, its beauty, its aspirations, and given in their stead naked fact,
mechanical order, pedestrian reason? It is true, rather, that each new
ideal, each new generalization, pushes out the old, ruthlessly tearing
the fair fabric of imagery and allegory which drapes it round. Man
cannot live without some ideal, any more than he can live without
some sense of beauty: but it is with the ideal as with beauty, for
beauty does not rest in untruth, nor is the loveliness of a landscape less appreciated by reason of a knowledge of perspective.
The knowledge which destroys false beauties enthrones new ones,
while it brings certain desirable and ideal conditions nearer present
realization.[5]

Aldous Huxley's maternal inheritance was as fruitful as that
which he received from his father's family. His mother's grandfather was the formidable Dr. Thomas Arnold of Rugby fame,
and one of her sisters was Mrs. Humphry Ward, a novelist with
puritan-like predilections; even more significantly, her uncle was
Matthew Arnold, who, among his many other activities, engaged
Thomas H. Huxley in debate over the relative values of science
and literature. Julia Arnold must have been a remarkably gentle
and spiritual creature. Besides founding a successful girls' school,
she seemed to influence her children, especially Aldous, far more
than their father:

> Possibly because of the extra care which had been given him [Aldous]
> as a child, possibly because his predilections ran back through his
> mother to the self-questioning Arnolds more naturally than through
> his father to TH [Thomas Henry Huxley]; possibly because his father
> tended to dehumanize scholarship and to arouse in his son a faint
> distaste—for whatever reasons, it was Julia Arnold who had occupied
> the centre of his world. Her death had not only cut down more
> deeply than it had cut into her other sons; it had also heightened
> Aldous's sensitivity, increased his awareness, added to the differences
> which already tended to set him apart from his companions.[6]

With such a genetic inheritance, little wonder then that Sir
Julian and Aldous became as illustrious as they did. And yet, with
typical Huxleyan skepticism, Aldous sometimes wondered whether
the parental influence was always beneficial:

My parents, for example, had no great love for the Oxford Movement; but I was brought up in the strait and narrow way of Ruskinism; and so strict was my conditioning that it was not till I was at least twenty and had come under the influence of the aestheticians of a newer school that I could perceive the smallest beauty in Saint Paul's cathedral. Till then, its dome and its round arches had acted on me like a Pavlovian bell: at the sight of them I had shuddered and the thought, "How ugly!" had immediately presented itself to my consciousness.[7]

From birth, Huxley was always rather frail, "with poor heart and a head so big that he was unable to walk before the age of two."[8] At Eton, he was struck with a temporary blindness that stopped him "from becoming a complete public-school English gentleman. Providence is sometimes kind even when it seems to be harsh. My temporary blindness also preserved me from becoming a doctor, for which I am also grateful. For seeing that I nearly died of overwork as a journalist, I should infallibly have killed myself in the much more strenuous profession of medicine."[9]

Huxley's poor eyesight did not prevent him from studying at Oxford and getting a First in English literature. He read with a magnifying glass at first, but, by using the Bates system, which he explains in *The Art of Seeing*, he could later read without glasses. After having been rejected by the army as physically unfit, he taught for a while at Eton but soon left the school to devote his time to writing. He was on the editorial staff of *The Athenaeum* from 1919 to 1920. His unhappiness with both teaching and newspaper writing can be seen from his disparagement of the public school system in *Antic Hay* and from his remark about his drama-critic days: "Once, in the course of an ill-spent life, it was my fate to go to the theatre some two hundred and fifty times in one year. On business, I need not add; one would hardly do that sort of thing for pleasure. I was paid to go."[10]

His first literary attempts, in poetry, reveal a nature romantically inclined both in its melancholy and its attachment to the soothing influences of the past and Nature:

> Old ghosts that death forgot to ferry
> Across the Lethe of the years—
> These are my friends, and at their tears

I weep, and with their mirth am merry.
On a high tower, whose battlements
Give me all heaven at a glance,
I lie long summer nights in trance,
Drowned by the murmurs and the scents
That rise from earth, while the sky above me
Merges its peace with my soul's peace,
Deep meeting deep. No stir can move me,
Nought break the quiet of my release!
In vain the windy sunlight raves
At the hush and gloom of polar caves.[11]

Although he continued to publish poetry from time to time until 1931 (*The Burning Wheel*, 1916; *Jonah*, 1917; *The Defeat of Youth and Other Poems*, 1918; *Leda*, 1920; *Selected Poems*, 1925; *Arabia Infelix and Other Poems*, 1929; *The Cicadas and Other Poems*, 1931), he candidly admitted in *Texts and Pretexts* that the writing of poetry was not his forte: "in company with all but about half a dozen of the men and women who have lived in the last thousand years, I lack these abilities [of a good poet]" (p. 4). He therefore turned to prose and began publishing a multitude of books of fiction, travel journals, essays.

His romantic predilections did not abide with him. As he began turning his searching eye on the world about him, he became more and more disturbed at what he saw. In *Along the Road* he declared, "I could give many excellent reasons for my dislike of large dinner-parties, soirées, crushes, routs, conversazioni and balls. Life is not long enough and they waste precious time . . . " (p. 25). Travel for a time served to keep him amused but not satisfied. The sight of people spending their lives in soulless work, deadening entertainments, brutish love-making was repulsive to him. "I often think it would be best not to attempt the solution of the problems of life . . . . The wisest thing, perhaps, is to take for granted the 'wearisome condition of humanity, born under one law, to another bound,' and to leave the matter at that, without an attempt to reconcile the incompatibles."[12]

But Huxley did not take his own advice not to attempt "to reconcile the incompatibles"; he continued to be both fascinated and appalled by the fact that "Thousands are drunk, thousands have over eaten, thousands have not had enough to eat. And they are all alive, all unique and separate and sensitive, like you and me. It's a horrible thought" (*Antic Hay*, p. 77). Having decided that social entertainments, ephemeral pursuits of pleasure, and sensual love-making were not to his taste, Huxley followed his inclinations to be a spectator rather than an actor in what seemed to him life's sardonic paradoxes. And yet this comparative detachment did not always seem as satisfying as he had first imagined: "occasionally, I must confess, I regret the chains with which I have not loaded myself. In these moods I desire a house full of stuff, a plot of land with things growing on it; I feel that I should like to know one small place and its people intimately . . ." (*Jesting Pilate*, p. 173).

This regret is not characteristic of Huxley during his first period of development. For the most part, up to 1926, Huxley was a disillusioned spectator, indignantly savage at life's paradoxes and apparent futility. This period of despair and philosophical negation lasted until he met D. H. Lawrence in 1926, when he embraced Lawrence's belief in instinctive and integrated living until Lawrence's death in 1930.

Even after he met Lawrence, however, Huxley approved Lawrence's belief in the instinctive life only intellectually and theoretically. It is significant that the character in *Point Counter Point* who personifies the integrated, instinctive personality is Mark Rampion, based on Lawrence, whereas the character in the novel who represents Huxley is Philip Quarles, who is still the detached spectator in life, emotionally uninvolved, and interested only intellectually in what his encyclopedic mind grasps. As Huxley says in Philip Quarles's notebook, "The chief difference between us, alas, is that his [Rampion's] opinions are lived and mine, in the main, only thought. Like him, I mistrust intellectualism, but intellectually" (p. 378).[13]

A life of negative futility could not go on indefinitely. Both in the novels and nonfiction books that he wrote in the 1930's, a note of sadness and mysticism seeps in. The sardonic element is still there, but it is now somewhat tempered by metaphysical and philosophical considerations. "I prefer Spinoza's freedom through knowledge and understanding to emotional bondage, however deliciously creepy with 'unknown fears' " (*Beyond the Mexique Bay*, p. 286). It was still, in the words of the character Anthony Beavis, "A senseless world, where nothing whatever can be done—how satisfactory!" (*Eyeless in Gaza*, p. 115). But now Huxley began to create characters like Dr. Miller to show the way to salvation—a life of mysticism, of nonattachment to the ego and its animal desires.

Despite his inclusion of a mystic character in all his novels beginning with *Eyeless in Gaza,* it is revealing that the characters who most closely resembled Huxley in those novels (people like Anthony Beavis in *Eyeless in Gaza* and Sebastian Barnack in *Time Must Have a Stop*) were not the mystics but those Hamlet-like individuals who were frozen into inaction by their excessive cerebration. The mystic characters, it would seem, typified the person whom Huxley would have liked to emulate. He still remained the person who found conflict between his ideals and reality; who preferred to detach himself from the torrent of life's paradoxes; who, essentially, seemed like the kind of person he thought Maine de Biran was:

> Such persons are as a rule sensitive to excess and have a tendency, in mere self-protection, to turn inwards, away from their surroundings, which they experience as a standing menace to their well-being. Like the world of all extreme cerebrotonics, Biran's universe was primarily that of his own inner experiences and only secondarily that of other people and autonomous objects. (*Themes and Variations*, p. 17)

The last years of his life Huxley spent largely in the United States, making his home in California. His observations of life in the United States did not in any way make him more optimistic about the condition of the world.[14] More and more, he was inclined to detach himself from the world and to take refuge in his mystical search for a unitive knowledge of the divine Godhead. This desire for withdrawal from life was further evidenced in *The Doors of Perception* (1952), in which he describes his reactions to mescalin, a drug which, he claims, helps one to achieve complete nonattachment and union with the oneness of life.

It is his temperament, he says in *Texts and Pretexts*, that has been largely responsible for this inability to take active part in the world about him:

> The earthly paradise, the earthly paradise! With what longing, be-tween the bars of my temperament, do I peer at its bright landscape, how voluptuously sniff at its perfumes of hay and raspberries, of honeysuckle and roast duck, of sun-warmed flesh and nectarines and the sea! But the bars are solid; the earthly paradise is always on the further side. Self-hindered, I cannot enter and make myself at home. (P. 78)

Yet this desire for withdrawal was counterbalanced by an almost equally keen desire to help ameliorate the world's proliferating problems. Huxley became a popular lecturer on college campuses and continued to offer his solutions for the achievement of a saner world and "the earthly paradise."

Judging Huxley solely on the basis of his writings, one might conclude that he was an aloof person, equally amused and appalled by the world's paradoxes and cruelties, expressing some compassion for its millions of victims, but somehow more analytic than compassionate. And yet this view is belied by the letters gathered and edited by Lester Grove, and by the reminiscences collected by his brother, Julian Huxley, in *Aldous Huxley, 1894–1963: A Memorial Volume.* His letters are often intimate, humorous, and considerate; similarly, all those who knew Huxley personally speak in his brother's memorial volume of his essential kindness, warmth, and humaneness. Even allowing for the inevitable hyperbole occasioned by the grief over his death, the portrait is that of a compassionate rather than a dispassionate individual. The sardonic wit and cynicism that so frequently appear in his writings could well have been the shield by which he fended off the hurts he felt in his own life and in the lives of those about him. When a fire destroyed nearly all his valuable books and letters and manuscripts a few years before his death, he remarked to Anita Loos, "It was quite an experience, but it did make one feel extraordinarily clean." When his second wife, Laura Archera Huxley, in a moment of restlessness and anxiety impulsively asked him for a divorce, "Aldous looked at me with such deep love, with such dissolving tenderness. He took my hand and kissed it. 'I caught a nymph,'

he said. 'I must let her go,' and released my hand."[15] Mrs. Huxley
also tells us that shortly before his death, he told an audience, "It
is a little embarrassing that, after forty-five years of research and
study, the best advice I can give to people is to be a little kinder
to each other."[16] These personal testaments do not picture a man
who lacked emotion; his temperament was such, however, that
he preferred to channel his emotions into intellectual outlets.
The question, nevertheless, remains whether it is solely his temperament, presumably hereditarily rooted, which determined his
outlook on life.

In the second book of John Galsworthy's *The Forsyte Saga*,
Soames Forsyte, paying his last respects to Queen Victoria upon
her death in 1901, reflects upon the changes that have taken place
in England since the ascension of the Queen in 1837:

> Well-nigh two generations had slipped by—of steamboats, railways,
> telegraphs, bicycles, electric light, telephones, and now these motor
> cars—of such accumulated wealth, that eight percent. had become
> three, and Forsytes were numbered by the thousand! Morals had
> changed, manners had changed, men had become monkeys twice-
> removed, God had become Mammon—Mammon so respectable as to
> deceive himself. Sixty-four years that favoured property, and had
> made the upper middle class; buttressed, chiselled, polished it, till
> it was almost indistinguishable in manners, morals, speech, appear-
> ance, habit, and soul from the nobility. An epoch which had gilded
> individual liberty so that if a man had money, he was free in law and
> fact, and if he had not money he was free in law and not in fact. An
> era which had canonised hypocrisy, so that to seem respectable was
> to be. A great Age, whose transmuting influence nothing had escaped
> save the nature of man and the nature of the Universe.[17]

The surface changes that had taken place were obvious: cities had
grown larger and dirtier; people were now using all the gadgets
of transportation and communication brought about by technological advances; the middle class had assumed more economic power
and were molding and sanctioning "a bourgeois morality." But
more important than merely listing these changes is finding out
why these transformations had occurred.

Perhaps the most compelling motivation in the changing world

sprang from a scientific conception of the universe, with its attendant mechanistic and materialistic philosophy of the universe. To
Lewis Mumford, "The materialist creed by which a large part of
humanity had sought to live during the last few centuries confused
the needs of survival with the needs of fulfillment; whereas man's
life requires both."[18] To Basil Willey, finding similarities between
the problems confronting the seventeenth and twentieth centuries,
the Renaissance is to blame for causing men's minds to be preoccupied with materialistic considerations; the world should be
purged "of these sloppy dregs of the Renaissance."[19] Professor
Alfred North Whitehead, on the other hand, says that "All the
world over and at all times there have been practical men, absorbed
in 'irreducible and stubborn facts' . . . ."[20] In *Essays New and Old*,
Aldous Huxley asserts that the scientific and industrial revolutions
aggravated a kind of futility which had its roots in the French
Revolution's political disappointments (pp. 52–53).

By the beginning of the twentieth century, a reexamination of
earlier sources of value had already begun:

> In the first place the young were being taught by their elders to prize
> "the things of the spirit" above worldly prosperity, but when they
> went out into the world they realized (as Gissing could show them)
> that the former was almost unattainable without the latter. Studious
> leisure, travel, and even healthy surroundings were expensive as well
> as necessary advantages. They had learnt to value pensive as well as
> necessary advantages. They had learnt to value the morals and man
> ners of the gentleman, but social intercourse (together with Mere
> dith's and Hardy's novels, and Wilde's comedies) soon convinced
> them that this cult had become a caste, and one easily to be imitated
> again, by the help of money.[21]

World War I intensified the reexamination of the social, economic, and physical bases of society. Aside from the crippling loss
of lives, the failure of the war to achieve its avowed goals of saving the world for democracy and ending the threat of future wars
only aggravated the pessimism and loss of faith in the traditional
concepts of conduct.

The reexamination of the traditional sources of value affected
both society in general and writers in particular. "The nineteenth
century has bequeathed to us a cult of disillusion, a nightmare of

an alien world, from which we find it extraordinarily difficult to recover."[22] This disillusion manifested itself in various ways. To some, there was a loss of faith in traditional religion and an attendant cynicism directed toward the ministers:

> The B. E. F. were in general irreligious; they had reduced morality to the single virtue of loyalty. The Seven Deadly Sins of Pride, Envy, Lust, Avarice, Intemperance, Anger and Sloth were venial, so long as a man was courageous and a reasonably trustworthy comrade. God as an all-wise Providence was dead; blind Chance succeeded to the Throne.[23]

Even before the corroding effects of war were felt, there were already signs of the decay of religion as a source of value. Bertrand Russell, in his credo published in *Living Philosophies,* writes that the first dogma he came to disbelieve was that of free will.[24] H. G. Wells, in his autobiography, reflects that although he was "scared by Hell," and although he "did not at first question the existence of Our Father . . . no fear nor terror could prevent my feeling that his All Seeing Eye was that of an Old Sneak and that the Atonement for which I had to be so grateful was either an imposture, a trick of sham self-immolation, or a crazy nightmare."[25] Graves and Hodge report that in World War I, the British soldiers were particularly bitter against the clergy (except the Catholic priests, who gave them comfort at the battle lines, rather than words of encouragement from the safety of England) and voiced their resentment in cynical outbursts against religion.[26]

The loss of faith in religious values was not the only disintegrating force at the beginning of the twentieth century. There was also loss of faith in family solidarity as a saving determinant in life: "when the ideal of the gentleman declined, the sentiment for the family circle declined also."[27] Young men and women began to feel the need of financial independence. As they went out to become liberated from economic limitations, they also grew independent of the moral restrictions of the home, which they regarded as stifling. The drifting from parental guidance made them respond eagerly "to the half understood promptings of sex, gathering hints from scientific gossip. So love became much less of a romance and much more an experience."[28]

In trying to incorporate this seeming disintegration of the traditional sources of value, the writers of the early twentieth century experimented with new techniques of writing:

> more significant for an understanding of the literature of the postwar period is the widespread dissatisfaction with the restrictive theories of romanticism, realism, and naturalism, and the tendency to experiment in literature, under the influence of similar movements in the pictorial and plastic arts, in the direction of increasing abstraction and the evolution of new genres.[29]

There was a rebellion, then, against the "romanticism" of such writers as Dickens, Tennyson, and Swinburne; against the "realism" of such Edwardian writers as Conrad and Bennett (although certainly there is a basic difference between the psychological realism of Conrad and the sociological realism of Bennett); and against the "naturalism" of writers like George Moore, who tried to write novels in the manner of Zola.

The writers who followed the Edwardians, people like Wells (who wrote utopias, attacked social and economic injustices, and brought to all his works the detached, though amused, spirit of scientific inquiry), Shaw (who favored "reason against emotion in romantic love, marriage, and domestic and economic relations"),[30] and Galsworthy (who, in his novels and plays, attacked the apotheosis of property and the poisons of snobbery, irresponsibility, and insensitivity), continued the questioning of the traditional sources of value. They exposed realistically some of the flaws exhibited in the cherished concepts of religion, the family life, and the romanticized belief in love.

It is with the second group of writers in the twentieth century—people like James Joyce, D. H. Lawrence, Virginia Woolf, and E. M. Forster—that the concrete results of the effects of science, increased mechanization, and Freudian psychology are most clearly felt. David Daiches's study of twentieth-century fiction has led him to observe that "One of the most outstanding features of Western civilization in the twentieth century—and especially after the World War—has been the drying-up of traditional sources of value and the consequent decay of uniform belief."[31]

What are these values that some of the leading twentieth-
century writers attacked and what are some of the credos that they
finally developed? James Joyce, in his *A Portrait of the Artist as a
Young Man*, wrote: "You talk to me of nationality, language,
religion. I shall try to fly by those nets."[32] Joyce wished to escape
into an unrestricted examination of all the facets of life: "Welcome,
O life! I go to encounter for the millionth time the reality of experience and to forge in the smithy of my soul the uncreated
conscience of my race."[33] E. M. Forster attacked the narrowness
of the traditional public school education of England and urged
a return to a life that would emphasize the release of "natural"
instincts. In *A Passage to India*, the solution to the problems created
by the British upper class's unregenerate snobbery was voiced by
Aziz, who urged, "Kindness, more kindness, and even after that
more kindness. I assure you it is the only hope."[34] Forster's hope
for the regeneracy of the "undeveloped heart" was a dim one,
however; the book ends with a pessimistic note: " 'No, not yet,' and
the sky said, 'No, not there.' "[35] The pessimism Forster voiced in
the end of the book was never alleviated; we find Forster writing
in 1949: "Works of art, in my opinion, are the only objects in the
material universe to possess internal order, and that is why, though
I don't believe that only art matters, I do believe in Art for Art's
Sake."[36] Virginia Woolf similarly found little comfort in the values
of a civilization that seemed to put a greater emphasis on material
well-being than on the emotional and aesthetic appreciation of
the experiences of life. Bernard Blackstone expresses Mrs. Woolf's
conclusions: "She is not to be overawed by size or prestige, by
societies or codes of law. Life is sacred, and life alone. The great
duty of the individual is to be himself, and to be honest with
himself, and not to judge others. Tolerance is the supreme virtue."[37]
D. H. Lawrence rejected the way of life that emphasized money,
convention, and false spirituality. He advocated the life of the
instincts, as expressed in the following passage: "My great religion
is a belief in the blood, the flesh, as being wiser than the intellect.
We can go wrong in our minds. But what our blood feels and
believes and says, is always true. The intellect is only a bit and
a bridle. What do I care about knowledge. All I want is to answer

to my blood, direct, without fribbling intervention of mind, or moral, or what-not."[38]

Exactly how all these environmental and literary influences affected Huxley is, of course, difficult to determine with even comparative accuracy. In his works, it is true, there are references to Freud, Ford, Lawrence, Joyce, Shaw (one of the few writers that the New Society in *Brave New World* has allowed to be kept), and Havelock Ellis.[39] But there are as many references to the seventeenth-century writer William Law, to Chaucer, to Blake, to Wordsworth, to ancient Buddhist, Hindu, and early Christian writers, to Spinoza.[40] His eclectic mind and omnivorous reading precluded his being forced into Procrustean beds of specialization.

One would not be justified, however, in concluding that Huxley's intellectual and spiritual journey was completely uncharted. The times in which he lived did help shape his thinking; and, as pointed out earlier, his genetic inheritance also left its mark on him. It was his grandfather, Thomas H. Huxley, who had coined the term *agnostic*, but it was his mother who, in her farewell message to Julian Huxley, showed some gnostic tendencies: "It is very hard to leave you all—but after these weeks of quiet thought, I know that all life is one—and that I am only going into another room 'of the sounding labour-house vast of being' [quoting from Matthew Arnold's "Rugby Chapel"]."[41] This dual strain of agnosticism and gnosticism was evident throughout Huxley's life, as he admitted in a letter to Reid Gardner a few months before his death: "It is, of course, quite true that I undervalue myth and indeed have a certain prejudice against it—the product, I suppose, of a rationalist upbringing. I remain an agnostic who aspires to be a gnostic— but a gnostic only on the mystical level, a gnostic without symbols, cosmologies or a pantheon."[42]

It would seem, then, that Huxley's life was a script coauthored by heredity and environment, but it should be emphasized that Huxley himself made considerable revisions in this script. He had written to Mrs. Naomi Mitchison in 1933 that his temporary blindness "shaped and shapes me; and I in my turn made and make use of it."[43] It could be also said that Huxley's forebears and environment shaped him, but he in his turn made use of them.

"The real thing?" Will shook his head. "Is there such a thing? I wish I could believe it." "You're not being asked to believe it," said Dr. Robert. "The real thing isn't a proposition; it's a state of being. We don't teach our children creeds or get them worked up over emotionally charged symbols. When it's time for them to learn the deepest truths of religion, we set them to climb a precipice and then give them four hundred milligrams of revelation. Two first-hand experiences of reality, from which any reasonably intelligent boy or girl can derive a very good idea of what's what."

—ALDOUS HUXLEY, *Island*

Basic to any interpretation of Huxley's quest for values is an understanding of Huxley's conception of reality, for therein lie the causes for his seeming inconsistencies, his sardonic irony, his rejection of many of the traditional sources of meaning in life, his plunge from the fetters of self, time, and space into self-transcendent mysticism, and finally, his attempt in his last novel (*Island*) to attain heaven on earth by embracing the knowledge of science along with the wisdom of religion. One wonders, however, whether this embrace was the mutually loving one of David and Jonathan or the antagonistic interlocking of David and Goliath.

Huxley's search for reality assumed three seemingly different directions. Until the 1930's, Huxley's books (both fiction and non-fiction) examined a world in which the traditional sources of value (Judeo-Christian religion, patriotism, the conventional frameworks of private and public morality, the "progress" concept derived from the findings of science) were either replaced by a moral vacuum or else privately violated while publicly espoused. Such books as *Crome Yellow, Antic Hay,* and *Point Counter Point* indicate Huxley's disillusionment with Western society. In the second stage, approximately from the publication of his *Eyeless in Gaza*

(1936) through *The Perennial Philosophy* (1945), Huxley tried to embrace the reality offered by mysticism, especially that preached by Buddhism. Then, in the last decade and a half of his life, Huxley tried to incorporate Buddhism within the framework of science. Thus, Huxley's search for meaning in life and for the attainment of the ultimate reality has been characterized by constant change and adaptation. In this chapter, my approach will be essentially chronological, although it should be fairly obvious that a mind as restless and inquisitive as Huxley's will not be bound by rigid stratifications.

That Huxley was always fascinated and puzzled by the apparent paradoxes of reality is evident from his earliest works. In 1925, his *Selected Poems* contained the following selection, entitled "Two Realities":

> A waggon passed with scarlet wheels
>   And a yellow body, shining new.
> "Splendid!" said I. "How fine it feels
> To be alive, when beauty peels
>   The grimy husk from life." And you
>
> Said, "Splendid!" and I thought you'd seen
>   That waggon blazing down the street;
> But I looked and saw that your gaze had been
> On a child that was kicking an obscene
>   Brown ordure with his feet.
>
> Our souls are elephants, thought I,
>   Remote behind a prisoning grill,
> With trunks thrust out to peer and pry
> And pounce upon reality;
>   And each at his own sweet will
>
> Seizes the bun that he likes best
> And passes over all the rest.[1]

This realization that reality is not absolute, that it is determined by the viewer's limitations and predilections, was the cause of much of Huxley's early discomfort. At first, he tried to insist that there is objective reality, regardless of the persons who sought either to deny it or to escape it into flights of romanticized abstractions. Strangely enough, this objective reality appeared at first to Huxley as the world of ugliness, of biological and economic determinism. He criticized Swift for not accepting the reality of the world of bowels and armpits:

> Swift's greatness lies in the intensity, the almost insane violence of that "hatred of bowels" which is the essence of his misanthropy and which underlies the whole of his work. As a doctrine, a philosophy of life, this misanthropy is profoundly silly. Like Shelley's apocalyptic philanthropy, it is a protest against reality, childish (for it is only the child who refuses to accept the order of things), like all such protests, from the fairy story to the socialist's Utopia.[2]

And yet this objective reality of ugliness and purposeless determinism could not very well satisfy Huxley for long. He admitted in *Proper Studies* that "Reality is so immeasurably complicated that it is impossible for us to comprehend it synthetically in entirety" (p. 35). His admiration for Chaucer was due primarily to Chaucer's ability to accept life's crudities and paradoxes without complaint and without need to escape. His criticism of Swift and Shelley was caused by Swift's perverse refusal to give man's instincts their due satisfaction and Shelley's etherealized conceptualizations of those same instincts. But Huxley argued in *Do What You Will* that since we cannot understand reality, the wisest policy would be to accept it as we find it without trying to plumb its teleological implications:

> the purpose of life, outside the mere continuance of living (already a most noble and beautiful end), is the purpose we put into it; its meaning is whatever we may choose to call the meaning. Life is not a cross-word puzzle, with an answer settled in advance and a prize for the ingenious person who noses it out. The riddle of the universe has as many answers as the universe has living inhabitants. Each answer is a working hypothesis, in terms of which the answerer experiments with reality. The best answers are those which permit the answerer to live most fully, the worst are those which condemn him to partial or complete death. (Pp. 101–102)

Similarly, in *Jesting Pilate,* Huxley told us that we should accept the world without worrying too much over the purpose of existence. Everybody accepts the existence of cows and elephants without speculating over the reasons for their being there. "There is as little *reason* why we should be here, eating, drinking, sleeping, and in the intervals reading metaphysics, saying prayers, or collecting dung" (p. 84). His juxtaposition of prayers and dung is significant, however, for it reveals a state of mind more sardonic than resigned; it is doubly significant that at the end of the passage from which this quotation is taken he says, "Still, in spite of the consolations of philosophy, I remained pensive" (p. 85).

His pensiveness led him to speculate further about the nature of reality. Recognizing in *Themes and Variations* that "our existence is intrinsically contradictory and paradoxical" (p. 155), Huxley nevertheless continued to delve into the abstruse essences of reality. Science, he at first believed, is adequate for only a limited perception of reality. Science is capable of classifying and measuring external phenomena but incapable of explaining either aesthetic or moral considerations. Science can describe everything about a flower but cannot explain its beauty. It is similarly inadequate in interpreting the significance of "intuitions of value and significance, . . . love, beauty, mystical ecstasy, intimations of godhead" (*Ends and Means*, p. 309). This inability of science to incorporate aesthetic and axiological judgments in its findings has been responsible for much of the meaninglessness that has characterized society since science's ascension to importance in the world:

> We are living now, not in the delicious intoxication induced by the early successes of science, but in a rather grisly morning-after, when it has become apparent that what triumphant science has done hitherto is to improve the means for achieving unimproved or actually deteriorated ends. In this condition of apprehensive sobriety we are able to see that the contents of literature, art, music—even in some measure of divinity, and school metaphysics—are not sophistry and illusion, but simply those elements of experience which scientists chose to leave out of account, for the good reason that they had no intellectual methods of dealing with them. (*Ends and Means*, p. 310)

Early in his career, Huxley stated that scientists soon realized their inadequacies; unfortunately, the masses, suffering inevitably from a time lag, continued to cling to the meaninglessness of the world brought about by the science which excluded values from their *Weltanschauung*. Nature, however, abhors a vacuum; consequently, the masses, "to satisfy their hunger for meaning and value," turned to nationalism, fascism, and revolutionary communism.[3] A valid and complete understanding of reality, Huxley believed, is therefore necessary for a balanced and satisfying life.

If science was inadequate in giving us a complete understanding of the nature of reality, would philosophy help? Huxley was not satisfied with existing philosophies either (except the nonpersonal mystical variety which he embraced after he discarded all the others):

> Philosophies are devices for making it possible to do, cooly, continuously and with good conscience, things which otherwise one could do only in the heat of passion, spasmodically and under the threat of subsequent remorse. Unsophisticated by thought, anger soon dies down; but supply a man with a philosophy proving that he is right to be angry, and he will go on performing in cold blood the acts of malice which otherwise he could have performed only when the fit was upon him. Philosophies, which their authors devised in order to justify some relatively harmless craving, have been subsequently made the excuse for monstrous iniquities. (*Olive Tree*, p. 157)

Unless philosophy is guided by self-transcendence, it is inadequate, Huxley believed, because it is, in most instances, merely a rationalization of selfish behavior. Furthermore, it is more dangerous than merely sporadic acts of animalism because it codifies under the guise of pseudologicality all kinds of lunacy; its codification is fortified by semblances of principle; it is the sanction of principles which gives acts of lunacy and violence their motivation and their continuity. Therefore, philosophy (unless of the self-transcendent variety) is also inadequate in giving us a complete and meaningful understanding of reality.

Although Huxley thus found both science and philosophy by themselves to be inadequate, he nevertheless seriously pondered the question of causality. This question, he found, is also beset with complications. He realized that "To over-simplify is fatal, and it is impossible to determine fully and correctly all the practically significant causes of complex events."[4] Nevertheless, Huxley attempted to determine the causes of men's actions. Causality he considered from three frames of reference: heredity, environment, and free will. He did not discuss heredity to any great extent, although in *Music at Night* he considered it more important than environment: "For though we can prevent one man from having more money than another, we cannot equalize their congenital wealth of wits and charm, of sensitiveness and strength of will, of beauty, courage, special talents" (pp. 76–77).[5] In *Point Counter Point,* he had both Rampion and Spandrell express the point of view that "Everything that happens is intrinsically like the man it happens to" (p. 342). He expressed a similar point of view in *Music at Night*: salvation in this world "is the fruit of certain inborn qualities of spirit . . . ; in other words, it is the result of favouritism and predestination" (p. 79).

Even though, at first, he did not regard environment so important in molding a man as heredity, we find more extensive discussion of the influence of environment. The kind of training one gains in childhood is significant. In *The Olive Tree,* he argued that if people behave well, "it is not because they have read about good behaviour and the social or metaphysical reasons for being virtuous; it is because they have been subjected, during childhood, to a more or less intensive, more or less systematic training in good behaviour" (p. 7).[6] Next to the influence of childhood, the state of our digestion is also important in determining our state of mind and our outlook on life. He agreed in *Texts and Pretexts* that our ancestors were quite right in trying to explain man's misery in physiological terms "as the spleen or the black bile . . . . They may have been wrong in their choice of the offending organ . . ." (p. 276). Pascal, Huxley felt, had a pessimistic outlook on life because he was a sick man. Similarly, Maine de Biran "had a very delicate and capricious digestion" (*Themes and Variations,* p. 72). When de Biran's digestion worked well, he considered life worth living and faced problems with healthy optimism; conversely, when he suffered indigestion, he became broodingly pessimistic and was incapable of doing any kind of intellectual labor. In *After Many a Summer Dies the Swan,* Dr. Obispo remarks that if the Romantic poets had taken proper care of their physical ailments, they would not have been so prone to compose agonized lamentations.

Digestion is not the only physical conditioning influence: our state of mind is discontinuous—different physical states affect our minds; hunger breeds irritability; good food effects euphoria. Similarly, our states of mind are determined by our sex life and the condition of the weather. Money is also a factor not to be overlooked:

> There can be no higher living that is not based solidly upon the income. Gregory's soul was able to soar, because the monastery provided his body with food and clothing, and because numerous peasants and artisans toiled in the welter of things corruptible in order to provide the monastery with the means to provide Gregory. These are facts which, however deep out of devotion to the things of the spirit, we must never forget. Spirituality can so easily be made an excuse for the most shocking sins, both of omission and commission. (*Texts and Pretexts*, pp. 299–300)

In *Eyeless in Gaza*, Anthony Beavis is envious of the youths who are going to a party; he cannot go because he does not have enough money to buy himself a dinner jacket. He is not only envious but somewhat perturbed by the seeming injustice of it: "By the mere force of social and economic circumstances, these ignorant barbarians found themselves quite naturally behaving as he did not dare to behave even after reading all Nietzsche had said about the Superman, or Casanova about women" (p. 88).[7]

Despite Huxley's belief that man's actions are molded by hereditary and environmental influences, he nevertheless asserted, early in his career, that man can overcome almost any obstacle by force of will power. As early as in 1923, in *Antic Hay*, this assertion of the power of free will is evident: "In the midst of pestilences, wars and famines, he builds cathedrals; and a slave, he can think the irrelevant and unsuitable thoughts of a free man."[8] Again, in *After Many a Summer Dies the Swan*, Mr. Propter, the mystic, reflects that the disasters and hatreds that have befallen mankind are, in part, caused by the people themselves, "Directly, by the commission of stupid or malicious acts. Indirectly, by the omission to be as intelligent and compassionate as they might be" (p. 79). The choice,

Propter comments, is entirely the individual's. Economic, social, political changes may be important, but the most fundamental change is to be brought about by the individual: "there must be more than a mere deflection of evil; there must be suppression at the source, in the individual will" (*End and Means*, p. 26). Similarly, Dr. Miller, the mystic in *Eyeless in Gaza*, "can see, for example, either irremediable senselessness and turpitude, or else actualizable potentialities for good—whichever one likes; it is a question of choice" (p. 350). Toward the end of his life, however, Huxley came to realize that the will to transcend the limitations of one's ego is fairly well confined to saints alone.

There seems to be some ambivalence in Huxley's claim that free will can change our lives. In several of his works he demonstrated how our lives are shaped beyond our control. For example, he wrote in *Themes and Variations* that Maine de Biran could not discover the "true nature of mystical salvation" because de Biran "was, congenitally, who he was, because of his body, his mind, his character, because of his profession and his social commitments" (p. 150). Similarly, in *Proper Studies*, Huxley had shown why a man is not completely the master of his own fate: "When he comes to the age of self-consciousness he has already been moulded by his parents, by his teachers, by all the ideals and prejudices of the society into which he happens to have been born" (pp. 231–32). And yet, in *The Perennial Philosophy*, he suggests that man does have within him the power to achieve self-transcendence, that what man "craves and thinks, what he believes and feels—this is, so to speak, the Logos, by whose agency an individual's fundamental character performs its creative acts."[9] Since he had earlier stated that what a man feels, thinks, and wants is largely determined by his hereditary and environmental forces, Huxley's assertions on free will seem ambivalent, if not circular. One is tempted to ask what determines the assertion of free will or self-transcendence. As he said in *Themes and Variations*, it may be that "the truth that saves is that which every individual has to realize in and for himself" (p. 103), but one gets the impression that Huxley's reflections on free will prior to the 1960's are more wishful thinking than clearly proved convictions. Little wonder that there is a fusion of optimism and pessimism in many of Huxley's later works: "Pessimism about the world at large and human nature as it displays itself in the majority of men and women. Optimism about the things that can be achieved by one who wants to and knows how" (*After Many a Summer Dies the Swan*, p. 199).

If contemplation of his own world offered little opportunity for optimism, perhaps a study of historical causality would lend more hope. Unfortunately, Huxley found little comfort in a study of history: "We see the past through the refractive medium of our prejudices, our tastes, our contemporary fears and hopes. The facts of history exist; but they hardly trouble us. We select and interpret our documents till they square with our theories" (*Olive Tree*, p. 139).

People, Huxley found, do not differ radically from generation to generation. In the days of Homer, there were introverts and extroverts, intellectuals and practical men. Hereditary and environmental forces have always been fairly much the same. "The form of institutions and philosophies may change; but the substance that underlies them remains indestructible, because the nature of humanity remains unaltered."[10] Furthermore, the course of history, Huxley found, is undulatory. One age is merely a reflection of, and in some instances, a reaction to another. In the ancient world "separatist patriotism" destroyed Greece; today fanatic nationalism is fast destroying an entire planet. "As Athens and Sparta died of idolatry and flag waving and jingoism, so we shall die of idolatry and flag waving and jingoism" (*Science, Liberty and Peace*, pp. 44–45). Our civilization has not purged itself of the barbaric cruelties found in earlier primitive societies.[11] And yet a study of historical causality does have its use:

> though it is impossible to foresee the remoter consequences of any given course of action, it is by no means impossible to foresee, in the light of past historical experience, the sort of consequences that are likely, in a general way, to follow certain sorts of acts. Thus, from the records of past experience, it seems sufficiently clear that the consequences attendant on a course of action involving such things as large-scale war, violent revolution, unrestrained tyranny and persecution are likely to be bad. Consequently, any politician who embarks

on such courses of action cannot plead ignorance as an excuse. (*Grey Eminence*, p. 295)

Let us briefly review the path Huxley took before he embarked on the road to the ultimate reality as revealed by mysticism. He first found objective reality (the world of matter as measured and interpreted by science) both ugly and incomplete. Subjective reality (as explained by most philosophies of the Western world) he found equally objectionable because in most instances these philosophies were merely rationalizations of basic ugliness and selfishness. On the question of teleology, he found little to write about. On the problem of causality, he felt that hereditary and environmental forces are influential; at the same time, he believed, or at least hoped, that an assertion of will can do much to combat the determinism of heredity and environment. Looking at history, he found that the mistakes of the past tend to be repeated. This concept of reality led Huxley first to a kind of bitter cynicism. In *Antic Hay*, one character, Coleman, comments about absolute reality:

> I remember once, when I was sitting there, quietly poring over the entrails, in came the laboratory boy and said to the stinks usher: "Please, sir, may I have the key of the Absolute?" And, would you believe it, that usher calmly put his hand in his trouser pocket and fished out a small Yale key and gave it him without a word. What a gesture! The key of the Absolute. But it was only the absolute alcohol the urchin wanted—to pickle some loathsome foetus in, I suppose. God rot his soul in peace! (P. 70)

Even the mystics found in Huxley's early works are somewhat cynical. Mr. Propter, in *After Many a Summer Dies the Swan*, tells Pete: "Most of the things that we're all taught to respect and reverence— they don't deserve anything but cynicism" (p. 97). It was almost inevitable, therefore, that the vacillations from despair to hope, from hope to cynicism again, vacillations which both objective and subjective reality engendered in Huxley, should yield to an attempt to find an absolute reality. This absolute reality Huxley found synonymous with the divine reality, or the divine Godhead. "Ultimate reality is at once transcendent and immanent. God is the creator and sustainer of the world; yet the kingdom of God is also within us . . ." (*Grey Eminence*, p. 59). It is characterized by self-transcendence, that is, by a negation of the world of the ego, of animal desires, or carnal and material aspirations. The philosophy of this absolute reality is the perennial philosophy:

> *Philosophia perennis*—the phrase was coined by Leibnitz; but the thing—the metaphysic that recognizes a divine Reality substantial to the world of things and lives and minds; the psychology that finds in the soul something similar to, or even identical with, divine Reality; the ethic that places man's final end in the knowledge of the immanent and transcendent Ground of all being—the thing is immemorial and universal. (*Perennial Philosophy*, p. vii)

This self-transcendence and loss of personality is the only effective cure for a world suffering from idolatry, stupidity, and cruelty. In the ultimate reality, we can find true salvation. This attainment of the divine Godhead, Huxley felt, can be facilitated by a strong determination to do so. "Whatever we will to do, whether it be to come to the unitive knowledge of the Godhead, or to manufacture self-propelled flame-throwers—that we are able to do, provided always that the willing be sufficiently intense and sustained" (*ibid.*, p. 17).

Huxley did not minimize the obstacles to the attainment of this absolute reality. First of all, as he pointed out in *Grey Eminence*, there is selfhood. "Selfhood is a heavy, hardly translucent medium which cuts off most of the light of reality and distorts what little it permits to pass" (p. 70). Secondly, there is man's preoccupation with time, that is, with ephemeral pursuits. In *Time Must Have a Stop*, Huxley depicts the truth of Shakespeare's quotation that "life's time's fool" and shows that men's troubles arise because they are busy with either the past or the future:

> True religion concerns itself with givenness of the timeless. An idolatrous religion is one in which time is substituted for eternity—either past time, in the form of a rigid tradition, or future time, in the form of Progress towards Utopia. And both are Molochs, both demand human sacrifice on an enormous scale. Spanish Catholicism was a typical idolatry of past time. Nationalism, Communism, Fascism, all the social pseudo-religions of the twentieth century, are idolatries of future time.[12]

In *Brave New World*, Huxley again illustrated the misery which the limitations of time and space impose. "And it was morning. Bernard was back among the miseries of space and time."[13] In *Beyond the Mexique Bay*, he similarly deprecated the limitations that time places on man's grasp of divine reality: "any possible conception of time must be depressing. For any possible conception of time entails the recognition and intimate realization of the flux of perpetual perishing; and to be made aware of the flux—the flux in relation to one's own being; worse, as a treacherous and destructive element of that being—is intolerable" (p. 197).[14]

Selfhood, time, space—these are the obstacles to attainment of self-transcendence. And yet, unless we achieve this state, Huxley warned us in *Themes and Variations*, we are slaves to sorrow, wars, barbarism, futility. "Sorrow is the unregenerate individual's life in time, the life of craving and aversion, pleasure and pain, organic growth and decay" (p. 83). By self-transcendence, we become part of eternity and part of divinity. Eternity and infinity are the elements of the divine reality; eternity and infinity, being limitless, cannot possibly impose the human limitations under which at present most of mankind suffers.[15]

Huxley did not believe that very many people are capable of achieving this self-transcendence, although there has always been yearning for self-transcendence because human beings are tired of themselves, their dreary lives, and their responsibilities. This drive for self-transcendence has had three different manifestations: alcohol and drugs, elementary sexuality when debased into debauchery, and herd intoxication. Of these three drives toward self-transcendence, herd intoxication was regarded by Huxley as the most dangerous. In *Devils of Loudun* he said, "A crowd is the social equivalent of a cancer" (p. 319), capable, when whipped by a demagogue, of great cruelty. By a process of elimination, therefore, Huxley found, prior to the last decade of his life, that the only satisfactory manifestation of self-transcendence is that which seeks identification with the divine Godhead.

Despite Huxley's passionate belief that the divine reality is the only reality that can bring salvation, he was sufficiently pragmatic to recognize the limited appeal of such a philosophy of reality for most people. With the exception of the people in *Island*, all the mystics in his novels are, significantly enough, either old or else completely without any family responsibility. Furthermore, when he talks in *The Perennial Philosophy* about the qualities necessary for achieving this divine self-transcendence, he is describing the qualities of a saint:

> The saint is one who knows that every moment of our human life is a moment of crisis; for at every moment we are called upon to make an all-important decision—to choose between the way that leads to death and spiritual darkness and the way that leads towards light and life; between interests exclusively temporal and the eternal order; between our personal will, or the will of some projection of our personality, and the will of God. (P. 43)

It may be that the saint knows how to gain this self-transcendence, and, yet, is not Huxley's endorsement of the saint's grasp of reality just as subjective as any of the other interpretations he refused to believe in? Each philosopher tends to feel that what he believes in is the truth; very few philosophers add the qualifying phrase, the truth as it appears to them. One is tempted to refer Huxley to a statement he himself made in *Proper Studies*: "Does the Dean [Inge] know what the real essence of religion is—or of anything else for that matter? If he does, he is to be congratulated; for he knows something which nobody on this earth ever has known or ever will know, until humanity learns to look without human eyes, and to understand with some other instrument than the human mind" (p. 172). Again, how workable a philosophy and conception of reality is it? Although the truth of a philosophy has not always a necessary connection with its functional success, it is important to note that Huxley is offering his philosophy of self-transcendence not only as a demonstration of truth, but also as policy to be followed. In regard to its workability, in *The Perennial Philosophy* Huxley has offered perhaps the most pungent observation: "There are many good soldiers, few saints" (p. 43).

Possibly because Huxley realized that the life of self-transcendence could not be attained by very many people if will power were the only means utilized, Huxley began experimenting with certain drugs like mescalin. He found that the mystic euphoria could be reached not merely by a saintly self-transcendence, but by the taking of these drugs as well. Consequently, the books he wrote during the last decade of his life (*The Doors of Perception, Heaven and Hell, Brave New World Revisited, Island,* and *Literature and Science*) show an increasing respect for science as a means of ordering the chaos of reality into a sane existence. In the utopian society of Pala that he created in his last novel, *Island,* chemistry, physics, physiology, and other sciences are no longer satirized as they were in *Brave New World.* There is still, however, an occasional cynical echo from Huxley's early period. Thus, the guilt-ridden Will Farnaby still remembers "his little joke about the chemistry of purgatory and paradise. Purgatory is tetraethylene diamine and sulfureted hydrogen; paradise, very definitely, is symtrinitropsibutyl toluene, with an assortment of organic impurities—ha-ha-ha! (Oh, the delights of social life!) And then, quite suddenly, the odors of love and death gave place to a rank animal smell—a smell of dog" (p. 272).

But the book does not end on a note of cynical despair. The Palanese take "*moksha*-medicine," grown from a type of mushroom, and this drug is "the reality revealer, the truth-and-beauty pill" (p. 157).[16] There is still talk here of the values of religion, especially the values of Mahayana philosophy and Tantrik Buddhism and the yoga of love. Religion, however, has now to be fortified by the drugs of science. In this marriage of Buddhism and science, it is quite evident that science is the dominating partner. Religion is talked about, but it is science which is looked to for specific guidance.[17]

Huxley's quest for values is now ended. Reality for him had assumed many faces. He began by mocking what he felt to be the limitations offered by both science and Western religions on the ultimate reality. He ended by embracing both science and Eastern religion. It should be fairly obvious, however, that Huxley's return to science and religion does not mean that he finally succeeded in his quest for truth. At the end of *Island,* in the midst of his thankfulness "for these gifts of luminous bliss and knowledgeless understanding," Will Farnaby is still exposed to the unbeatific spectacle of insects copulating and the female insect killing the male after the physical consummation. Whatever bliss he may be enjoying is not provided by the insights of religion, but by the euphoria of drugs.

Huxley began by trying to attain "Shanti." He ended by embracing the hallucinatory bliss of "*moksha*-medicine." On his pilgrimage to reach the shrine of understanding the ultimate reality, he ended by embracing not reality but an escape from it. The jesting Pilate had become a narcotic-seeking Narcissus; as Othello commented to Iago, "But yet the pity of it."

... oft it chances in particular men,
That for some vicious mole of nature
    in them,
As, in their birth—wherein they are
    not guilty,
Since nature cannot choose his
    origin—
By the o'ergrowth of some
    complexion,
Oft breaking down the pales and
    forts of reason,
Or by some habit that too much
    o'erleavens
The form of plausive manners, that
    these men,
Carrying, I say, the stamp of one
    defect,
Being nature's livery, or fortune's
    star,
Their virtues else—be they as pure
    as grace,
As infinite as man may undergo—
Shall in the general censure take
    corruption
From that particular fault.

—*Hamlet*, I, iv

*The first and indispensable condition
of systematic thought is classification.*

—ALDOUS HUXLEY, "Who Are You?" *Harper's*

The tendency to classify human beings according to types is almost as old as the history of man himself. The association between certain kinds of temperament and imbalances in the four humors and the four elements goes back to Hippocrates and the ancients. The sanguine, the phlegmatic, the choleric, and the melancholy types appear in the works of the writers of the Middle Ages and the Elizabethan period. Curiously enough, however, people's belief that one could not be held completely accountable for his temperament did not prevent them from making judgments or forming preferences.

Along with the tendency to classify people in accordance with their humors, one sees a corresponding penchant for classifying people into certain moral categories. Character-writing goes back to that ancient Greek, Theophrastus. It was revived in the seventeenth and eighteenth centuries by such writers as Bishop Joseph Hall in his *Characters of Virtues and Vices* (1608), by Sir Thomas Overbury, and by John Earle. Furthermore, whether we take such types as found in the comedies of Ben Jonson or those found in the comedies of Molière later on; whether we take the character sketches in the essays of Addison and Steele or the moral types in Bunyan's *The Pilgrim's Progress,* one clearly sees the transition among writers from a purely diagnostic attempt to ascertain the causes of the human personality to subjective evaluations of the types of the human personality. Character types thus became symbols of virtue and vice. The miracle and morality plays of the Middle Ages, the characters of humors of Jonson and others in the Elizabethan and Stuart eras, Milton's epics and Bunyan's works are all forerunners of the character types taken over by the English novelists in the eighteenth, nineteenth, and twentieth centuries. Such titles as Richardson's *Pamela or Virtue Rewarded,* Jane Austen's *Sense and Sensibility, Pride and Prejudice,* Meredith's *The Egoist,* Thackeray's *Vanity Fair* are indicative of the symbolic nature of the novels. Dickens' novels are replete with character types who have since become symbols of the particular trait of the characters personified; thus, Fagin, Little Nell, Scrooge, Uriah Heep, Pecksniff, and others are today spoken of as representative of certain characteristics of the human personality. Aldous Huxley's use of character types in his novels helped to maintain this tradition.

There are many character types in Huxley's novels. Charles J. Rolo writes that "Huxley's characters, though individualized by satiric detail, are essentially embodiments of an attitude, mouthpieces for a set of ideas."[1] Rolo lists nine types: the ineffectual intellectual, "the sentimentalist in reverse," "the disenchanted siren," the "Victorian materialist," the hypocritical scholar, the maternal female, the female *"bête noire,"* the sentimental romanticist, and the admirable man of wisdom. It is quite accurate to say that these types do exist in Huxley's novels, but it is also true that these nine types can be considered simply variations of four major character types that Huxley found among people: three of these four general types correspond to Dr. William Sheldon's categories of the cerebrotonic, the viscerotonic, the somatotonic; the fourth is the "ideal" character.[2] It is with these four groups of characters that this chapter will be concerned.

Before I continue the presentation of Huxley's character types, a few words about my adaptation of the Sheldonian classification are in order. Dr. William Sheldon, the American behavioral scientist, and his associates found definite correlation between the kind of bodily structure a person had and the temperament he developed. Huxley has given us an excellent analysis of the Sheldonian findings in the *Harper's* article. He tells us that the three kinds of bodily structure are endomorphy (characterized by fatness and emphasis on the digestive tract), mesomorphy (featured by a muscular bodily structure), and ectomorphy (distinguished by leanness and nervous sensitivity). From these types of bodily structure there result corresponding temperaments. Thus, the endomorph is the viscerotonic (a person who loves eating, comfort, and company); the mesomorph is the somatotonic (a person who loves action, danger, and controlling the lives of other people); the ectomorph is the cerebrotonic (an individual who prefers the inner world of privacy to the external world of action and other people). Although a person is born with his bodily structure and thus with a certain kind of temperament, Huxley emphasizes that what the individual does with his innate tendencies is not only the result of his upbringing and the social environment in which he finds himself but also the consequence of his own free will. Thus a somatotonic person may determine whether he uses his innate tendency toward power for good or evil; he decides whether to become a business executive, a vigorous military man, or a gangster.

Now it is important to keep in mind that Huxley has transferred the Sheldonian classification from science to ethics. Although he admits in the *Harper's* article that one should learn to tolerate temperamental differences that are essentially innate, nevertheless, he emphasizes that these temperaments can be used for either good or evil; it is the individual's free will which determines to what use he will put his temperament.[3] It should also be kept in mind that Huxley's character types appear in his novels long before the Sheldonian classifications were published in 1940 and 1942. What Sheldon did was to provide a general theory concerning the types that Huxley (and other artists before him) had already created. It was not the first time that the artist had sensed intuitively what the scientist and social scientist later codified with objective data. Since these types appear as moral rather than physical types, we do not find the kind of physical description that should accompany the delineation of the Sheldonian classifications. Sometimes, as in the case of Gumbril Junior (*Antic Hay*), Huxley will include a fake beard to satirize the concept of the "Complete Man"; sometimes, as in the case of Illidge, the frustrated Communist in *Point Counter Point*, Huxley will describe Illidge's freckles, his sandy complexion, "the sandy-brown eyes, the sandy-orange eyebrows," to emphasize the character's feeling of inadequacy, but, generally, Huxley is not very concerned with physical description. What does concern him is the moral emptiness and spiritual bankruptcy of the types I shall be describing in this chapter.

I must also emphasize that I shall not be using *viscerotonic*, *cerebrotonic*, and *somatotonic*, in the strict Sheldonian sense; Huxley, in *The Perennial Philosophy*, speaks of Hamlet and Ivan Karamazov as cerebrotonics, Hotspur as a somatotonic, and Pickwick as a viscerotonic; in *Literature and Science*, he refers to two characters from Shakespeare's *Troilus and Cressida* as "the two hulking mesomorphs, the idiot Ajax and the brighter but hardly less odious Achilles." Similarly, in *Island*, his last published novel, one of his characters speaks of "cat-people," "sheep-people," and "marten-people"—types that correspond closely to the cerebrotonic, viscerotonic, and somatotonic. Obviously, Huxley could not justify such Sheldonian designations by physical measurement. What Huxley is concerned with is using this classification of different kinds of temperament as a springboard for making psychological and moral observations; consequently, when I use the Sheldonian terms, I too shall be more concerned with their moral connotations than with their scientific denotations.

The cerebrotonic is the individual whose life is lived chiefly on an intellectual plane. It is in the world of ideas, books, and thoughts that the cerebrotonic feels most at home. When he enters the world of emotions and action, he is lost. He is the writer, the painter, the scientist, the research scholar. Generally, he is democratic at heart and idealistic in principle, but when he tries to act upon his principles, he is often uncomfortable at the vulgarity and ugliness he experiences in the world of actuality. He tends to consider the opposite sex in romanticized terms and often feels frustrated when he finds that his idealized conception is at variance with reality.

The cerebrotonic characters in Huxley's novels are Denis Stone (*Crome Yellow*); Shearwater (*Antic Hay*); Calamy (*Those Barren Leaves*); Philip Quarles, Walter Bidlake, Lord Tantamount

(*Point Counter Point*); Bernard Marx and the Savage (*Brave New World*); Anthony Beavis and Brian Foxe (*Eyeless in Gaza*); Pete (*After Many a Summer Dies the Swan*); Sebastian Barnack (*Time Must Have a Stop*); and Will Farnaby (*Island*). It will be noticed that these are all male intellectuals. Denis is an incipient poet who also occasionally writes novels; Shearwater is a scientist; Calamy is not sure of what he is going to do, although he considers himself "a pure contemplative" who has a right to one of the 84,000 paths (he does not enumerate these paths, luckily) open to people; Philip Quarles is a novelist; Walter Bidlake is a book critic for a literary magazine; Lord Tantamount is a scientist; Bernard Marx is one of the Alphas in the world of the future, whose intellectual power has made him one of the leaders; the Savage is kept on in the new world as a memento of the times when people read Shakespeare and performed innumerable other curious acts before the era of Our Ford; Anthony Beavis is a sociologist; Brian Foxe commits suicide before he has had time to be anything but he, too, is intellectual and romantic; Pete is a scientist; Sebastian Barnack is a poet; and Will Farnaby is a poet turned journalist.

What all these characters have in common is a sense of frustration. They wish to consider the world as a place where equality, liberty, and fraternity should rule, but they all feel a sense of discomfort in the presence of the masses:

> The proximity of the poor always made him [Sebastian Barnack] feel uncomfortable, and to discomfort was added, when they worked and he apparently did nothing, a sense of shame. These were feelings which ought, he supposed, to have made him want to follow in his father's footsteps. But politics always seemed so futile and unimportant. His ordinary reaction from the shame and discomfort was a flight from the situation which had occasioned them. (*Time Must Have a Stop*, p. 184)

Similarly, Walter Bidlake in *Point Counter Point* "wished that he could personally like the oppressed and personally hate the rich oppressors" (p. 16), but the sight of a member of the oppressed class spitting on the floor of the subway car nauseates him. Pete, before he joined Dr. Obispo to find ways of scientifically prolonging human life, had helped the Spanish Loyalists in their cause, but he too feels more comfortable in the company of intellectuals like Mr. Propter.

The frustration of the cerebrotonics is further intensified by their inability to act upon their desires. They are Hamlet-like characters suffering from indecision and inability to execute their plans. Calamy typifies this trait when he says:

> When I do something stupid or dirty I can't help feeling that it is stupid or dirty. My soul lacks virtues to make it wise or clean. And I can't dissociate myself from what I do. I wish I could. One does such a devilish number of stupid things. Things one doesn't want to do. If only one could be a hedonist and only do what was pleasant! But to be a hedonist one must be wholly rational; there's no such thing as a genuine hedonist, there never has been. Instead of doing what one wants to do or what would give one pleasure, one drifts through existence doing exactly the opposite, most of the time—doing what one has no desire to do, following insane promptings that lead one, fully conscious, into every sort of discomfort, misery, boredom, and remorse . . . . (*Those Barren Leaves*, p. 71)

Sebastian Barnack also typifies this inability to do what he wants to do. At the beginning of *Time Must Have a Stop*, a strange woman presents him with a box of chocolates; he wants to refuse but ends up taking it anyway. Later on in the book, he wants to tell everybody that it is he who has sold one of his uncle's paintings and not the innocent Italian girl who is suspected; he keeps delaying the decision until it is too late. Similarly, Philip Quarles wants to tell his wife that he loves her and wants to show more affection toward her, but he too is unable to carry out his intentions.

It is in their relationships with women that the cerebrotonics suffer their greatest frustration. Thus, Denis loves Anne passionately but does not quite know how to declare his love. He writes a poem to her, expecting her to divine his love from the poem, but she never even alludes to it. Pete is equally fumbling in his efforts to make known his love to Virginia; Sebastian Barnack is intensely enamored of the widowed Mrs. Thwale, but it is she who finally effects a consummation of his desire. The cerebrotonics who are married are equally ineffective in their relationships with their women. Philip Quarles is so detached in his love for his wife that she is seriously contemplating having a love affair with another man just to provoke some kind of feeling in her husband. Shearwater and Lord Tantamount are blissfully unaware of their wives' infidelity while they are making scientific experiments. Walter Bidlake buries his head in a pillow as he reads a letter from his mistress, Lucy Tantamount, in which she gleefully describes her affair with another man. Brian Foxe, perhaps the most pathetic of the cerebrotonics, is unable to declare his love to his girl and commits suicide when he thinks that she has had an affair with his best friend. The relationships of cerebrotonics with women bring either unfulfilled desire, passive consummation, infidelity, or pain.

The intellectuality of the cerebrotonic is further indicated by the fact that many of them keep diaries or notebooks. Philip Quarles keeps a notebook in which he jots down his impressions of life; never, his own actions. He is the observer, not the actor. Similarly, Anthony Beavis keeps a diary in which he records his reactions to his own experiences and his growing admiration for the mystic Dr. Miller. Again, Sebastian Barnack keeps a diary so that he too can recollect his experiences in passive tranquillity. These cerebrotonics do not keep a calendar of things to do; they keep diaries and notebooks of thoughts and actions, frequently undone. Little wonder that Huxley occasionally finds this kind of life unsatisfying. In one of his earliest poems, entitled "The Life Theoretic," he gives us his reactions to the life of the cerebrotonic:

> While I have been fumbling over books
> And thinking about God and the Devil and all,
> Other young men have been battling with the days,
> And others have been kissing the beautiful women.
> They have brazen faces like battering rams.
> But I who think about books and such—
> I crumble to impotent dust before the struggling,
> And the women palsy me with fear.
> But when it comes to fumbling over books
> And thinking about God and the Devil and all,
> Why, there I am.
> But perhaps the battering-rams are in the right of it,
> Perhaps, perhaps ... God knows.[4]

Thus, the cerebrotonic is hardly the type of person whom Huxley would consider an ideal character. Two (Brian Foxe and the Savage) commit suicide; the fate of the others is hardly any better —they suffer either frustration or a merciful ignorance of what is going on. Only three manage to escape this Ixion-like wheel of futility. Calamy, at the end of *Those Barren Leaves,* retires to the hills to seek a life of mystical contemplation; Will Farnaby, at the end of *Island,* seems to be enjoying the yoga of love with Susila, but this bliss is interrupted as the militarists take over the island; Anthony Beavis, at the end of *Eyeless in Gaza,* is determined to address a group of pacifists despite threats to his own life if he goes through with his speech. Significantly, however, the novel ends not with completion of his intention, but with merely statement of it.

Next we come to the viscerotonic; he is the person who lives his life chiefly on the plane of the emotions. "There is the emotional sociable extraversion of the viscerotonic endomorph—the person who is always seeking company and telling everybody just what he feels" (*Perennial Philosophy,* p. 150). His chief characteristic is love of food, comfort, luxury, and sensuality. In other words, he is basically an epicurean, a hedonist, a man of the senses. In this group we find Barbecue-Smith (*Crome Yellow*); Mercaptan and Boldero (*Antic Hay*); Burlap and Sidney Quarles (*Point Counter Point*); Henry Foster (*Brave New World*); Pordage (*After Many a Summer Dies the Swan*); Eustace Barnack (*Time Must have a Stop*); and Dr. Poole (*Ape and Essence*).

Perhaps the best-drawn portrait of the viscerotonic is Eustace Barnack in *Time Must Have a Stop.* Eustace had married a widow years before the main action of the novel. When she died five years after the marriage, she left him a huge fortune which has enabled Eustace to follow a life of indulgence in sensual pleasures. He likes good food, fine drinks, and affairs with all sorts of women— from countesses to cheap courtesans. He buys books and paintings, not for any intrinsic love for them but as a means of "Just keeping out of mischief—it's the greatest of all the virtues" (p. 53). He thinks all attempts at reform are nonsense and that under the cloak of idealism, the reformers are merely trying to get to power. He has a knack of making up limericks about all people and all occasions. In the presence of Bruno Rontini, the mystic, he feels somewhat uncomfortable. He refers to God as the "Gaseous Vertebrate." His advice is that one should gather one's rosebuds while one may; the thought of death is extremely depressing to him, and he shuns all mention of it. And yet he is not completely without philosophical justification for his kind of life:

> The moral codes have always been framed by people like your [Sebastian Barnack's] father—or, at the very best, people like Bruno. People like me have hardly been able to get a word in edgeways. And when we do get our word in—as we did once or twice during the eighteenth century—nobody listens to us seriously. And yet we demonstrably do much less mischief than the other fellows. We don't start any wars, or Albigensian crusades, or Communist revolutions. "Live and let live"—that's our motto. Whereas *their* idea of goodness is "die and make to die"—get yourself killed for your idiotic cause, and kill everybody who doesn't happen to agree with you. Hell isn't merely paved with good intentions; it's walled and roofed with them. Yes, and furnished too. (P. 122)

What seems to characterize the viscerotonic, besides his obvious sensuality, is his unawareness, in most instances, that there may be something wrong or hypocritical with the kind of life he is leading. Thus, Barbecue-Smith sees nothing wrong with always quoting from his own "inspirational" column; Sidney Quarles, similarly, has no conception of his hypocritical position in trying to make his wife believe that all the time he is spending in London is being spent on research in the London Museum for his contemplated *magnum opus*, while actually he is enjoying himself with his mistress. Jeremy Pordage, a scholar who has been hired by the opulent Mr. Stoyte to edit the Hauberk papers, always carries a book of Wordsworth's poems with him, likes to visit the London Library, enjoys listening to the Vespers at the Westminister Cathedral "if they happened to be singing Palestrina, and every alternate week, between five and six-thirty he would spend an hour and a half with Mae or Doris in their flat in Maida Vale. Infinite squalor in a little room, as he liked to call it; abysmally delightful" (*After Many a Summer Dies the Swan*, p. 89). Burlap, the editor of a literary magazine, is always talking about believing in "Life" and spirituality; talk of Susan, his dead wife, brings tears to his eyes. Yet despite his saintly poses, he keeps a careful eye on the market securities and is engaged in trying to seduce as many innocent women as he can. *Point Counter Point* ends as he and Beatrice pretend to be little children and take a bath together: "The bathroom was drenched with their splashings. Of such is the Kingdom of Heaven" (p. 514).

The curious feature about Huxley's viscerotonics is that they are all either literary critics, writers, scholars, or dilettantes in the arts, but unlike the cerebrotonics, they are committed to the arts only superficially. They are all expert either in quoting their own sapience or the wisdom of others. They collect books, buy paintings, and are otherwise patrons of the arts. What Huxley seems to be saying about these characters is that an assumed spirituality or intellectual or aesthetic refinements are no guarantee against the encroachments of sensuality.

It is quite obvious that the viscerotonic individual is also not to be set up as a source of value. Either the character is obviously satirized (as in the case of Burlap, Barbecue-Smith, Sidney Quarles) or else his way of life is expressly criticized as a failure. Thus, in *After Many a Summer Dies the Swan*, as the mystic Mr. Propter looks at Jeremy Pordage, he thinks, "A comic spectacle, . . . except, of course, that it was so extremely depressing" (p. 89). Similarly, Huxley indicates the futility of hedonism as a way of life when he depicts Eustace Barnack, who, after gorging himself on food and drink, suffers a fatal heart attack, significantly enough, in the lavatory. Even before his death, Eustace had confessed to his nephew the futility of girls, parties, and life in general.

There are not very many somatotonic characters in Huxley's novels, possibly because he is least familiar with men of action. There are enough, however, to lead us to believe that the somatotonic is likewise unable to live a profoundly satisfying life. The somatotonic's extraversion is that "of the engineer who works off his lust for power on things, of the sportsman and the professional blood-and-iron soldier, of the ambitious business executive and politician, of the dictator, whether in the home or at the head of a state" (*Perennial Philosophy*, p. 151). He is the man who "can bend people to his will and shape things to his heart's desire" (*ibid.*). The characters in Huxley's novels who can be classified as somatotonics are Webley (*Point Counter Point*); Mr. Stoyte (*After Many a Summer Dies the Swan*); Mustapha Mond (*Brave New World*); John Barnack (*Time Must Have a Stop*); and Colonel Dipa and Lord Aldehyde (*Island*). Webley is the leader of the British Fascists; Mr. Stoyte is the millionaire industrialist and real estate magnate who owns half of California; John Barnack is a radical Socialist, dedicated to bringing about a utopia by overthrowing the present system; and Colonel Dipa and Lord Aldehyde are characters we never meet directly in the novel, but their somatotonic presence is felt throughout the book. Colonel Dipa wants political control and Lord Aldehyde wants economic power. In both cases, their lust for power is felt to be sinister.

All the somatotonics are thorough extroverts, with their thoughts directed to mastering those around them. Thus, Webley is the fearless leader whose commands are obeyed without question; all his followers cringe before him. He hates democracy and believes that government should consist of the rule of the aristocracy —the aristocracy consisting, of course, of his followers and himself. He has great faith in himself, in his followers, and in the destiny of his movement, which is featured by unquestioning discipline. Yet despite some show of a flamboyant kind of courage, he is made out to be a tin-pot Mussolini, with his uniform, his ringing voice, and lust for power. Near the end of *Point Counter Point*, he is assassinated by Spandrell and Illidge.

Jo Stoyte is the man who owns half of California. All fly to do his bidding. He has Dr. Obispo and Pete investigate ways of prolonging life. He hires Jeremy Pordage to edit the Hauberk papers. He contributes generously to Tarzana College, to hospitals, to needy people. He is affectionately known by children as "Uncle Jo." And yet despite the success of his ruthless business ventures, he is pathetic in his hysterical anxiety to prolong his life and in his futile love affair with his mistress Virginia, a former show girl. He maintains Mr. Propter on his estate because Mr. Propter is the only one who has understood that Stoyte's lust for power is merely a psychological compensation for his feelings of inferiority at being fat and clumsy when he was a child.

John Barnack, the crusading radical in *Time Must Have a Stop*, is an equally ineffectual somatotonic type. He wants to bring the socialist revolution to the world so as to rid it of its social and economic injustices. By profession a lawyer, he is also a writer for a left-wing paper. As a father, he again demonstrates his unorthodoxy; he refuses to buy his son a dinner jacket because, to him, it is a symbol of capitalist exploitation; dinner parties are a sinful waste of time when the threat of fascism is to be met. All his brave talk about changing the world notwithstanding, at the end of the book we see a tired, broken man who still mouths the same words, but without quite the same conviction. He admits to his son that perhaps he was mistaken in regarding the mystic, Bruno Rontini, as ineffectual; and he no longer thinks optimistically of the imminence of the proletarian revolution:

> The main result of the war, he went on gloomily, would be the acceleration of processes which otherwise would have taken place more gradually and therefore less catastrophically. The process of Russia's advance towards the domination of Europe and the Near East; of China's advance towards the domination of the rest of Asia; and of all Asia's advance towards industrialism. Torrents of cheap manufactures flooding the white men's markets. And the white men's reactions to those torrents would be the *casus belli* of the impending war of color. (P. 306)

Mustapha Mond is the somatotonic who has achieved the greatest power of all. He is one of the world's twelve controllers; his word is absolute law. Even the Alpha pluses, the cream of the new world's aristocracy, tremble before his utterances. He has the power to determine how many shall be born in his domain, and what kind of life they shall lead. Significantly enough, however, he has (in a locked safe, to be sure!) books by Shakespeare and other writers of the pre-Ford era (all these writers are proscribed to everybody else); and it is to these writers that he occasionally refers, for spiritual sustenance, it would seem. It is almost wistfully that he relates to the Savage how he chose power over freedom when, in his youth, he was given the choice to make.

Even though later on, in *Literature and Science,* he was to realize that modern psychologists and physiologists added blood type to Sheldon's physical measurements as predisposing one to certain kinds of behavior, it was still the moral consequences of behavior that concerned Huxley. The cerebrotonic, the viscerotonic, and the somatotonic were all found to be inadequate as sources of value. It is no surprise then that Huxley had to resort to a search for the ideal character. That Huxley was long troubled by the absence of the ideal man in our society is evident in his early books:

> The Ideal Man of the eighteenth century was the Rationalist; of the seventeenth, the Christian Stoic; of the Renaissance, the Free Individual; of the Middle Ages, the Contemplative Saint. And what is our Ideal Man? On what grand and luminous mythological figure does contemporary humanity attempt to model itself? The question is embarrassing. Nobody knows. (*Texts and Pretexts,* pp. 4–5)

Huxley's first ideal character is a fusion of Greek culture and the ideals of D. H. Lawrence. This individual integrates all the instincts into a harmonious combination. As Mark Rampion (the only integrated character in Huxley's novels before the mystics enter into the picture) says: "To be a perfect animal *and* a perfect human—that was the ideal" (*Point Counter Point,* p. 133). He is against the inroads made by false spirituality, materialistic science, and deadening industrialism. As Rampion states it, "It's Jesus's and Newton's and Henry Ford's disease. Between them, the three have pretty well killed us. Ripped the life out of our bodies and stuffed us with hatred" (p. 139). In his essay "Pascal," in *Do What You Will,* is perhaps the best expression of the kind of individual Huxley had in mind:

> Briefly, then, these are my notions of the life-worshipper into whose likeness I myself should be prepared to bovaryze the diversities of my personality. His fundamental assumption is that life on this planet is valuable in itself, without any reference to hypothetical higher worlds, eternities, future existencies. "Is it not better, then, to be alone and love Earth only for its earthly sake?" It is, particularly if

you have Blake's gift for seeing eternity in a flower and for "making the whole creation appear infinite and holy . . . by an improvement of sensual enjoyment." The life-worshipper's next assumption is that the end of life, if we leave out of account for the moment all the innumerable ends attributed to it by living individuals, is more life, that the purpose of living is to live. God, for the life-worshipper, is of course life, and manifests himself in all vital processes, even those which, from our point of view, are most repulsive and evil. (P. 276)

Thus, the ideal individual for Huxley in the 1920's was the person who lived instinctively, spontaneously, realistically, intuitively, fully. As he said in "Wordsworth in the Tropics," if this spontaneity occasionally resulted in inconsistency, no harm resulted. "Too much consistency is as bad for the mind as it is for the body. Consistency is contrary to nature, contrary to life" (*ibid.*, p. 125). Huxley admired the Greek way of life because it included realistically all the phases of life. The Greeks realized that a man had a mind to think with; but he also had senses to enjoy with, passions to succumb to occasionally, beauty to worship. "Man is multifarious, inconsistent, self-contradictory; the Greeks accepted the fact and lived multifariously, inconsistently, and contradictorily. Their polytheism gave divine sanction to this realistic acceptance" ("Spinoza's Worm," *ibid.*, p. 81).

Since realism was one of the ingredients of this integrated personality, Huxley was sufficiently realistic to recognize that modern society made it extremely difficult to live this kind of life at all times. The answer, therefore, was a compromise:

> The only satisfactory way of existing in the modern, highly specialized world is to live with two personalities. A Dr. Jekyll that does the metaphysical and scientific thinking, that transacts business in the city, adds up figures, designs machines, and so forth. And a natural, spontaneous Mr. Hyde to do the physical, instinctive living in the intervals of work. The two personalities should lead their unconnected lives apart, without poaching on one another's preserves or inquiring too closely into one another's activities. ("Wordsworth in the Tropics," *ibid.*, p. 125)

If people only tried to emulate the principles of this integrated personality, what grief would be spared them! Baudelaire, for example, might have spared himself much self-torture if he had lived instinctively; unfortunately, "We may doubt whether he ever embraced a woman he respected, or knew what it was to combine desire with esteem, and tenderness with passion" ("Baudelaire," *ibid.*, p. 188). Similarly, in discussing Dostoevsky's *The Possessed,* Huxley writes that if Stavrogin "could have gone to bed with women he liked," and "if Kirillov had had a wife and a job of decent work; if Pyotr Stepanovitch had ever looked with pleasure at a landscape or played with a kitten" (*ibid.*, p. 174), they would have been normal, happy individuals instead of the morbidly miserable creatures they were. Both Robert Burns and Chaucer, on the other hand, understood the inconsistencies of life and lived their lives instinctively and realistically and so avoided the pitfalls of life's tragedies.

Huxley's espousal of the integrated life of the life-worshiper did not last very long. Even before Lawrence's death in 1930 there were signs that Huxley was not irrevocably committed to worshiping at the shrine of the integrated personality. In *Those Barren Leaves*, published in 1925, he wrote: "To be torn between divided allegiances is the painful fate of almost every human being. Pull devil, pull baker; pull flesh, pull spirit; pull love, pull duty; pull reason and pull hallowed prejudice. The conflict, in its various forms, is the theme of every drama" (p. 57). In *Point Counter Point*, he sees that the ideal personality is rarely found—"a few perhaps in Spain, in Greece, in Provence. Not elsewhere in modern Europe" (p. 379). Also, he realizes the great difficulty of attaining this ideal. Indulging in intellectual pursuits, writes Philip Quarles, is much easier than "learning the art of integral living" (p. 380). Philip wonders whether he will ever be strong enough to break himself away from intellectual pursuits. "And even if I did try to break these habits, shouldn't I find that heredity was at the bottom of them and that I was congenitally incapable of living wholly and harmoniously?" (p. 381).

We now come to the second of Huxley's "ideal" characters. Even before Lawrence's death in 1930, Huxley created a character, Calamy, in *Those Barren Leaves*, who turns to mysticism at the end of the book. The drift to mysticism, temporarily suspended by Huxley's endorsement of Lawrence's life-worshiping aspirations, became a permanent shift with Huxley after Lawrence's death. The mystic characters in Huxley's novels are Dr. Miller (*Eyeless in Gaza*); Mr. Propter (*After Many a Summer Dies the Swan*); Bruno Rontini (*Time Must Have a Stop*); the Narrator (*Ape and Essence*); and a host of characters in *Island* who try to enhance their mysticism with the assistance of science.

What are the personal characteristics of these mystics? First of all, none of them are youthful men. It seems to take many years of mellowing for a person to realize the folly of most of life's activities. The exceptions are the characters in *Island*, who are artificially trained rather than developed through maturing experiences. As for the other personal characteristics, perhaps what Sebastian Barnack writes about Bruno Rontini in *Time Must Have a Stop* can best represent these traits:

> There were so many things one could mention. That candor, for example, that extraordinary truthfulness. Or his simplicity, the absence in him of all pretensions. Or that tenderness of his, so intense and yet so completely unsentimental and even impersonal—but impersonal, in some sort above the level of personality, not below it, as his own [Sebastian's] sensuality had been impersonal. Or else there was the fact that, at the end, Bruno had been no more than a kind of thin transparent shell, enclosing something incommensurably other than himself—an unearthly beauty of peace and power and knowledge. (P. 310)

This mystic is, in many respects, like "Jesus's ideal personality" (*Eyeless in Gaza*, p. 98). He is not influenced by the rigidities of convention, but at the same time he is neither proud nor ostentatious, because he is never led into thinking that he is better than others; he is humble and is not concerned with material well-being. He realizes that the world's improvement must begin with the individual, and thus he tries to exemplify the ideal life. At the same time, as Huxley points out in *Grey Eminence*, the mystic has to be conscious of the role that he is to have in effecting the world's salvation; his program of altruism should include the following:

1. Helping others to attain a unitive knowledge and love of God either through his disciples or by writing about his experiences.

2. Helping to down economic evils—as did the Benedictines when they revived agriculture and drainage systems.

3. Improving the educational system—as did the Benedictines.

4. Doing good works, as, for example, performed by St. Vincent de Paul, a contemporary of Father Joseph in the seventeenth century, and by George Fox and the Quakers.[5]

All of Huxley's mystic characters are prone to give both a diagnosis of and prognosis for the world's evils. Thus, in *Eyeless in Gaza*, Dr. Miller tells Anthony that one of the reasons for the world's troubles is the eating of meat. "I eat like a Buddhist, because I find it keeps me well and happy; and the result is that I think like a Buddhist—and, thinking like a Buddhist, I'm confirmed in my determination to eat like one" (p. 379). The greatest enemy of Christianity, according to Dr. Miller, is frozen meat. It makes people skeptical and pessimistic. The cure, obviously, is vegetarianism. Another bit of practical advice that Dr. Miller dispenses concerns muscular use: by straightening out his back, one would restore the soul's vigor. "(Note the typically bad physical posture of neurotics and lunatics. The stooping back, the muscular tension, the sunken head.) Re-educate. Give back correct physical use. You remove a keystone of the arch constituting the neurotic personality" (p. 224). It would seem that at least in the character of Dr. Miller it is the body that determines the temperament.

With most of the mystics, however, the advice is not quite so pragmatic. Bruno Rontini's cure in *Time Must Have a Stop* is expressed somewhat more lyrically:

Apotheosis—the personality exalted and intensified to the point where the person ceases to be mere man or woman and becomes god-like, one of the Olympians, like that passionately pensive warrior, like those great titanesses brooding, naked, above the sarcophagi. And over against apotheosis, deification—personality annihilated in charity, in union, so that at last the man or woman can say, "Not I, but God in me." (P. 253)[6]

The mystic, in Huxley's novels, is not merely a man of contemplation, but a man of action as well. Mr. Propter, in *After Many a Summer Dies the Swan*, tries to make work easier for the impoverished peasants who labor on Stoyte's fruit farms. Rontini, rather than implicate his friend Sebastian Barnack, goes to jail because he is suspected of aiding the anti-Fascist struggle in Italy. Dr. Miller tries to help the natives in South America by giving them medical advice. Thus, the mystic realizes that after he has gained a knowledge and love of God by annihilating the desires of the ego, he must help others.

It is to be remembered that Huxley seldom views people as either cerebrotonics, or viscerotonics, or somatotonics, or ideal characters. He knows that most people probably fuse some of the characteristics of all these types; at the same time, it is for purposes of clarity and simplicity that he has chosen to consider a person as belonging chiefly to one of these groups; his gauge of classification has been to determine whether an individual is mainly a man of intellect, or a man of feeling, or a man of action, or a life-worshiper, or a mystic. He knows that most people are gray characters, but white and black are much easier to discern.

Huxley's admission that such an arbitrary classification of human beings leads to artificiality serves but to emphasize that an analysis of human types is not synonymous with an analysis of human beings; consequently, what is gained in clarity by oversimplification is lost through lack of profundity. The creation of types is inextricably intertwined with the tendency toward exaggeration; exaggeration helps to focus more sharply on what is being viewed, but it has the disadvantage of distorting reality. Furthermore, the ideal character that Huxley evolved in the creation of the mystic is also defective in some ways. I have already noted that most of the mystics in his novels tend to be old men without any family responsibilities. The experience of a mystical union with God, Huxley reminds us often, is both intuitive and ineffable; and yet what frequently characterizes these mystics in his novels is their garrulity. One is tempted to agree with Huxley's comment in *Point Counter Point* about "The profound silliness of saintly people; their childishness" (p. 377). Even if the "saintliness" of these mystics is expressed more by action than by talk, Huxley has himself admitted that there are likely to be more soldiers than saints. Consequently, the ideal character remains an ideal devoutly to be wished rather than a goal likely to be achieved.

It can also be seen that my discussion of Huxley's character types has been confined to males; it is not that there are no females in Huxley's novels, but rather that his females are seen chiefly in relationship to the males. Elinor Quarles (*Point Counter Point*) serves mainly to reinforce her husband's cerebrotonic tendencies. Susila (*Island*) is brought into the picture to help Will Farnaby attain the yoga of love. Lenina Crowne (*Brave New World*) intensifies the picture of the dehumanization of experience in a technologically manipulated society. Women in Huxley's novels occupy a satellite position. There is no Molly Bloom or Emma Bovary to grace his pages; on the other hand, there is no Leopold Bloom either.

And yet, despite these criticisms, Huxley's analysis of these character types does help us to appraise twentieth-century writers and their evaluation of the world about them. Huxley has often been called by critics the novelist who best represents his generation; in his character types, one can detect several of the traits one sees in the characters created by Huxley's contemporaries. James Joyce, D. H. Lawrence, Virginia Woolf, and E. M. Forster may not have used the same satiric approach in the creation of their characters, but certainly one can see the viscerotonic tendencies of Molly Bloom (Joyce's *Ulysses*), or the cerebrotonic quality of Stephen Dedalus (Joyce's *A Portrait of the Artist as a Young Man*) and Rupert Birkin (Lawrence's *Women in Love*), or the somatotonic ambitions of Mr. Pembroke (Forster's *The Longest Journey*) and Gerald Crich (Lawrence's *Women in Love*). Huxley's diagnosis of these tendencies in human beings is perceptive and meaningful if one applies the caution which should be extended to any presentation of stereotyped characters.

V   HUXLEY AMONG THE MUSES

His Philosophy of the Arts and Literature

That the arts have played a dominant role in Huxley's thinking
and writing since the beginning of his career is evident from the
preponderance of writers and painters in his novels and from the
abundance of comments in them concerning literature, painting,
music, the role of the artist in society, the status of the arts in
modern times, the relationship between art and life, and between
art and religion. It will be noted that the central figure in his first
novel, *Crome Yellow,* is a poet and that the chief figure in his last
published novel, *Island,* is a poet turned journalist. His last published work, *Literature and Science,* and the essay he finished the
day before his death, "Shakespeare and Religion," reaffirm his life-
long immersion in the creative springs of the Muses.

In *Jesting Pilate,* published in 1926, Huxley wrote, "Art and the
artist have become tremendously important in our modern world"
(p. 264). The reason for this increasing importance of the artist,
Huxley feels, lies in the need to "fill the vacuum created in the
popular mind by the decay of established religion" (p. 265). The
priest, according to Huxley, has now been supplanted to a large
degree by the doctor, the lawyer, and the artist. What is this at-

traction that the artist and the arts have exercised over modern man? For one thing, as Huxley writes in *Point Counter Point*, art does not contain the irrelevancies and impurities of life: "there's no hiccoughing or bad breath, no fatigue or boredom, no sudden recollections of unpaid bills or business letters unanswered, to interrupt the raptures. Art gives you the sensation, the thought, the feeling quite pure—chemically pure, I mean . . . not morally" (p. 9).

Furthermore, the best works in literature, music, and painting not only furnish us with pleasure but enlighten us about the nature of the world. Artistic creations such as Beethoven's Mass in D and Shakespeare's *Macbeth* "tell us, by strange but certain implication, something significant about the ultimate reality behind appearances" (*Ends and Means*, p. 331). The beneficent illumination which Wordsworth spoke of when he wrote of Nature's revealing "something far more deeply interfused," Huxley now ascribes to the masterpieces of the arts. At least upon occasion, as in his essay "Meditation on El Greco" in *Music at Night*, he even equates beauty and truth, and echoes Keats's aesthetic theory when he writes, "every significant artist is a metaphysician, a propounder of beauty-truths and form-theories . . ." (p. 57).[1]

The arts, at least in the early stages of Huxley's works, offer solace and illumination not only to people individually, but to society as well:

> We tend to think and feel in terms of the art we like; and if the art we like is bad, then our thinking and feeling will be bad. And if the thinking and feeling of most of the individuals composing a society is bad, is not that society in danger? To sit on committees and discuss the gold standard are doubtless public-spirited actions. But not the only public-spirited actions. They also serve who only bother their heads about art. (*Texts and Pretexts*, p. 1)

If people do "bother their heads about art," what will they discover about the interrelationship between art and life, about the reasons for qualitative differences among different nations and eras, and the conditions which make for superior art? First of all, Huxley believes that "The life of an epoch is expressed by, and at the same time is itself an expression of, the art of that epoch" (*Beyond the Mexique Bay*, p. 248). Vulgarity in the emotional and intellectual life of the people will produce vulgarity in art. This vulgarity is inevitable, Huxley finds, if the people are wealthy, superficially educated, and dedicated to attaining quantitative abundance. "Vulgarity is the price we must pay for prosperity, education and self-consciousness" (*ibid.*, p. 259).

It is to be remembered, however, that although art, in a general sense, does reflect the attributes of the periods in which it is germinated, the greatest art will transcend the limitations of a particular epoch and will follow the dictates of the artist's "talent and the inner logic of the tradition within which he works" ("Art and Religion," *Themes and Variations*, p. 161). In other words, the greatest artists belong to no particular period, but the incompetent artists will, in a way, be bound by the limitations of the period in which they work. At the same time, Huxley believes that the modern era has encouraged vulgarity and incompetence in the arts because it has encouraged catering to the dictates of the masses, rather than to the compulsions of individual expression. The trouble with arts in our times, he tells us in "Art and the Obvious," is that we are given only those "truths" which the consumer-public wants, and that these truths are handled by incompetent artists. Mechanization has created more leisure and therefore a greater demand for more art; consequently, there are now more bad artists catering to the vulgar demands of the masses than previously:

> It is possible, also, that the break-up of all the old traditions, the mechanization of work and leisure (from both of which creative effort has now, for the vast majority of civilized men and women, been banished), have had a bad effect on popular taste and popular emotional sensibility. But in any case, whatever the causes, the fact remains that the present age has produced a hitherto unprecedented quantity of popular art (popular in the sense that it is made *for* the people, but not—and this is the modern tragedy—*by* the people) . . . . (*Music at Night*, p. 25)

Although "geographical, climatic and economic factors play their part" in the differences among artistic traditions, and although the vulgarity of the times may influence incompetent artists, Huxley asserts in *Beyond the Mexique Bay* that the really great artist is the result of accident, "the accident of an unusual combination of chromosomes and the consequent birth of an unusually gifted person" (p. 56).[2] It is also pure accident, Huxley feels, if the artist is sufficiently fortunate to be born into the kind of environment that encourages his artistic development.

Occasionally, Huxley is guilty of assigning to the artist an excessively influential role. He tells us in *Texts and Pretexts* that "Nations are to a very large extent invented by their poets and novelists" (p. 52). In the same section of the book, he writes that the "curious uncertainty and artificiality of character displayed by so many of the Germans whom one meets in daily life" are explained by "the inadequacy of German drama and the German novel." Furthermore, Frenchmen and Englishmen are more fortunate in knowing how they should behave because they have had superior dramatists and novelists.

If we were to accept as valid these highly dubious generalizations, we would still need to ask, what is it about the artist and his art which brings about this influence? In "Tragedy and the Whole Truth," Huxley said it is the artist's intuitive powers of perception and his consummate powers of expression: "Good art possesses a kind of super-truth—is more probable, more acceptable, more convincing than fact itself. Naturally; for the artist is endowed with a sensibility and a power of communication, a capacity to 'put things across,' which events and the majority of people to whom events happen, do not possess" (*Music at Night*, p. 5). Besides his powers of intuition and his ability at communicating his preceptions, the artist must also have sincerity. This sincerity is attained not by moral intention, but by talent. "A man may desire with all his soul to write a sincere, a genuine book and yet lack the talent to do it" ("Sincerity in Art," *Essays New and Old*, p. 303). If he does not possess the sincerity (that is, the talent), then for all his earnestness, his work will be "unreal, false and conventional."

The artist's powers of intuition and expression flourish best when the artist is faced with conflict himself, or when the society in which he lives is beset with struggle. The painter Lypiatt, in *Antic*

Hay, stresses this need for suffering: "Can an artist do anything if he's happy? Would he ever want to do anything? What is art, after all, but a protest against the horrible inclemency of life?" (p. 102). Mustapha Mond, one of the leaders of the utopia in *Brave New World*, also expresses the interdependence between great art and conflict, except that to Mond, the state of comfort without great art is infinitely preferable to the state of misery accompanying great art:

> You can't make flivvers without steel—and you can't make tragedies without social instability. The world's stable now. People are happy; they get what they want, and they never want what they can't get. They're well off; they're safe; they're never ill; they're not afraid of death; they're blissfully ignorant of passion and old age; they're plagued with no mothers or fathers; they've got no wives, or children, or lovers to feel strongly about; they're so conditioned that they practically can't help behaving as they ought to behave. And if anything should go wrong, there's *soma*. (Pp. 263–64)[3]

And yet the instability and the conflict which seem to Huxley to offer the conditions from which great art springs are the very conditions he sometimes bewails:

> The towers rise, the palaces, the temples, the dwellings, the workshops; but the heart of every beam is gnawed to dust even as it is laid, the joints are riddled, the floors eaten away under the feet.
>
> What poetry, what statues—but on the brink of the Peloponnesian War! And now the Vatican is painted—just in time for the sack of Rome. And the Eroica is composed—but for a hero who turns out to be just another bandit. And the nature of the atom is elucidated—by the same physicists as volunteer in war-time to improve the arts of murder. (*After Many a Summer Dies the Swan*, p. 218)

Art without God, Huxley concludes in *Ends and Means*, is useless: "Science and art are only too often a superior kind of dope, possessing this advantage over booze and morphia: that they can be indulged in with a good conscience and with the conviction that, in the process of indulging, one is leading the 'higher life'" (p. 320).[4]

Huxley feels comfortable in roaming among all the Muses; however, it is to literature that he devotes most of his attention. To understand Huxley's preferences in literature and his use of satire in his novels, it is first necessary to analyze his philosophy of literature. In his essay on T. H. Huxley in *The Olive Tree,* he states that "all verbal communications whatsoever are literature," but he qualifies this by adding: "Some kinds of literature, however, are more widely accessible than others. Also, certain classes of experience give more artistic scope to those who communicate them than do certain other classes of experience" (p. 58). For example, experiences of love and pain lend themselves more adequately to the artist's purpose than his observations of the habits of deep-sea fish. At the same time, Huxley believes that the artist should be aware of the seeming paradoxes in and multiplicity of influences on people and their experiences. Even though a person may be experiencing grief, he is nevertheless subject to the physiological needs of satisfying his hunger or getting some sleep. According to Huxley, there is no such phenomenon in life as unalloyed grief, or joy, or spiritual exaltation. Experiences are not chemically pure, and those writers who seek to make them such are guilty of distortion of reality:

> Mark, at dinner, said he'd been re-reading *Anna Karenina.* Found it good, as novels go. But complained of the profound untruthfulness of even the best imaginative literature. And he began to catalogue its omissions. Almost total neglect of those small physiological events that decide whether day-to-day living shall have a pleasant or unpleasant tone. Excretion, for example, with its power to make or mar the day . . . . Then the small illnesses—catarrh, rheumatism, headache, eye-strain. The chronic physical disabilities—ramifying out (as in the case of deformity or impotence) into luxuriant insanities . . . . In life, an empty cigarette-case may cause more distress than the absence of a lover; never in books. Almost equally complete omission of the small distractions that fill the greater part of human lives. Reading the papers; looking into shops; exchanging gossip; with all the varieties of day-dreaming, from lying in bed, imagining what one would do if one had the right lover, income, face, social position, to sitting at the picture palace passively accepting ready-made day-dreams from Hollywood. (*Eyeless in Gaza*, pp. 354–55)[5]

In his essay "Tragedy and the Whole Truth," he indicates his preference for what he calls "Wholly Truthful art" to tragedy. To create tragedy, the artist must single out one experience from the mass of experiences in life; what is gained in intensity of feeling is lost in distortion of reality. Tragedy has unity of expression and unity of emotion; life, however, contains a multitude of mutually contradictory states; Huxley's preference is for realism rather than for purity. He agrees that a pure tragedy results in a more powerful emotional catharsis, but he also believes that although works which reproduce the paradoxes and inconsistencies of life do not give the reader this mood of "heroic exultation," the mood obtained in reading these realistic works is one of "resignation, of acceptance." Thus, Huxley concludes in this essay, the effects of works which are truthful are more enduring, even though less intense.

Once we have understood that Huxley is not a devotee of pure aestheticism or of purely imaginative literature, then we can more readily understand his literary preferences and his employment of satiric counterpoint as a literary device. He greatly admires those writers who are fully conscious of the curious blending of paradoxical currents in the experiences of life. In "Tragedy and the Whole Truth," he singles out a passage from Homer's *Odyssey:* "When they had satisfied their thirst and hunger, they thought of their dear companions and wept, and in the midst of their tears sleep came gently upon them." Huxley praises this passage as typical of Homer's wonderful powers of realism. To Huxley, only a realist like Homer would have his characters take care of their physical needs before they wept; only an artist like Homer would have his characters go to sleep after weeping; less realistic writers would not bring in these physiological irrelevancies—irrelevancies which, however, constitute the web of life. It is for the same attribute of realism that Huxley praises Fielding's *Tom Jones,* especially the creation of the character of Sophia Western. Characters who do not incorporate the influences of physiological and emotional needs, Huxley feels, are more representative of their authors' subjective imagination than objective reality: "We are accustomed to thinking of ourselves as thinking entirely with our heads. Wrongly, as the physiologists have shown. For what we think and feel and are is to a great extent determined by the state of our ductless glands and our viscera" ("Meditation on El Greco," *Music at Night,* p. 60).

Among the nineteenth- and twentieth-century novelists, Huxley expresses admiration for Tolstoy, Dostoevsky, D. H. Lawrence, Henry Miller (especially his *Tropic of Cancer*), and Norman Mailer (especially his *The Naked and the Dead,* which he describes in *Themes and Variations,* p. 178, as "that most horrifyingly truthful of war books"). It is to be remembered that although he admires these writers as novelists, he nevertheless feels that a good novelist does not necessarily give us the ultimate answers to all of life's problems. Thus, he calls Tolstoy's *The Death of Ivan Ilyitch* "one of the artistically most perfect . . . books ever written . . . [because] Tolstoy is never emphatic, indulges in no rhetorical flourishes, speaks simply of the most difficult matters and flatly" (*ibid.,* p. 177); yet he tells us in Philip Quarles's notebook (*Point Counter Point*) that Tolstoy's excellence as a novelist should be no reason "for regarding his ideas about morality as anything but detestable, or for feeling anything but contempt for his aesthetics, his sociology, and his religion" (p. 377). Similarly, although he was a disciple of Lawrence for several years, he nevertheless felt that Lawrence did not know enough about science; consequently, he believed that Lawrence's philosophy of life was based too much on intuition and not enough on an objective grasp of scientific truths.[6] At the same time, Huxley is aware that a scientific interpretation of life is not sufficient by itself. In *Texts and Pretexts,* he tells us that "the psychological analyst" breaks reality into parts but fails to synthesize these parts into a meaningful totality:

> Under his [the psychological analyst's] pen, two islands grow where only one grew before. He is perpetually recognizing new states, emphasizing the distinction between those already known. In the modern novel psychological analysis has been carried to a point never reached before. With what results? That "characters," in the accepted sense of the word, have disappeared, to be replaced by a succession of states. We know each state very well; but what precisely is the sum of the states? What, finally, is the character of the man under analysis? Of that, as analysis goes further and further, we become less and less certain. (Pp. 48–49)

Shakespeare, Huxley tells us in the same essay, looked at life "macroscopically," that is, synthetically; Lawrence looked at life "microscopically," that is, analytically. As individuals, we are morally responsible for our actions; as successive states, we tend to become morally irresponsible. Huxley concludes in "Crébillon the Younger" in *The Olive Tree* that perhaps a combination of the synthetic and analytical approaches to the novel is the ideal solution: "There is much to be said for both methods of presentation; most of all, perhaps, for a combination of the two" (p. 142).

In his own novels, we see that he himself had leaned to the analytical rather than to either the synthetic approach or the combination of the two. Sometimes, in the manner of Virginia Woolf's *Mrs. Dalloway,* he will observe what several characters are doing at a particular moment; at other times he will chronicle with scientific and yet amused detachment the succession of states his characters are undergoing. This fugue-like technique as he describes it in "And Wanton Optics" in *Music at Night* results in ironic counterpoint but almost never in tragic intensity:

> Juxtapose two accounts of the same human event, one in terms of pure science, the other in terms of religion, aesthetics, passion, even common sense; their discord will set up the most disquieting reverberations in the mind. Juxtapose, for example, physiology and mysticism . . . ; juxtapose acoustics and the music of Bach (perhaps I may be permitted to refer to the simultaneously scientific and aesthetic account of a concert in my novel, *Point Counter Point*); juxtapose chemistry and the soul (the ductless glands secrete among other things our moods, our aspirations, our philosophy of life). . . . We live in a world of *non sequiturs*. Or rather, we would live in such a world, if we were always conscious of all the aspects under which any event can be considered. But in practice, we are almost never aware of more than one aspect of each event at a time. Our life is spent first in one watertight compartment of experience, then in another. The artist can, if he so desires, break down the bulkheads between the compartments and so give us a simultaneous view of two or more of them at a time. So seen, reality looks exceedingly queer. Which is how the ironist and the perplexed questioner desire it to look. (Pp. 37–38)

Huxley, it will be seen, chose to look at life in his novels through the eyes of the ironist who sees reality as composed of a mixture of mutually contradictory states. Thus, for example, we have, at the end of *Point Counter Point,* the assassination of Spandrell as Beethoven's A-Minor Quartet is heard. Jeremy Pordage (*After Many a Summer Dies the Swan*) can think of Wordsworth and his mistress at the same time. Anthony Beavis (*Eyeless in Gaza*) can think about helping to solve the world's problems while he is helping to bring about his friend's suicide by having an affair with his friend's fiancée. Similarly, the scene of the public mating in *Ape and Essence* is accompanied by the music from Wagner's *Parsifal.* This same predilection for ironic incongruity can be seen in this description from *Point Counter Point:* "The bar began to fill up with men in quest of spiritual relaxation" (p. 263).[7]

Huxley thus looks at man and finds him both angel and beast, both hero and devil. It is the juxtaposition of these seemingly contradictory traits that makes for his irony. It is important, however, to bear in mind two points: first, Huxley's irony and satire are serious in intention and tragic in implication; in *Jesting Pilate,* he has stated that "The finest comedy . . . is the most serious, the most nearly related to tragedy" (p. 160). Secondly, irony as the sole way of looking at life came to be regarded by Huxley as inadequate; consequently, it was later supplemented by mysticism. Irony as a technique of showing the discrepancies between the nature of appearance and the nature of ultimate reality was not completely discarded, however; he still employed it as an auxiliary weapon in his arsenal with which to expose sham and superficiality. In *The Genius and the Goddess,* Huxley maintains his ironic perspective: John Rivers discusses reality as it appears in novels; when asked whether reality ever makes any sense at all, he replies:

> Maybe from God's point of view . . . . Never from ours. Fiction has unity, fiction has style. Facts possess neither. In the raw, existence is always one damned thing after another, and each of the damned things is simultaneously Thurber and Michelangelo, simultaneously Mickey Spillane and Thomas à Kempis. The criterion of reality is its intrinsic irrelevance.[8]

It is perhaps Huxley's dissatisfaction with the "intrinsic irrelevance" of the reality interpreted in fiction and seen by people limited by temporal and material considerations that made him turn to the ultimate reality revealed by mysticism; he never, however, completely abandoned his sense of irony.

Huxley's preferences in poetry are also for those poets who write about life as it is, rather than about life as they would like to see it. He particularly admires Chaucer who, he writes, took life for what it is, without complaining; enjoyed all the delights of Nature without assigning to it any beneficent powers; did not allow his breadth of vision to be circumscribed by contemporary events; wrote realistically and humorously; did not believe in self-mortification, was tolerant and understanding, and was master of creating three-dimensional characters ("Chaucer," *Essays New and Old*, pp. 249–72). Similarly, in *Time Must Have a Stop*, Huxley has Eustace Barnack express his preference of Chaucer to Dante: "how infinitely one would prefer to be Chaucer! Living through the forty disastrous years after the Black Death with only one reference to the troubles in the whole of his writings—and that a comic reference!" (p. 126).

Huxley's other preferences in poetry include Homer, Shakespeare,[9] Blake, and some of the French symbolists such as Baudelaire (some of whose poetry he has translated) and Rimbaud. His reason for admiring these poets is that they all looked at life wholly and treated it realistically in their writings. It is the lack of realism, on the other hand, that he deprecates among the Romantic poets. Wordsworth, after the French Revolution and his affair with Annette, lived only the life of Dr. Jekyll (the metaphor is Huxley's), and not as formerly, the life of Dr. Jekyll and Mr. Hyde alternately. The Dr. Jekyll-Mr. Hyde life may not be perfect, but "it is, I believe now (though once I thought differently), the best that, in the modern circumstances, can be devised" (*Do What You Will*, p. 126).[10] In *The Olive Tree*, Huxley also criticizes Wordsworth's Preface to *The Lyrical Ballads* because in it Wordsworth made too sharp a distinction between literature and science:

> "The remotest discoveries of the chemist, the botanist, or the mineralogist will be as proper objects of the poet's art as any upon which he is now employed, if the time should ever come, when these things shall be familiar to us, and the relations under which they are con-

templated shall be manifestly and palpably material to us as enjoying and suffering beings." But who, we may inquire, are the people whom Wordsworth calls "us"? Is it not obvious that the more intelligent a man is, and the more highly cultivated, the wider will be the range of things which are "material to him as an enjoying and suffering being"? (P. 57)[11]

The comments that Huxley's characters make about Shelley are likewise derogatory. In *Point Counter Point,* Mark Rampion, discussing Shelley, states: "Oh, exquisite and all that. But what a bloodless kind of slime inside! No blood, no real bones and bowels. Only pulp and a white juice" (p. 143). Similarly, Dr. Obispo, in *After Many a Summer Dies the Swan,* says that Shelley's "chronic tuberculous pleurisy" was responsible for his melancholy poetic moods. "And most of the other *Weltschmerz* boys were either sick men or alcoholics or dope addicts. I could have prevented every one of them from writing as he did" (p. 190).

Specifically, what Huxley finds objectionable among some of the Romantic poets is their failure to live and write realistically, that is, their failure to realize that living involves experience with evil as well as aspiration toward beauty:

> The poet's place, it seems to me, is with the Mr. Hydes of human nature. He should be, as Blake remarked of Milton, "of the devil's party without knowing it"—or preferably with the full consciousness of being of the devil's party. There are so many intellectual and moral angels battling for rationalism, good citizenship, and pure spirituality; so many and such eminent ones, so very vocal and authoritative! The poor devil in man needs all the support and advocacy he can get. The artist is his natural champion. When an artist deserts to the side of the angels, it is the most odious of treasons. (*Do What You Will,* p. 126)

Huxley makes a similar point in *Texts and Pretexts* when he writes that most of the "nature-poets" fail to consider that reality occasionally involves "a quality of supernatural evil, supernatural ugliness" as well as the quality of "supernatural beauty" (p. 28). These poets frequently forget to write about "the dark malignities of jungle and swamp and arctic desert" and confine their lyrical outbursts to the loveliness of Nature. Thus, their picture of reality is, at best, but a limited vision. Even though he concedes among the Romantic poets a sense of creative imagination, he cautions that the "religion of imagination is a dangerous faith, liable to the most deplorable corruptions" (*ibid.*, p. 59).

As Huxley developed his espousal of mysticism, he found even the greatest poets inadequate unless they could transcend the limitations of selfhood and embrace "the divine Ground":

> The poet, the nature lover, the aesthete are granted apprehensions of Reality analogous to those vouchsafed to the selfless contemplative; but because they have not troubled to make themselves perfectly selfless, they are incapable of knowing the divine Beauty in its fulness, as it is in itself. The poet is born with the capacity of arranging words in such a way that something of the quality of the graces and inspirations he has received can make itself felt to other human beings in the white spaces, so to speak, between the lines of his verse. This is a great and precious gift; but if the poet remains content with his gift, if he persists in worshipping the beauty in art and nature without going on to make himself capable, through selflessness, of apprehending Beauty as it is in the divine Ground, then he is only an idolater. True, his idolatry is among the highest of which human beings are capable; but an idolatry, none the less, it remains. (*Perennial Philosophy*, p. 138)

Huxley's distress at much of what he has found in literature emanates not only from his finding many writers not writing about life with complete truth, but also from his failure to find in literary works a virtuous model upon which readers could base their concept of values. Here again, Huxley may be somewhat inconsistent, but inconsistency he would explain is part of reality. Thus, while on the one hand, he chastises the Puritans for trying to mold literature and the other arts in accordance with their rigid morality,[12] he writes in *Ends and Means* that there has been "a singular lack, as well in imaginative as in biographical literature, of intelligently virtuous, adultly non-attached personages, upon whom young people may model their behaviour" (p. 242).[13] It is not, therefore, didacticism that Huxley objects to in literature so much as the wrong kind of didacticism. Literature should not be a value in itself, but rather a valuable means in the attempt to gain the supreme value: a life of nonattachment to the limitations of selfhood and attachment to the divine Godhead. Thus, Huxley has evolved from the writer who espoused living a life dedicated to experiencing all of the sensations of corporal, spiritual, and emotional reality to a moralist who advocates embracing a life in which the individual detaches himself from selfhood and strives for union with God.

Yet Huxley, realizing that a transcendent union with God was an ideal not likely to be attained by most people, returns in his last published work, *Literature and Science,* to somewhat less utopian objectives. Here he maintains that literature should not be enjoyed merely for its own sake, but that the greater emotive power of the language of literature should be used to achieve a life of greater sanity on this earth:

> First and most important, the writer must perform to the best of his ability the tasks for which his talents uniquely qualify him—namely, to render in words purer than those of his tribe, his own and other people's more private experiences; to relate these experiences in some humanly satisfying way to public experiences in the universes of natural facts, linguistic symbols and cultural conventions; and to get on with the job of making the best of all the worlds in which human beings are predestined to do their living and their dying, their perceiving, feeling and thinking. Literature gives a form to life, helps us to know who we are, how we feel and what is the point of the whole unutterably rummy business. Our immediate experiences come to us, so to say, through the refracting medium of the art we like. If that art is inept or trivial or overemphatic, our experiences will be vulgarized and corrupted. Along with unrealistic philosophy and religious superstition, bad literature is a crime against society. (Pp. 71–72)

Thus it can be seen that Huxley's literary muses have turned out to be essentially moral ones. The struggle waged by Huxley's paternal grandfather, Thomas Henry Huxley, and his maternal granduncle, Matthew Arnold, has been resolved in Aldous Huxley by a symbiotic accommodation.

The Uses and Abuses of Language

*Thought is crude, matter unimag-
inably subtle. Words are few and
can only be arranged in certain
conventionally fixed ways; the
counterpoint of unique events is
infinitely wide and their succession
indefinitely long. That the purified language of science, or even
the richer purified language of
literature should ever be adequate
to the givenness of the world and
of our experience is, in the very
nature of things, impossible.
Cheerfully accepting the fact, let
us advance together, men of letters
and men of science, further and
further into the ever-expanding
regions of the unknown.*

—Aldous Huxley, *Literature and Science*

Huxley's life can be viewed as an attempt to bring greater sanity into a civilization showing increased symptoms of mass inanity and insanity. In this conflict between the forces of reason and the powers of irrationality and greed, Huxley found language to be a powerful instrument. From his earliest books to his last published work, *Literature and Science*, his books contain numerous references to language; as a matter of fact, it is Mallarmé's line "donner un sens plus pur aux mots de la tribu," which underlies much of what Huxley says in his last work. Although not a professional semanticist, Huxley has many perceptive comments about language and its effects on people.

It is in the inadequacy of both imaginative and functional literature that Huxley finds much of the cause of the world's difficulties. He writes in *Texts and Pretexts,* "All literature is a mixture, in varying proportions, of magic and science" (p. 228). At one extreme, he finds those works of literature in which the language is characterized by the objectivity of scientific terminology: "Text-books are almost unadulteratedly scientific" (*ibid.*). At the other extreme are writers like Joyce (he singles out "Anna Livia Plurabelle" from *Finnegans Wake*) and Virginia Woolf, in whom "the principal, sometimes almost the sole, ingredient is magic. The great bulk of literature is a compromise lying between the two extremes" (*ibid.,* p. 229).[14] Not all languages, however, contain this potential for magic in equal proportions:

> From the time of Chaucer onwards almost all our writers have turned, by a kind of infallible instinct, like swallows, towards the South—

towards the phantoms of Greece and Rome, towards the living realities of France and Italy. On the rare occasions when, losing their
orientation, they have turned eastward and northward, the results
have been deplorable. The works of Carlyle are there, an awful
warning, to remind us of what happens when the English forget that
their duty is to be mongrels and go whoring, within the bounds of
consanguinity, after German gods. (*Olive Tree*, pp. 296–97)

The magic of language, however, is not enough. The artist should
not leave out the scientific contributions to his comprehension of
reality. Even the poet can use science if he uses it to modify his
intellectual and emotional grasp of life, the grasp which Gerard
Manley Hopkins, Huxley reminds us, called the artist's "inscape."

Once we leave the world of literature, then the inadequacies of
language become much more pronounced and more profoundly
damaging. The inadequacies are many and varied. As he points
out in *After Many a Summer Dies the Swan*, first, we do not have
enough kinds of words to describe the various shades of difference
of experiences: "We don't even make the simple Greek distinction
between *erao* and *philo*, *eros* and *agape*. With us, everything is just
love, whether it's self-sacrificing or possessive, whether it's friendship or lust or homicidal lunacy" (p. 133).[15] Second, words have
the power to move us more strongly than the things or people that
they represent. Words expressing longing may be more intensely
effective than the presence of the person who is object of the longing. Similarly, "The hatred we feel at the sight of our enemies is
often less intense than the hatred we feel when we read a curse
or an invective" (*Olive Tree*, p. 41). Third, words, if euphemistically employed, tend to hide the basic cruelty and ugliness of the
phenomena which they represent. Because it is this third inadequacy which Huxley finds most dangerous, the euphemistic use
of language deserves to be examined a little more carefully.

The savagery of war, Huxley finds, is frequently hidden from
the people by the use of euphemistically laden abstractions. Thus,
for example, a phrase such as "a war of attrition" shields the
mind from "the particular realities of mangled flesh and putrefying
corpses" (*Texts and Pretexts*, p. 171). Similarly, the word *force* is
a rather convenient abstraction which, by its ambiguity, conceals

the specific elements of force, such elements as "thermite, high explosives and vesicants."[16] And when we employ such words as *in-
fantry* and *enemy* we lose sight of the individuals involved and
become embroiled in a miasma of confusion which facilitates the
waging of war: "What is absurd and monstrous about war is that
men who have no personal quarrel should be trained to murder one another in cold blood. By personifying opposing armies
or countries, we are able to think of war as a conflict between
individuals" (*Olive Tree*, p. 88).

The abstractions in terminology which facilitate the waging of
war also help dictators to keep control over their semantically
naive people. Words like *nation, state, party, freedom, unity* tend
to make people oblivious of concrete reality and lull them into
a state of gullible acceptance of the dictator's policies. Eustace
Barnack, in Huxley's novel *Time Must Have a Stop*, comments
that under the name of "Idealism," politically ambitious men
"drape over the will-to-power" and make their ambition "look
respectable" (p. 55). Similarly, Anthony Beavis, in *Eyeless in
Gaza*, writes in his diary: "There ought to be some way of dry-
cleaning and disinfecting words. Love, purity, goodness, spirit—
a pile of dirty linen waiting for the laundress" (p. 10).[17] Symbol-
ically enough, in *Eyeless in Gaza*, when Anthony Beavis' mother
dies, it is Brian Foxe who is the only one who manages successfully
to convey his sympathy, not by his fluency, but by his stuttering.
Dr. Obispo, in *After Many a Summer Dies the Swan*, perhaps gives
the most sardonic comment about the inadequacies of language:

> What drivel it all is! . . . A string of words called religion. Another
> string of words called philosophy. Half a dozen other strings called
> political ideals. And all the words either ambiguous or meaningless.
> And people getting so excited about them they'll murder their neigh-
> bours for using a word they don't happen to like. A word that prob-
> ably doesn't mean as much as a good belch. Just a noise without even
> the excuse of gas on the stomach. (P. 48)

Little wonder, then, that Mark Rampion, in *Point Counter Point*,
escapes from the confusions of language by turning to painting:
"one prefers the genuine country outside. Painting, I find, puts
you in real touch with it. I can say what I want to say" (p. 250).

If words are inadequate in a person's comprehending the reality of the world of pain, love, wars, they then are doubly inadequate in helping him to achieve an understanding of ultimate reality:

> Ultimate reality is incommensurable with our own illusoriness and imperfection; therefore it cannot be understood by means of intellectual operations; for intellectual operations depend upon language, and our vocabulary and syntax were evolved for the purpose of dealing precisely with that imperfection and illusoriness, with which God is incommensurable. Ultimate reality cannot be understood except intuitively, through an act of the will and the affection. (*Grey Eminence*, pp. 64–65)

What then is the solution to the problem? In *The Perennial Philosophy*, Huxley notes that never before have so many talented writers and semanticists written so much about the dangers of intemperate and ambitious language; at the same time, he sadly reflects that never have words been employed so dangerously by so many politicians with such ominous success. Although he cites this as proof that the problem remains "to all appearances, insoluble" (p. 129), he nevertheless does outline in various places in his writings what can be done to counteract the inadequacies of language. First of all, he recommends that all pupils in high schools be given careful instruction in the complexities of language. Second, he urges both leaders and their followers to try to use language which deals with specific, concrete reality, and not to employ ambiguous abstractions. Rather than such a word as *force,* he would employ such words as *high explosives.* In other words, he would urge people to try to eliminate euphemisms, abstractions, generalizations from language. Instead of saying that a country should use "force" to conquer "the enemy," Huxley suggests with Swiftian irony that that nation say that it will use H-bombs to kill millions of men, women, and children of the particular nation with whom it intends to wage war. People should also attempt to use words which are rational rather than emotional: "let us make the best of rational speech" (*Music at Night,* p. 96). But to speak rationally, people must first think rationally. "To think correctly is the condition of behaving well. It is also in itself a moral act; those who would think correctly must resist considerable temptations" (*Olive*

Tree, p. 103). Restraining one's language is difficult, but this
"guard of the tongue . . . the most difficult and searching of
all mortifications . . . is also the most fruitful" (*Perennial Philosophy*, p. 217).

Advertising also tends to debase language, and Huxley frequently levels many of his satiric shafts at this multimillion-dollar
industry. In his early novel, *Antic Hay*, he points out the lack of
integrity and common sense in advertising. Boldero, the advertising genius, maps an advertising campaign with Gumbril Junior
for the proposed plan to sell pneumatic trousers. Conceding that
sex will not be able to be played up in the advertisements for these
trousers, he is not discouraged. He proposes to appeal to the
masses' social instincts, their love for newness, their sense of thrift
(pneumatic pants will last longer than other kinds), their gullibility for medical jargon. If all this fails, there is always a recourse
to patriotism. Their slogan could well be "English trousers filled
with English air, for English men" (p. 170).

At least in two of Huxley's other novels, he satirizes advertising
because it tends to make people oblivious of more significant values.
As Anthony Beavis, in *Eyeless in Gaza*, is riding in a train, he bewails the loss of the beauty of the countryside as he sees it
dotted with advertisements: "Pills, soaps, cough drops and—more
glaringly inflamed and scabby than all the rest—beef essence, the
cupped ox" (p. 17). Similarly, in *After Many a Summer Dies the
Swan* Huxley gives a satiric glimpse of some of the advertisements
which he found in California:

> Go to church, and feel better all the week.
> What is good for business is good for YOU.
> YOU too can have abiding youth with thrill-phorm brassieres.
> Beverly Pantheon, the cemetery that is DIFFERENT. (P. 12)

In *Literature and Science*, Huxley wrote: "As a medium of literary expression, common language is inadequate. It is no less inadequate as a medium of scientific expression" (p. 12). What
Huxley tried to accomplish was to make people aware of the
potential that language has for either good or evil; what he also
attempted was to fuse the findings of science with the aesthetic

and emotional effectiveness of the language of literature. In trying to facilitate a saner world, Huxley probed the effects of language on people; it is to his credit that this probing is both morally ameliorative and linguistically effective. In his best moments he has indeed achieved Mallarmé's goal of "rendering a purer meaning to the words of the tribe."

Painting

Oh, these words! I'm thankful to have escaped from them. It's like getting out of a prison—oh, a very elegant, fantastic sort of prison, full of frescoes and tapestries and what not. But one prefers the genuine country outside. Painting, I find, puts you in real touch with it. I can say what I want to say.

— ALDOUS HUXLEY, *Point Counter Point*

Huxley's comments on painting strongly resemble those about literature. At first, he felt that the painter should not only paint an isolated experience or a spiritual abstraction, but should also incorporate the manifold experiences of a life-worshiper. There is no inherent irreconcilability between the representation of the corporeal and that of the spiritual or the abstract. In *Along the Road* he cites Michelangelo, who found it possible "to have a complete realization of breasts and also an interest in the soul," and Rubens, who also thought it not incompatible "to have a sentiment for human greatness as well as for human rumps" (p. 139).

Among the painters he admires are Breughel the Elder, Goya, El Greco. He has particularly high praise for Piero della Francesca's fresco of the Resurrection and, early in his life, proclaimed it the best picture in the world. Significantly enough, he admires not only the technical skill of these painters but also their interpretation and criticism of life. Thus, he tells us that Breughel was "the first landscape painter of his century, the acutest student of manners, and the wonderfully skilled pictorial expounder or suggester of a view of life" (*ibid.*, p. 144). As early as 1925, he already took morality as his yardstick for gauging the significance of a work of art:

> It is all a matter of personal taste. And up to a point this is true. But there does exist, none the less, an absolute standard of artistic merit.

And it is a standard which is in the last resort a moral one. Whether a work of art is good or bad depends entirely on the quality of the character which expresses itself in the work. Not that all virtuous men are good artists, nor all artists conventionally virtuous . . . . Bad art is of two sorts: that which is merely dull, stupid and incompetent, the negatively bad; and the positively bad, which is a lie and a sham. Very often the lie is so well told that almost every one is taken in by it—for a time. In the end, however, lies are always found out. (P. 179)

Although Huxley writes, in the manner of Matthew Arnold, that painting, like any other art, must be a criticism of life, it must be a criticism of life which also suggests both immanent and transcendent reality. It must comment not only upon things as they are, but as they are reflected in the mirror of eternity. In this respect, he finds that Oriental art is superior.

His admiration for Oriental art did not develop until he embraced mysticism. Earlier, he had found Oriental art lacking in credibility. In 1926, in *Jesting Pilate*, he criticized Hindu art for not being content with representing "things human" and for adding "the superhuman, the spiritual, the pure metaphysical idea . . . . the Hindus have evolved a system of art full of metaphysical monsters and grotesques . . ." (p. 107). To Huxley, in the 1920's, art was not supposed to delve into the abstruse depths of reality;[18] art was supposed to create order out of the chaos of the daily paradoxes of life. After he embraced mysticism, he began to accept the spiritual significance of the same Oriental art which he formerly found difficult to endorse. Thus, in 1950, in *Themes and Variations*, he writes that the artist who painted scenes from Christendom in the Middle Ages did not get far beyond the superficial backgrounds "whereas those of the Far East painted landscapes that are the equivalent of mystical poetry—formally perfect renderings of man's experiences of being related to the Order of Things" (p. 181). Similarly, although he admires Goya, he comments that Goya was too circumscribed by the ugliness of the world around him and did not penetrate to the essence of transcendental reality. Again, when he writes of El Greco in *Themes and Variations*, he notes that great as El Greco is, he would have been even greater if he had infused his paintings with a more spiritual significance:

Landscape and the human figure in repose—these are the symbols through which, in the past, the spiritual life has been most clearly and powerfully expressed. "Be still and know that I am God." Recollectedness is the indispensable means to the unitive knowledge of spiritual reality; and . . . it is most effectively symbolized by a body in repose and a face that expresses an inner serenity. . . . It seems strange that El Greco, who received his first training from Byzantine masters, should not have recognized the symbolical values of repose, but should have preferred to represent or, through his accessory abstractions, to imply, an agitation wholly incompatible with the spiritual life of which he had read in the pages of Dionysius. (P. 196)

It should be recalled that Huxley did not highly regard much of either contemporary literature or contemporary music. His distaste for contemporaneity extends to modern art as well. As early as 1921, in his first novel, *Crome Yellow*, he criticized the modern abstractionists. He has a character comment wryly that one of these abstractionists is growing increasingly abstract every day; he had already given up the third dimension and was contemplating giving up the second also. "Soon, he [the abstractionist] says, there'll be just the blank canvas. That's the logical conclusion. Complete abstraction" (p. 116).

In his last published novel, *Island*, he again has his chief character, Will Farnaby, express a preference for the spiritual quality of Oriental art. As Will goes into "the meditation room," he is impressed with a large oil painting, painted by a local painter on the island of Pala, who had studied "with a Cantonese painter who was living in Pala" and who had "seen plenty of reproductions of Sung landscapes." The painting represents a "manifestation of Mind with a large M in an individual mind in relation to a landscape, to canvas and to the experience of painting." The features of the landscape are also metaphysically meaningful:

They mean precisely what they are. And so do the mountains, so do the clouds, so do the lights and darks. And that's why this is a genuinely religious image. Pseudoreligious pictures always refer to something else, something beyond the things they represent—some piece of metaphysical nonsense, some absurd dogma from the local theology. A genuinely religious image is always intrinsically meaningful.

So that's why we hang this kind of painting in our meditation room.
(P. 212)

Jacob Israel Zeitlin notes in his reminiscence of Huxley that "the
bibliography of Eschelbach and Shober lists forty-two separate essays by Aldous Huxley which one can definitely recognize as dealing with art."[19] What is important to consider, however, is not
merely the extent of Huxley's criticism of art and artists, but the
intuitive correctness of his perceptions. In Huxley's house, there
are many mansions; his comments on art lend distinction to the
edifice.

Popular Culture

Although an intellectual aristocrat by nature, Huxley was democratic in his interests. When we turn to Huxley's analysis of the
modern forms of popular culture, we find him intensely critical. He
fears that the extension of leisure to the average person will but
swell the flood of mediocrity prevalent in the movies, radio, television, music, and other forms of "entertainment."

For Hollywood films, he has almost no sympathy at all. They
have produced, he finds, either inanity or criminality or cheap
sentimentality:

> The world into which the cinema introduces the subject peoples is a
> world of silliness and criminality. When its inhabitants are not steal-
> ing, murdering, swindling or attempting to commit rape (too slowly,
> as we have seen, to be often completely successful), they are being
> maudlin about babies or dear old homes, they are being fantastically
> and idiotically honourable in a manner calculated to bring the great-
> est possible discomfort to the greatest possible number of people,
> they are disporting themselves in marble halls, they are aimlessly
> dashing about the earth's surface in fast-moving vehicles. (*Jesting
> Pilate*, p. 225).

In 1928, when his essay "Movies Moving?" appeared in *Essays New
and Old*, he wrote that the silence of the films makes hideously
nightmarish the explosive action in them. When sound was added
to film, he found the results even more distressing. In his *Brave*

New World, he bitterly attacks the technological innovations in the movies which enable the almost drugged observer to participate vicariously in the emotions being purveyed on the screen. In more recent years he allowed his short story "The Gioconda Smile" and his novelette *The Genius and the Goddess* to be made into films, but his opinion of the movies did not appreciably change— although he did declare his appreciation for the fine acting he found in *The Genius and the Goddess.*

What he objects to in the movies, besides their obviously inane and violent subject matter, is that they exercise such a profound hold on millions of people and thus incapacitate these people from viewing life with any sense of reality: "Can it be that the standard of intelligence is lower now than it was three hundred years ago? Have newspapers and cinemas and now the wireless telephone conspired to rob mankind of whatever sense of reality, whatever power of individual questioning and criticism he once possessed? I do not venture to answer" (*Essays New and Old,* p. 94).

The criticism he has leveled against the movies he has also directed against newspapers. In addition to finding in them the customary violence, inanities, gossip, and carnality, he maintains that their advertising inculcates their readers' minds with the soul-decaying credo that only those entertainments are valuable which are mechanized, standardized, and paid for: "newspapers are always suggesting that a good time can be enjoyed only by those who take what is offered them by entertainment manufacturers" (*Olive Tree,* p. 131). He finds that the "Dickensian Christmas-at-Home" has now been replaced by an economically motivated campaign to induce people to find joy not in themselves, but in mechanized entertainment. The result has been that people have lost their creativity and desire to search for more enduring values in life. They have become robots reacting mechanically to external stimuli. And yet despite people's feverish anxiety to have a good time, Huxley concludes in his essay "Holy Face" in *Do What You Will* that they are still essentially bored:

> The prevailing boredom—for oh, how desperately bored, in spite of their grim determination to have a Good Time, the majority of pleasure seekers really are!—the hopeless weariness, infect me. Among

the lights, the alcohol, the hideous jazz noises, and the incessant movement I feel myself sinking into deeper and ever deeper despondency.
By comparison with a night-club, churches are positively gay. If ever
I want to make merry in public, I go where merry-making is occasional and the merriment, therefore, of genuine quality; I go where
feasts come rarely. (P. 204)[20]

Rather than spend their leisure time in being victims of the mechanized entertainments, people would be better occupied concen-
trating on their work. Unfortunately, the very standardization
which has taken the creativity from entertainment is also the bane
of work. Perhaps Spandrell, a character in *Point Counter Point*,
overstates the case, but essentially Huxley would agree that meaningless work "is no more respectable than alcohol, and it serves
exactly the same purpose: it just distracts the mind, makes a man
forget himself. Work's simply a drug, that's all" (p. 255).[21]

Modern man, therefore, is faced with the alternatives of the
Scylla of soulless work and the Charybdis of mechanized entertainment. Although Huxley has not deviated from his continuous
attack upon the mechanization of "our industrial-scientific civilization," his solutions for modern man's dilemma have evolved from
advocating the philosophy of the life-worshiper,[22] to favoring the
life of nonattachment and striving for unity with God.

Turning our attention to his comments on music, we find excori-
ating attacks on popular music. Huxley's references to music are
not so frequent in his novels and other writings as his comments on
literature or education or government, perhaps because, as he says
in *Music at Night*, efforts to convey verbally the thoughts and
images evoked by music are "necessarily doomed to failure. We
cannot isolate the truth contained in a piece of music; for it is a
beauty-truth and inseparable from its partner" (p. 47). Nevertheless, Huxley does use music in his novels to serve as a contrast with
the ugliness of the experience he is describing. Even when his character is being purposely sardonic, the beauty of the music he is
hearing remains unsullied. For example, in *Antic Hay* as Gumbril
Junior is listening to Mozart's G-Minor Quintet, he reflects: "How
pure the passion, how unaffected, clear and without clot or pre-
tension the unhappiness of that slow movement which followed!

. . . In the name of earwig. Amen. Pure, pure" (p. 206). Music again serves in *Point Counter Point* to heighten the difference between the celestial beauty of Beethoven's A-Minor Quartet and the squalidness of the murder of Spandrell by a group of British Fascists. First, Huxley lyrically describes the music:

> It was an unimpassioned music, transparent, pure, and crystalline, like a tropical sea, an Alpine lake. Water on water, calm sliding over calm; the according of level horizons and waveless expanses, a counterpoint of serenities. And everything clear and bright; no mists, no vague twilights. It was the calm of still and rapturous contemplation, not of drowsiness or sleep. It was the serenity of the convalescent who wakes from fever and finds himself born again into a realm of beauty. But the fever was "the fever called living" and the rebirth was not into this world; the beauty was unearthly, the convalescent serenity was the peace of God. The interweaving of Lydian melodies was heaven. (Pp. 508–509)

After the murder of Spandrell, "then suddenly there was no more music; only the scratching of the needle on the revolving disc" (p. 512). The reader is catapulted from the music of Beethoven into the prosaic ugliness of the daily realities. Perhaps the most sardonic contrast between the spirituality of music and the corporeality of life is given in *Ape and Essence*. In one scene, there is a public mating orgy while in the background is heard the music from Wagner's *Parsifal*. Similarly, in *Island*, the beauty of Bach's Fourth Brandenburg Concerto is shattered by the presence of copulating insects.

Huxley's musical preferences are chiefly for Mozart, Bach, and Beethoven. He likes Mozart because of the pure, "civilized" quality in his music. It might be said that the very qualities of sentimentality and escape which he disliked in the Romantic poets are the traits he dislikes in the Romantic composers. Thus, he speaks disparagingly of Berlioz, Wagner, Rimsky-Korsakoff, Debussy, and Puccini. He considers their music vulgar and cheaply sensual. In *Along the Road* he compares the music of *The Beggar's Opera* with the music of contemporary composers and comments: "They differ as life in the garden of Eden differed from life in the artistic quarter of Gomorrah. The one is prelapsarian in its airy sweetness, the other is rich, luscious and loud with conscious savagery" (p. 247).

Sometimes his dislike for sentimental music reaches a pitch of intense denunciation:

> how deeply I distrust the judgment of people who talk about "Nature's passion-warbled plaint" and disparage the intricacies of musical art! They are the sort of people whose bowels yearn at the disgusting caterwaulings of Tziganes; who love to listen to Negroes and Cossacks; who swoon at the noises of the Hawaiian guitar, the Russian balalaika, the Argentine saw and even the Wurlitzer organ; who prefer the simpleminded sadness, the rustically trampling merriment of English folksongs to *Figaro* or the Mass in D. In other words, they are the sort of people who don't really like music. (*Texts and Pretexts*, p. 262)

Even good music should provide more than aesthetic pleasure, for when a person listens to it, he may experience "the thought-and-feeling processes of a man of outstanding intellectual power and exceptional insight" (*Ends and Means*, p. 236). Good music gives the listener a glimpse into the nature of ultimate reality. If a person likes the music "sensually and viscerally" (as did Maine de Biran, he tells us in his essay "Variations on a Philosopher," in *Themes and Variations*), then he becomes intoxicated with emotions evoked by the music, and he fails to apprehend its more profound significance. Music, thus, should be used not only to give us a momentary relief from the squalid irrelevancies of life; "the aesthetic experience might be an analogue of the mystical experience, bringing with it insight as well as rapture . . ." (p. 149). Music, like literature, should be not an end in itself, but another stepping-stone on the path of achieving the greatest of values: the union with God.

Huxley has always shown a moral preoccupation with the values, or more frequently, the lack of values, which the arts and popular culture have exercised upon mankind. To him, the arts offer a criticism and interpretation of life. When the arts betray their all-important purpose of giving meaning to the nature of reality, or when the arts become idolatrous ends in themselves, or when they lead to an atrophy of the soul, then Huxley hurls a Messianic warning that disaster is impending and "the Gadarene descent continues" (*Do What You Will*, p. 51).

Huxley's opinion of professional educators was never adulatory. Yet his voluminous writings contain innumerable references to both educators and education. Toward the end of his life, he gave talks to several colleges in the United States and, at different periods, held visiting professorships at the Menninger Foundation, the Massachusetts Institute of Technology, and the University of California, Berkeley. Since listening only to *ex cathedra* pronouncements of fellow educators may lead to intellectual sclerosis, examining what his encyclopedic and first-rate mind observed about education may prove illuminating.

Huxley's attendance at Eton and Oxford did not impress him with either their stated claims for education or their methodology. In *Along the Road*, he comments that he has always been fond of plane geometry "probably because it was the only branch of mathematics that was ever taught me in such a way that I could understand it" (p. 104). Although he criticizes the method of teaching at these schools, he also makes it clear that the methods do not really matter very much because "it is only those rare beings desirous of learning and possessing a certain amount of native ability who ever do learn anything" (*ibid.*). In *Antic Hay*, he utters the same sentiment, except this time he is more sardonic. In the follow-

ing passage, Gumbril Junior is talking about the educational system
in England:

> I have come to the conclusion . . . that most people . . . ought never
> . . . to be taught anything at all. . . . Lord have mercy upon us, they're
> dogs. What's the use of teaching them anything except to behave
> well, to work and obey. Facts, theories, the truth about the universe—
> what good are those to them? Teach them to understand—why, it
> only confuses them; makes them lose hold of the simple real appear-
> ance. Not more than one in a hundred can get any good out of a
> scientific or literary education. (Pp. 27–28)

Huxley clearly believes then that only very few people are intellectually equipped or temperamentally inclined to benefit from
their education. In *Along the Road* he even questions the advantage some people ascribe to knowledge: "Knowledge has brought
with it restlessness, uncertainty and the possibility of rapid and incessant change in the conventions of art" (p. 197). In *The Perennial Philosophy,* he again deprecates the overemphasis given to
culture and education as ends in themselves. Furthermore, those of
Huxley's characters who have been successful in achieving either
a literary or scientific education are anything but ideally adjusted
individuals. Denis, the aspiring poet in *Crome Yellow,* is completely
unsuccessful in pursuing the object of his love and is wafted from
indecision to futility. Theodore Gumbril, Jr., leaves the profession
of teaching to devote himself to the production and sale of pneumatic trousers. Philip Quarles in *Point Counter Point,* successful,
certainly, in profiting from his education, uses the world about him
merely as a source from which to extract philosophical generalizations. Lord Tantamount, the successful biologist in the same novel,
operates on tadpoles while his wife is making an adulterous mock-
ery of their marriage. Paul De Vries, in *Time Must Have a Stop,*
tries to save the world by bridging the misunderstandings in the
intellectual and educational circles: "he had been making a tour of
all the leading universities of Europe and Asia. Getting in touch
with the really significant people working in each. Trying to enlist
their cooperation in his great project—the setting up of an international clearing house of ideas, the creation of a general staff of

scientific-religious-philosophic synthesis for the entire planet" (p. 87).

And yet, while Paul De Vries, whose ambition is to become the *pontifex minimus*, the "bridge-building engineer" of this project, is trying to save the world by this educational and philosophical synthesis, he fails to realize that Veronica Thwale wants to marry him merely for his money, and that after she does marry him she is carrying on affairs with others.

If the people who have benefited from education turn out to be unsuccessful in leading harmonious, integrated lives, what are the effects on those upon whom education has been merely foisted and who have obviously no genuine love either for culture or scientific inquiry? The results, Huxley finds, in *Music at Night*, are sad to behold. "Stupidity-snobbery and ignorance-snobbery are the fruits of universal education" (p. 181). In *Time Must Have a Stop*, the "Triumph of Education" has resulted in "Northcliffe and advertisements for cigarettes and laxatives and whiskey. Everybody went to school, and everywhere the years of schooling had been made a prelude to military conscription. And what fine courses in false history and self-congratulation! What a thorough grounding in the religions of nationalism! No God any more; but forty-odd infallible Foreign Offices" (p. 194).

Obviously, since the educational systems have resulted in ineffectual, maladjusted individuals, or in a mass craving for cheap reading matter and mechanical soulless entertainment, or in inability to prevent periodic wars, Huxley believes that some improvements ought to be made. What is the nature of these improvements? First of all, Huxley finds that generally the kindergartens are doing a good job. They are performing their functions successfully because they teach the children things which concern them— teaching them to take care of their biological needs, taking them to places of interest in the community, making them conscious of the importance of working together on worthwhile projects, and treating them not as automatons, but as individuals who have different problems. Huxley finds little to criticize here; it is after the child leaves the kindergarten that the difficulty begins. The teachers now begin to impose theoretical knowledge on uninterested pupils and treat them all as if all the students were equally capable or equally eager to learn the mass of unrelated, compartmentalized data hurled at them. The result is that the child either never learns or else, if he does, he soon forgets what he has probably memorized, because the knowledge is meaningless to him and unrelated to his everyday world. Huxley recommends that teachers should avoid extremes of too much liberty and too much discipline. They should teach the children decency, fair play, nonmilitary goals. At the same time, the inculcation of these virtues is not effective unless the world into which these youngsters emerge also engages in nonmilitary pursuits and practices the qualities of decency and fair play. Physical education can facilitate the achievement of a well-integrated being if the sports stress not winning, but proper team cooperation. Physical education can, Huxley contends, be more successfully accomplished because the body is something we can see and work with. "We are unable to see the mind, and find it difficult in consequence to understand its nature . . . . What is the mind? The question is, of course, ultimately quite unanswerable."[1]

Huxley believes, in addition, that educators should recognize the individual differences among their students; not all of them are congenitally capable of receiving the same education and some would profit more from a vocational training than from a liberal arts curriculum. At the same time, those receiving a liberal education would benefit from some experience in vocational training as well. He finds it ironic that we have taken from the Hebrews all their "faults" and not adopted the worthwhile feature of their system of education, "the rabbinical tradition of an all-round education, at once academic and technical . . ." (*Ends and Means*, p. 235).

Furthermore, our educational system should stress the importance of inner resources rather than the tempting attractiveness of external stimuli. We should teach the "art of dissociating ideas" (*ibid.*, p. 252), that is, we should train students to be able to analyze the difference between the abstractions of language (as used in advertising and propaganda) and the essence of reality. They should learn to beware of the traps of metaphorical ambiguity, images and slogans—and this training in language could be given by only those individuals who are not under the direct control of the government. This necessity of freedom from control, Huxley finds, is one of the reasons it is vital to supplement state-aided education, wherever possible, with privately controlled schools.

Huxley disagrees with the Freudian slant given to education in some schools. First of all, he admits that childhood experiences are important, but not quite so traumatic as the Freudians would have us believe. Consequently, Huxley firmly believes that inhibition is not psychologically inadvisable:

> The technique of inhibition needs to be learned on all the planes of our being. On the intellectual plane—for we cannot hope to think intelligently or to practice the simplest form of "recollection" unless we learn to inhibit irrelevant thoughts. On the emotional plane—for we shall never reach even the lowest degree of non-attachment unless we can check as they arise the constant movements of malice and vanity, of lust and sloth, of avarice, anger and fear. On the physical plane—for if we are maladjusted (as most of us are in the circumstances of modern urban life), we cannot expect to achieve integration unless we inhibit our tendency to perform actions in the, to us, familiar, maladjusted way. (*Ibid.*, p. 257)[2]

University education should follow the principles outlined for secondary education. The colleges, like the high schools, should help the students learn for themselves. Lecturers, even the good ones, are no longer so necessary as in the past, inasmuch as books are much more readily available than they once were. As a matter of fact, Huxley (when attending Oxford, he did not attend more than two lectures a week, so he tells us) believes that lectures are almost an anachronism these days.

As for research, Huxley is very impatient with the kinds of dissertations written at many universities; "where research is not original, but consists in the mere rearrangement of existing materials, where its object is not scientific but literary or historical, then there is a risk of the whole business becoming merely futile" (*Proper Studies*, p. 134). Huxley affirms that research should be a contribution to the world's knowledge, not merely an addition to its unused book shelves, that it should be restricted to some original problem (especially in the physical and natural sciences).

The curriculum of the college should be well integrated to make the student a person mentally, physically, spiritually sound. Under this principle of integration, knowledge and experience would be so coordinated that the "network of significant relations would be, not material, but psychological, not indifferent to values but moral, not merely cognitive, but also effective and conative" (*Ends and Means*, p. 230).

Antioch College, as administered under the presidency of Dr. A. E. Morgan, is the kind of college that Huxley would have other colleges emulate. Academic study is alternated with "periods of labour in the factory, the office, the farm—even the prison and the asylum. Three months of theory are supplemented and illustrated by three months of practice" (*ibid.*, p. 234). As for the reading matter, the concentration should be on "the comparatively few books that have been written by men who lived, thought and felt with style" (*Texts and Pretexts*, p. 3). What specifically these books are, Huxley does not inform us, but if his selection in *Texts and Pretexts* is any indication, it would include the traditional classics. (Of the authors included, Shelley, Milton, Wordsworth, and Shakespeare are most often used.) Huxley believes that to be well informed, one should read "merely instructive books" in great quantity and in great haste; "To be cultivated, one must read slowly and with a lingering appreciation" the great books of the ages (*ibid.*).

What kind of teachers should be used to inculcate these desirable traits of integration, nonattachment, and wholesome individuality into the students? On the question of teachers, Huxley displays some inconsistency. In *Antic Hay*, he tells us that "Until all teachers are geniuses and enthusiasts, nobody will learn anything, except what they teach themselves" (p. 27). This is not the same opinion he offers in his essay on education in *Proper Studies*. Here he informs us that the clever teacher can do more harm than the stupid one; the enthusiastic and capable teacher makes things too easy for his students. Consequently, the students are tempted to learn (if they do learn) by rote, rather than by meaningful exploration on their own account. The stupid teacher, on the other hand, may be so completely incapable that the student may be driven by desperation into self-education.

For professors of teaching, Huxley's reactions have varied from sympathy to a fierce disparagement. Although in *Point Counter Point* it is Mark Rampion (whose character is based on D. H. Lawrence) who says, "Teaching . . . teaching! Does it surprise you that I should feel depressed?" (p. 128), we know that Huxley shares the same opinion about teaching as a profession. We recall the futile endeavors of Gumbril Junior in *Antic Hay* and Paul De Vries in *Time Must Have a Stop*—and we are forced to conclude that Huxley does not hold out much hope for the teaching profession. As for college professors, Huxley is not quite charitable. From Philip Quarles's notebook in *Point Counter Point,* we read that "it's obvious that excessive development of the purely mental functions leads to atrophy of all the rest. Hence the notorious infantility of professors and the ludicrous simplicity of the solutions they offer for the problems of life" (p. 377). In *After Many a Summer Dies the Swan*, Huxley draws a satiric portrait of a university president in Dr. Mulge, president of Tarzana College. His goal is to make Tarzana College "the living Centre of the New Civilization that is coming to blossom here in the West" (p. 62), a new Athens to accommodate religion, art, philosophy, science. Dr. Mulge's effectiveness is demonstrated in his eulogy of Mr. Stoyte, who owns half of California and who contributes generously to Tarzana College. He praises Mr. Stoyte as another Maecenas, ignoring Stoyte's demonstrable vulgarity and materialism.

Huxley saves his bitterest attack upon professors for his Introduction to the reissue of his *Brave New World*. He tells us that he was told by "an eminent academic critic" that he, Huxley, was "a sad symptom of the failure of an intellectual class in time of crisis." The following is Huxley's retaliation: "Let us build a Pantheon for professors. It should be located among the ruins of one of the gutted cities of Europe or Japan, and over the entrance to the ossuary I would inscribe, in letters six or seven feet high, the simple words: Sacred to the memory of the World's Educators. SI MONUMENTUM REQUIRIS CIRCUMSPICE" (p. xxi).

In his last novel, *Island*, Huxley offers some additional advice by describing the kind of education the utopian island of Pala gives to its children. Will Farnaby, the central character in the novel, is taken for a tour through an elementary school by the Under-Secretary of Education. The Under-Secretary asks, "what are boys and girls for in America? Answer: for mass consumption. And the corollaries of mass consumption are mass communications, mass advertising, mass opiates in the form of television, meprobamate, positive thinking, and cigarettes" (p. 235). Europe is following in the American path, Will is told. Russia and China are training children for service to the state. But in Pala, children are trained for "actualization, for being turned into full-blown human beings" (p. 236). To achieve this kind of ideal education, the children are classified early into the types they are likely to become. They may be "sheep-people" (i.e., that species likely to be gregarious) or they may be "cat-people" (i.e., they prefer being alone). They may prefer to do things (i.e., they may be "marten-people") or they may not. If they are doers, then the problem is to change their "driving aggressiveness into the Way of Disinterested Action." The stress on classification of types leads to encouragement of toleration of differences, whereas in Western countries, standardization rather than individualization is stressed. With those who are "somnambulists," time is deliberately distorted so that they can learn in one-thirtieth of the time it takes under conventional methods of teaching. The training of the children has always the aim of developing the well-adjusted individual with a sense of balance: "What we give the children is simultaneously a training in perceiving and imagining, a training in applied physiology and psychology, a training in practical ethics and practical religion, a training in the proper use of language, and a training in self-knowledge. In a word, a training of the whole mind-body in all its aspects" (p. 243).

Although presumably this kind of education is going to eliminate the "monstrosities" of Western-type specialized and dehumanized education, it does not seem vastly different from the kind of Pavlovian conditioning which Huxley had scathingly attacked in *Brave New World*.[3] Even Will, impressed as he is with this utopian society, feels that in a society where conflict and anxiety have been erased, where children are conditioned into a scientifically oriented euphoria, great literature (and all the creative arts) cannot flourish.

What can be concluded about Huxley's opinions on education?

First of all, it is not always clear whether he is criticizing the British or the American system of education. He talks somewhat fuzzily about "Western" education as if all the countries in Europe and the American continent can be discussed as an entity. There are obvious differences between the European and the American systems of education that are not clearly distinguished in Huxley's comments. Furthermore, especially when he talks about secondary education in the United States, he is unaware that there are vast regional differences which should prevent a discerning commentator from talking uncritically about the "American" system. He seems to be unaware that education in this country is a state, not a national responsibility, and that there are fifty states. It makes a difference whether one is talking about secondary education in New York or Mississippi. Even when he talks about college education, it is not always clear again whether he is fanning British or American coals; even assuming he is talking about American colleges, the existence of four thousand colleges (including the junior colleges) precludes making blithe observations about the entire college system.

And yet, in spite of these strictures against Huxley's criticism of the educational scene, his conclusions are worth one's attention. His was a vast and perceptive intelligence. He always wrote with lucidity and grace. Furthermore, his books have been read by millions of readers, and, quite possibly, his opinions could have influenced the thinking of many of them. He represents an attitude toward professional educators quite common among those intellectuals who tend to deride the people they refer to as "educationists." And yet, although Huxley may seem condescending at times in his attitudes on education, he is by no means entirely negative. Despite his occasional conclusion that both teachers and teaching are futile, Huxley, in his more constructive moments, outlines his plans for reforming the systems of education prevalent in the world. He would teach not unrelated abstractions of knowledge, but principles of living harmoniously, integrally, and meaningfully. He would adapt the kind of curriculum to be administered to the kind of student to be educated. And yet, he would have all students, regardless of whether their ultimate goal is cultural or vocational, combine education in the classroom with practical experience out-side the school. (It might be added parenthetically that some of these reforms have already been put into effect.) He would stress the principles of decency, fair play, and morality—but at the same time, he believes that these qualities would have meaningful effect only if the world outside the classroom were equally dedicated to those principles. It may seem inconsistent for Huxley to find education incapable of helping man achieve a better world and yet to offer constructive suggestions for improving education. Inconsistency in Huxley, however, is a quality that the reader may expect quite regularly. In this respect, Huxley shares Emerson's belief that "A foolish consistency is the hobgoblin of little minds, adored by little statesmen and philosophers and divines." Let us not add "educators" as well to this unholy Emersonian trinity.

There are essentially at least two Aldous Huxleys. One is the societal Huxley who feels keenly the outrages of history and the del-
eterious distortions inflicted upon man by political, technological,
and social-religious systems; this is the Huxley who looks at society,
finds it wanting, and offers prescriptive cures. There is also the
other Huxley who, with the weariness of Ecclesiastes, knows that
the more things change the more they remain the same, that man
is Sisyphus performing a futile and endless task, that involvement
with society tends to yield despair, and that one's quest therefore
should be directed toward self-transcendence in an attempt to gain
a unity with the Godhead. Self-realization becomes self-effacement
and the problems of society are solved through a dissolution of time
and place. In Huxley, as in Goethe's *Faust*, there are two forces con-
tending for supremacy: the corporeal and sentient societal self and
the transcendent self seeking unity with the spirit of divinity. Huxley wants to be a part of and apart from the human predicament.
In his concern for improving society he will occasionally comment
on politics through characters like Illidge, the Communist, and
Spandrell, the nihilist (both found in *Point Counter Point*)—although in no way can he be called a political novelist.[1]

Contemplation of the world of politics never gives Huxley any solace. His meditations on government have made him pessimistic; this pessimism is reflected in the many qualifications he attaches to his proposals for the eradication of the evils generated by government. He seems to endorse Henry Ford's dictum that "History is bunk" and the cliché that the only thing we learn from history is that we never learn from history.[2] And yet, Huxley believes that once we admit the difficulty, we are ready to begin discussing with comparative objectivity the problems of government, which

> are not solved, and . . . can never be definitely solved, for the simple reason that societies change, and that the forces of government must change with them. There is no absolutely right kind of government. Men have come at last to realize this simple but important fact, with the result that, for the first time in history, the problems of government can be discussed in a relatively scientific and rational spirit. Even the divine rights of parliamentarism and political democracy can now be questioned with impunity. (*Do What You Will*, p. 90)

Huxley firmly accepts Lord Acton's belief that the more absolute the power, the more absolute the corruption. As early as 1921, in his first novel, *Crome Yellow*, he already was concerned with the dangers implicit in a government in which the leaders gathered unto themselves too much centralized power. Scogan, one of the characters in the novel, talks about the "Rational State" of the future and predicts that ultimately society will be divided into three groups: the Directing Intelligences, the Men of Faith, and the Herd. This classification of society resembles the "utopian" state in his *Brave New World*, published eleven years later. In this state of the future, the power of the world has been centralized into the hands of ten directors. Every person is under the control of the government. Even his birth is carefully controlled so as to insure a proper proportion of Alphas, Betas, and so on down to the lowly Epsilons. Under this centralized government, everybody is "happy." There are no neuroses, no psychoses, no inhibitions, no diseases, no economic insecurity. Everything has become standardized and predictable. In this state of the year 2600, the only thing to fear is not fear itself, but the threat of unorthodoxy. All wisdom, all initiative, all creativity, all problems have been assumed by the directors of this super-government. If the individual has lost his

freedom and the nobility of individual action, and if the springs of
the creative arts have become desiccated in the process, we must
not shed too many idle tears. As Mustapha Mond, one of the directors, tells us, freedom, nobility, the arts, and religion have given
people in the past merely the right to be unhappy, "Not to mention
the right to grow old and ugly and impotent; the right to have
syphilis and cancer; the right to have too little to eat; the right to
be lousy; the right to live in constant apprehension of what may
happen to-morrow; the right to catch typhoid; the right to be tor-
tured by unspeakable pains of every kind" (p. 288).[3]

It is obvious, however, that Huxley would not have us barter the
trappings of happiness for meaning and value in life. He deprecates
the evils of totalitarianism of both the right and left not only in his
novels, but in his nonfiction works as well. In *Themes and Variations* and in *The Perennial Philosophy*, for example, he tells us that
the religion of totalitarianism is "only an idolatrous *ersatz* for the
genuine religion of unity on the personal and spiritual levels" (*Perennial Philosophy*, p. 11). Totalitarianism leads to privileges for
the few and enslavement of the many. The excessive privilege and
power which flow into the hands of the few encourage greed, vanity, and cruelty in the leaders, and abysmal dedication to false ideals
by the many. The greatest danger, moreover, is not the assumption
by the dictators of all political power: "Tyrants cannot be satisfied
until they wield direct psychological and physiological power. The
third revolution is that which will subvert the individual in the
depths of his organic and hyperorganic being, is that which will
bring his body, his mind, his whole private life directly under the
control of the ruling oligarchy" (*Themes and Variations*, p. 133).

Huxley is careful to indicate that there is no preferred system of
totalitarianism. He indicts communism, fascism, and socialism with
almost equal vehemence. Let us look more analytically at his comments on these three manifestations of centralization of power.
First, he tells us in *Do What You Will* that Karl Marx has been
proved wrong in many ways. "The Proletariat as he [Marx] knew it
had ceased—or, if that is too sweeping a statement, is ceasing—to
exist in America and, to a less extent, industrialized Europe" (p.
216). The working man is no longer the victim of callous capitalists.

Not only because of agitation by labor, but also because of employers' guilty feelings and their realization that a prosperous worker means a better consumer, the worker's salary has continued to increase until today the skilled and unskilled workers make as much as the professional people: "Given this transformation of the Proletariat into a branch of the bourgeoisie, given this equalization—at an unprecedentedly high level, and over an area unprecedentedly wide—of standard income, the doctrines of socialism lose most of their charm, and the communist revolution becomes rather pointless" (p. 220).

The diminution of economic exploitation and the growth of the bourgeoisie did not lead to the disappearance of communism and socialism, as one might have expected; dictatorial governmental leaders have insured the perpetuation of totalitarianism by adroitly manipulating largely chimerical grievances. Huxley, consequently, is more concerned with the more pragmatic problems of denouncing the evils springing from these forms of totalitarianism than with the comparatively academic question of exposing the obsolescence of Marxist predictions. In *After Many a Summer Dies the Swan*, Huxley objects to socialism because it "seems to be fatally committed to centralization and standardized urban mass production all round. Besides, I see too many occasions for bullying there—too many opportunities for bossy people to display their bossiness, for sluggish people to sit back and be slaves" (p. 122). Communism he finds even more objectionable chiefly because it resorts to violence whereas socialism presumably does not. In *Eyeless in Gaza*, he has several Communists among the characters: Giesebrecht, a refugee from Hitler, and two people who are influenced by Giesebrecht to embrace temporarily the tenets of communism—Helen Amberley and Mark Staithes. Huxley's attitude toward Communists is perhaps best expressed by his comments on Helen's dialectical arguments:

> Helen's was the usual communist argument—no peace or social justice without a preliminary "liquidation" of capitalists, liberals and so forth. As though you could use violent, unjust means and achieve peace and justice! Means intrinsically different from the ends proposed achieve ends like themselves, not like those they were meant to achieve. (P. 222)

Little wonder, then, that Huxley has Anthony Beavis, the chief character in the novel, characterize communism as "Organized hatred—it's not exactly attractive. Not what most people feel they really want to live for" (p. 412).

Huxley's attacks on fascism are relatively fewer in number than his criticism of the evil of mechanization in our society, for example. Their comparative rarity, however, should not be interpreted as a silence of consent. Certainly, the points he makes about totalitarianism apply to fascism as well as communism. Furthermore, in the character of Webley, whose prototype is the British Fascist Sir Oswald Mosley, Huxley expresses his low regard for fascism as a way of life and for Fascists as leaders of people. Like Communists, they use violence and hatred to achieve their "ideal" society; like Communists, they too should be looked upon as false Messiahs.[4]

Abhorrence of totalitarianism did not lead Huxley to a complete endorsement of democracy. Like E. M. Forster,[5] he has but two cheers for it. Whenever he mentions democracy in his books, he does so with comparatively little enthusiasm: "My prejudices happen to be in favor of democracy, self-determination, and all the rest of it. But political convictions are generally the fruit of chance rather than of deliberate choice. If I had been brought up a little differently, I might, I suppose, have been a Fascist and an apostle of the most full-blooded imperialism" (*Jesting Pilate*, p. 134). Similarly, in *Music at Night*, when he compares the democracy of today with the kind of democracy that Godwin, Shelley, and other utopians dreamed about, he finds that "Democracy in those days was not the bedraggled and rather whorish old slut she now is, but young and attractive" (p. 134).

Huxley gives several reasons for his reservations about democracy. These he outlines in his essay "Political Democracy," published in *Proper Studies* in 1927. First of all, he believes that most people in a democracy are politically lethargic; they seem to become interested in the problems of government only when the policies of their government affect them adversely. Second, according to Huxley's observations, it is generally the incompetent charlatans who get into office; if competent people do manage to get into office, they do so either through accident or through undemocratic manipulations. Third, the press in a democratic government usually wields tremendous power and sways the thinking and the votes of the electorate. Fourth, because in a democracy more people tend to be involved in the control of government than in other forms of political states, more individuals will be exposed to the opportunities for corruption.

Other causes for his rather mild endorsement of democracy can be inferred from his other works. Many of the major characters in his novels are somewhat uncomfortable when they try to practice the tenets of fraternity and equality. For example, Walter Bidlake in *Point Counter Point*, despite his liberal desire to help people, feels disgust as he mingles with some of the less savory representatives of the lower strata of society. Similarly, Anthony Beavis, in *Eyeless in Gaza*, suffers a rather rude jolt as he tries to spread the gospel of pacifism to the masses. There is something essentially aloof in Huxley's temperament (as in that of his characters) which renders him more sympathetic to the discriminating exclusiveness of aristocracy than to the equalitarian spirit of democracy.

And yet he finds that democracy does have some benefits. In *Themes and Variations*, he says with almost Whitmanesque glee that "Democracy is, among other things, the ability to say No to the boss" (p. 246). Similarly, in *Science, Liberty and Peace* he finds that in a democracy there are fewer opportunities for the few to exploit the many: "In countries where democratic institutions exist and the executive is prepared to abide by the rules of the democratic game, the many can protect themselves against the ruling few by using their right to vote, to strike, to organize pressure groups, to petition the legislature, to hold meetings and conduct press campaigns in favor of reform" (p. 4).

There is one twentieth-century aspect of both totalitarian and democratic governments which Huxley deprecates: the growth of the spirit of nationalism, which he finds responsible for many evils. In *Beyond the Mexique Bay*, he complains that nationalism has been responsible for endless and unnecessary red tape. "A mitigation of nationalism would save the world millions of hours of wasted time and an incalculable expense of spirit, physical energy, and money" (p. 186). There are other evils emanating from nationalism that are even more regrettable: "One of the great attractions of patriotism—it fulfils our worst wishes. In the person of our nation we are able, vicariously, to bully and cheat. Bully and cheat, what's more, with a feeling that we're profoundly virtuous. Sweet and decorous to murder, lie, torture for the sake of the fatherland" (*Eyeless in Gaza*, p. 155). Furthermore, nationalism has become a religion in itself. The internationalism of religion has been replaced by the tribalism of nationalism so that "in actual fact we worship, not one God, but fifty or sixty godlets each of whom is, by definition, the enemy, actual or potential, of all the rest" (*Themes and Variations*, p. 244). The state has now become a god; however, it is not a benign deity, but an idolatrous entity which encourages greed, bestiality, and sacrifice of the decencies of life. Not that nationalism did not exist before the advent of the twentieth century. In previous eras of history, however, nationalism was confined only to the sphere of politics. It did not hinder the exchange of ideas or the respect for artists of countries other than one's own:

> During the eighteenth century France and England exchanged ideas almost as freely as cannon balls. French scientific expeditions were allowed to pass in safety between the English fleets; Sterne was welcomed enthusiastically by his country's enemies. The tradition lingered on even into the eighteen hundreds. Napoleon gave medals to English men of science; and when, in 1813, Sir Humphry Davy asked for leave to travel on the Continent, his request was granted at once. He was received in Paris with the highest honours, was made a member of the Institute, and in spite of the intolerable rudeness and arrogance which he habitually displayed, he was treated throughout his stay in France with the most perfect courtesy. In our more enlightened twentieth century he would have been shot as a spy or interned. (*Along the Road*, pp. 215–16)

The chief evil caused by nationalism (although, as will be pointed out later, not by nationalism alone) is war. Huxley has never wavered in his opposition to war; he has changed his attitudes toward the arts, toward the life-worshiping philosophy of the Greeks, but never toward war. In his first novel, *Crome Yellow*, he writes sardonically that "Those who had lost relations in the war might reasonably be expected to subscribe a sum equal to that which they would have had to pay in funeral expenses if the relative had died while at home" (p. 181). In *Ape and Essence*, the horrors of atomic warfare are made palpably evident; man has reverted to the savagery of the ape and the only "hope" left is "the ultimate and irremediable / Detumescence."[6] War, Huxley finds, is the extreme evil because it has no redeeming qualities. "War always weakens and often completely shatters the crust of customary decency which constitutes a civilization" (*Themes and Variations*, p. 227). He urges us to look at Goya's *Desastres* to find out what war really means—if we need any reminders.

But it is not nationalism alone which brings about wars. The causes for wars are many and complex. Perhaps his fullest analysis of the intricate pattern of war is given in his essay "War" in *Ends and Means*. First of all, he tries to shatter the myth that war is an instinctive part of human nature; in other words, it is not inevitable. He reminds us that the religions of Buddhism, Hinduism, and Confucianism have all regarded war as evil and peace as desirable. He tells us that only the Western leaders (he singles out the Puritan Calvinists as being especially guilty in this respect) have preached a policy of "righteous indignation" and a consequent justification of war. War has existed only because human beings have wanted it to exist. They have encouraged the perpetuation of wars for a variety of reasons: war is an escape from the boredom of life—he notes that there are usually fewer suicides in times of war than in times of peace; war provides a psychological outlet in which the suppressed antisocial tendencies of the people get the opportunity for either direct or vicarious expression; war also provides the political leaders with the chance to secure strategic bases, additional armaments, and increased manpower; wars, like those waged by Islam or like the American Civil War, are fought for religious or political aggrandizement and for economic gains—more land, natural resources, and profit arising from the manufacture of armaments. It is clear, however, that war comes because of many interlocking factors; a single cause will not precipitate conflict.

Huxley notes that wars never achieve the goals for which they are allegedly fought. For example, in *Time Must Have a Stop*,

as Eustace Barnack thinks of the wars of history, he is both amused
and horrified at the futility of them all:

> He remembered his collection of Historical Jokes. A million casualties
> and the Gettysburg Address, and then those abject, frightened ne-
> groes one sees in the little towns of Georgia and Louisiana. The cru-
> sade for liberty, equality, fraternity, and then the rise of Napoleon;
> the crusade against Napoleon; and then the rise of German na-
> tionalism; the crusade against German nationalism, and now those
> unemployed men, standing, like half-animated corpses, at the corners
> of mean streets in the rain. (P. 193)

In placing the responsibility of wars upon the leaders of governments, Huxley does not absolve the people from guilt either. In
After Many a Summer Dies the Swan, he notes that so long as people "go on thinking exclusively in terms of money and regarding
money as the supreme good" (p. 124), so long as they continue to
worship false values and false gods, so long will they be subject to
the horrors of war. Similarly, in *Time Must Have a Stop,* he writes
that it is the gullibility and passivity of the bulk of people that have
been responsible for the evils of mankind:

> Without Susan and Kenneth and Aunt Alice and all their kind, so-
> ciety would fall to pieces. With them, it was perpetually attempting
> suicide. They were the pillars, but they were also the dynamite;
> simultaneously the beams and the dryrot. It was thanks to their
> goodness that the system worked as smoothly as it did; and thanks to
> their limitations that the system was fundamentally insane—so in-
> sane that Susan's three charming babies would almost certainly grow
> up to become cannon fodder, plane fodder, tank fodder, fodder for
> any one of the thousand bigger and better military gadgets with
> which bright young engineers like Kenneth would by that time have
> enriched the world. (P. 279)

What are the solutions which Huxley proposes to counteract the
evils of excessively powerful governments with their concomitants
of nationalism and war? His remedies appear in nearly all his works.
The cures call for action by individuals; by reform groups working
within a country; and by international movements.

The individual first needs to be reminded that he is a force by himself, and not merely a puppet of external circumstances. "What is needed is a restatement of the Emersonian doctrine of self-reliance . . ." (*Science, Liberty and Peace*, p. 56). The individual should, by exercising his will power, realize that he need not fall victim to the lure of false ideals. All of Huxley's ideal characters are self-sufficient. Thus, Mr. Propter, in *After Many a Summer Dies the Swan*, is skillful in farming and carpentry. Similarly, Bruno Rontini, in *Time Must Have a Stop*, owns a small bookstore, takes care of his own needs in his modest apartment, and does not fall victim to the temptations of the world of materialists. Furthermore, the individual should not shrink in the face of threats of brutal punishment. Anthony Beavis, in *Eyeless in Gaza*, knows that it is dangerous to continue his preaching of pacifism; yet, in spite of threats to his person, he continues his work. Similarly, Bruno Rontini, when faced with arrest by the Italian Fascists, does not flinch in the face of punishment and accepts his fate with the resignation befitting his mystic philosophy.

If the individual is sufficiently strong-willed, he can transcend the limitations of customs and laws. The pages of history, Huxley reminds us in *Themes and Variations*, are replete with examples of people who escaped from the fetters of their times:

> laws and precepts, ideals and conventions have a good deal less influence on private life than most educators would care to admit. Pepys grew to manhood under the Commonwealth; Bouchard, during the revival of French Catholicism after the close of the religious wars. Both were piously brought up; both had to listen to innumerable sermons and exhortations; both were assured that sexual irregularity would lead them infallibly to Hell. And each behaved like a typical case from the pages of Ellis or Ebbing or Professor Kinsey. (P. 75)

Huxley realizes, however, that strong-willed individuals like Pepys and Bouchard are the exceptions, that most people do succumb to the influences of their environment; he therefore outlines a program of reform, scattered throughout his works, since he recognizes that the individual cannot wrestle with the evils of a centralized, standardized, and violence-ridden civilization by himself. What strikes the reader as he reads Huxley's suggestions for reform is the tone of moderation. His is not the passionate denunciation of Lawrence, who perhaps hated more than he loved.[7] He cautions us that reform must be undertaken under certain conditions: (1) Only those reforms which are absolutely needed should be attempted; (2) no reform should be undertaken if it is likely to provoke violent opposition; (3) reforms have greater chances of succeeding if the people are already familiar with and approve of the methods used in achieving them.[8]

These collective reforms should be attempted in several directions. As Huxley suggests in *Themes and Variations*, one kind of reform might well be economic in nature:

> We need a new system of money that will deliver us from servitude to the banks and permit people to buy what they are able to produce; and we need a new system of ownership that will check the tendency towards monopoly in land and make it impossible for individuals to lay waste to planetary resources which belong to all mankind. But changes in social and economic organization are not enough, of themselves, to solve our problem. Production is inadequate to present population, and population, over large areas, is rapidly rising. A change in the laws governing the ownership of land will not change its quantity or quality. The equitable distribution of too little may satisfy men's desire for justice; it will not stay their hunger. In a world where population is growing at the rate of about fifty-six thousand a day, and where erosion is daily ruining an equal or perhaps greater number of productive acres, our primary concern must be with reducing numbers and producing more food with less damage to the soil. (P. 251)

In *Science, Liberty and Peace*, he outlines more specifically the kinds of economic reform he would like to see implemented. He advocates a small localized community in which the motivation would be mutual help, and not individual profit. He would like to see the establishment of credit unions so that the individual can borrow money without increasing the influence of "the state or of commercial banks"; he would also favor the creation of "legal techniques, through which a community can protect itself against the profiteer who speculates in land values, which he has done nothing whatever to increase" (p. 57).

Along with the decentralization of economic power there should also be the decentralization of political power. He favors "federations of local and professional bodies, having wide powers of self-government" (*Themes and Variations,* p. 58). The greater the power of the government, Huxley believes, the greater the opportunities of corruption (even though for fewer people than in a democracy), and the less likely the possibility that ethical values will supplant expediency and efficiency as bases for conduct.

The decentralization of economic and political power is best achieved under a sociological system where most of the people live on farms, rather than in cities. Cities, Huxley finds, breed the evils of mechanization and centralization of power; rural communities, on the other hand, encourage self-sufficiency and cooperation. In *After Many a Summer Dies the Swan,* Mr. Propter, expounding his suggestions for the achievement of a more meaningful human life, says that under the new system, society would consist of mostly peasants, "plus small machines and power. Which means that they're no longer peasants, except insofar as they're largely self-sufficient" (p. 122). All Mr. Propter hopes for is that if he does his share in effecting an improvement in society, there will be some people who will be sufficiently interested to cooperate with him; he is realistic enough to admit, however, that most people will not be content with living on small farms: "Frankly, then, I don't expect them to leave the cities, any more than I expect them to stop having wars and revolutions" (p. 123).

Although the "ideal" governmental unit should be small, Huxley recognizes that the increased complexity of the world and the augmented, centralized power of governments make possible, at best, something which he calls "goodness politics":

> The art of what may be called "goodness politics," as opposed to power politics, is the art of organizing on a large scale without sacrificing the ethical values which emerge only among individuals and small groups. More specifically, it is the art of combining decentralization of government and industry, local and functional autonomy and smallness of administrative units with enough overall efficiency to guarantee the smooth running of the federated whole. Goodness politics have never been attempted in any large society, and it may

be doubted whether such an attempt, if made, could achieve more than a partial success, so long as the majority of individuals concerned remain unable or unwilling to transform their personalities by the only method known to be effective. But though the attempt to substitute goodness politics for power politics may never be completely successful, it still remains true that the methods of goodness politics combined with individual training in theocentric theory and contemplative practice alone provide the means whereby human societies can become a little less unsatisfactory than they have been up to the moment. (*Grey Eminence*, p. 312)[9]

I have already mentioned Huxley's lukewarm endorsement of democracy and his penchant for a kind of Miltonian aristocracy. In his essay "Political Democracy," which appeared in *Proper Studies*, he writes that the weaknesses of a political democracy can best be overcome by a government characterized by an aristocracy of minds and character. Governmental positions should be restricted to those who could pass rigid educational and psychological tests. He indicates that in industry, we already have an aristocracy of leadership; why should we not have an equivalent aristocracy of talent in government? Furthermore, in this kind of government, every individual should have the position to which he is entitled by virtue of his mental and temperamental attributes:

That every human being should be in his place—this is the ideal of the aristocratic as opposed to the democratic state. It is not merely a question of the organization of government, but of the organization of the whole of society. In society as it is organized at present enormous numbers of men and women are performing functions which they are not naturally suited to perform. The misplacement of parts in the social machine leads to friction and consequent waste of power; in the case of the individuals concerned it leads to many varieties of suffering. (P. 166)

It would seem, from the tone of this passage, that Huxley, in 1927, was not aware of the dangers befalling a society that emphasized efficiency and competence at the expense of more human considerations. And yet he was conscious of the limitations of a societal organization that put a premium on efficiency alone. In the introduction to *Proper Studies*, he writes that "Institutions which deny the facts of human nature either break down more or less violently, or else decay gradually into ineffectiveness" (p. xii). Machine-like efficiency, therefore, is not the supreme good. Furthermore, his espousal of an aristocracy of minds and character is later subjected to much modification. In 1937, in *Ends and Means*, he writes that "disciplinary arrangements may be of various kinds, but that the most educative form of organization is the democratic" (p. 156). Huxley's belief in the virtues of aristocracy is hardly rigid; he realizes that "human nature" is such as to preclude absolute advocacy of any specific form of government; hence, his caution, spirit of moderation, and philosophical resignation to the unlikelihood of the adoption or success of the reforms he writes about.

This skeptical caution has made his attitude toward the adoption of a world government seem somewhat ambivalent. That he has been long conscious of the need to transcend the limitations of national boundaries is evident even in his earlier writings; in *Ends and Means*, he writes that "It is the business of educators and religious teachers to persuade individual men and women that bridge-building is desirable and to teach them at the same time how to translate mere theory and platonic good resolutions into actual practice" (p. 193).[10]

In *Science, Liberty and Peace*, published in 1946, he is not at all convinced that the bridge-building intended for the establishment of a world government will lead to an elimination of existing evils. He feels that even under a system of world government, "power lovers" will yield to the temptations of gratifying their lust for domination. In the essay "The Double Crisis," published in 1950 in *Themes and Variations*, he is willing to forego his opposition to the establishment of a world governnment if it will facilitate "the relief of hunger and the conservation of our planetary resources [a relief which] seems to offer the best and perhaps the only hope for peace and international co-operation" (pp. 266–67). It should be emphasized, however, that Huxley is more interested in feeding the hungry people of the world and in saving the world's natural resources than he is in the formation of a world government: "If . . . federation can be achieved by purely political means, so much the better. It does not matter which comes first, the political chick-en or the technological egg. What is important is that, in some way or other, we should get both, and get them with the least possible delay" (p. 268).

Although he never actually spells out in detail the kind of world government he would like to see established, he seems to be for it in principle because it would eliminate one of the primary causes of war—what he calls "the demographic and ecological crisis." His interest in a world government stems from his desire to bring about the conditions of peace. He is even willing to forget his objection to the increased centralization which the establishment of a world government would encourage; he feels that if it is a choice between world government and peace on the one hand, and no world gov-ernment and decentralization and war on the other hand, he would prefer the first alternative.

War, in other words, must be avoided at all costs. It is the mainte-nance of peace which is all important. And yet Huxley is not so naive as to believe that peace is the result of mere political federa-tion. When Mr. Barnack, in *Time Must Have a Stop*, asks his son under what conditions peace can become a reality, his son replies: "peace doesn't come to those who merely work for peace—only as the by-product of something else." That "something else," we are told, is "a metaphysic, which all accept and a few actually succeed in realizing" (p. 308). Furthermore, this "metaphysic" is obtained only by "direct intuition."

Because very few people are capable of obtaining peace through direct intuition, Huxley, in his other books, outlines other remedies for the achievement of peace. First of all, we cannot have inter-national peace unless we conduct our interpersonal relationships peacefully. Global struggles are facilitated by the "hypocrisy and stupidity of those who advocate peace between states, while con-ducting private wars in business or the family" (*Eyeless in Gaza*, p. 284). Secondly, pacifism is not enough; it must be what he calls in *Eyeless in Gaza* "positive pacifism." It is true, as Huxley explains in the book, that in times of unemployment people are not easily swayed to fight wars; however, in such times, the people are easily persuaded to embrace either communism or fascism. It is therefore important to establish conditions of a more positive nature—not the condition of hunger and peace followed by the encroachment of totalitarianism, but a state of relative prosperity and peace.

A materialistic prosperity by itself is not sufficient for the permanence of peace. Materialistic pursuits themselves sometimes produce the conditions of war. As Huxley says in *After Many a Summer Dies the Swan*, what is needed above all is that philosophy of life which recognizes the ephemeral importance of material well-being and the permanence of a unitive knowledge and love of God:

> you can't preserve people from the horrors of war if they won't give up the pleasures of nationalism. You can't save them from slumps and depressions so long as they go on thinking exclusively in terms of money and regarding money as the supreme good. You can't avert revolution and enslavement if they *will* identify progress with the increase of centralization and prosperity with the intensifying of mass production. You can't preserve them from collective madness and suicide if they persist in paying divine honours to ideals which are merely projections of their own personalities—in other words, if they persist in worshipping themselves rather than God. (P. 124)[11]

Although Huxley has offered many suggestions to effect an ideal government and the establishment of peace, what underlies all his statements for reform is a current of pessimism about the ultimate efficiency of any attempt to ameliorate the evils of our society. This undercurrent of pessimism is perhaps responsible for the paradoxical juxtaposition of offering a cure in one book, and then satirizing it in the next. For example, although he will advocate the creation of bridge-builders to bring about a better understanding of the various countries and philosophies in the world, he will satirize such a bridge-builder as De Vries in *Time Must Have a Stop*. Similarly, although he mildly favors the establishment of a world government, he will say, in *The Perennial Philosophy*, that what is needed is more decentralization: "since genuine self-government is possible only in very small groups, societies on a national or supernational scale will always be ruled by oligarchical minorities, whose members come to power because they have a lust for power" (p. 125). Again, while admiring the efficiency of a government in which the elite would rule, he realizes that efficiency by itself is not the supreme good. Similarly, although he will criticize the apparent inefficiency of democracy, he will mildly cheer its ability to withstand the tyranny of totalitarianism. And although he will preach the necessity of feeding the hungry people of the world, he will caution us that preoccupation with the material needs of life will lead to an atrophy of the soul and ultimately to the greedy savagery of war. He advocates reforms, but he admits that the achievement of reforms—universal education, for example, or public ownership of the means of production—sometimes leads to other evils:

> Universal education has proved to be the state's most effective instrument of universal regimentation and militarization, and has exposed millions, hitherto immune, to the influence of organized lying and the allurements of incessant, imbecile and debasing distractions. Public ownership of the means of production has been put into effect on a large scale only in Russia, where the results of the reform have been, not the elimination of oppression, but the replacement of one kind of oppression by another—of money power by political and bureaucratic power, of the tyranny of rich men by a tyranny of the police and the party. (*Grey Eminence*, pp. 305–306)

Despite the lack of finality and absolute certitude in the reforms he suggests, the impression that clearly emerges from the reading of his works written prior to *Island* is that government per se cannot possibly serve as a source of permanent value; he may be critical of the groping attempts of democracies to solve the ills of mankind, but he would hardly advocate looking to a centralized government as the god at whose shrine people should worship in self-abasement. Certainly, that is the message not only of *Brave New World* but the message of his other books as well. Granted that if we look at human affairs, we are faced with an almost insoluble dilemma: "In human affairs the extreme of messiness is anarchy; the extreme of tidiness, an army or a penitentiary" (*Themes and Variations*, p. 204). When faced with such a dilemma, the best that can be achieved is a compromise between two extremes: "The good life can be lived only in a society where tidiness is preached and practiced, but not too fanatically, and where

efficiency is always haloed, as it were, by a tolerated aura of mess"
(*ibid.*). Little wonder that Huxley tried to resolve the mess of human problems by detaching himself from them; consequently, his
penultimate solution for the problem which a consideration of government, war, and peace engenders is a life of mystical nonattachment and a striving for a unitive knowledge and love of God.

This gnawing pessimism that seems to erode many of his am023eli-
orative suggestions also underlies his last published novel, *Island*.
The very technological schemes that Huxley mocks in his 1932
novel, *Brave New World*, now become the altars before which he
worships—almost. *Soma* has become the *moksha*-medicine, "the
reality revealer, the truth-and-beauty pill" (p. 157). Love-making,
satirized in *Brave New World*, becomes one of the paths to a luminous bliss. In *Island*, on Pala, there are birth control, artificial insemination, classification of people into extroverts ("sheep-people"),
introverts ("cat-people"), and activists ("marten-people")—reminis-
cent of the earlier classification of people into Alphas, Betas, and
Epsilons. Again, people are conditioned for happiness in Pavlovian
style: "Pharmacology, sociology, physiology, not to mention pure
and applied ontology, neurotheology, metachemistry, mycomysti-
cism, and the ultimate science . . . the science that sooner or later
we shall all have to be examined in—thanatology" (pp. 163–64).
The guilt-oriented patterns for which St. Paul and Freud are held
responsible have been exchanged for the guilt-free lives in which
mind, body, and spirit are artificially synthesized into a harmonious
unity. Yet somehow one realizes that "Pala-dise" is not Paradise.
The book begins with the old cynicism of Huxley: "A moment later
the bird on her shoulder joined in with peal upon peal of loud de-
monic laughter that filled the glade and echoed among the trees,
so that the whole universe seemed to be fairly splitting its sides
over the enormous joke of existence" (p. 15). The book ends on a
similarly disturbing note. In spite of Will Farnaby's belief that he
has gained "knowledgeless understanding and luminous bliss" as
he enjoys the triune blessing of the *moksha*-medicine, Bach's
Fourth Brandenburg Concerto, and the yoga of love that Susila
offers him, his eyes still see the ugliness of a lizard, the copulation
of two insects, and his ears hear the noise of "heavy vehicles" and

"a few rifle shots," indicating that Pala's government has now been taken over by the Western-oriented politicians, with all the attendant greed, materialism, and war the Palanese had tried to eliminate. The last words in the book are *"Karuma, Karuma . . .* Compassion." *Karuma* means "compassion," but "compassion" etymologically means "suffering with." The Utopia of Pala turns out to be a *moksha*-inspired dream that vanishes when eyes are once again opened. Under the influence of *moksha* and the love of Susila, Will Farnaby thinks that "What he was seeing now was the paradox of opposites indissolubly wedded, of light shining out of darkness, of darkness at the very heart of light" (p. 327). The reader emerges, however, feeling not that he has attended a wedding of indissoluble opposites, but that he has witnessed rather a reaffirmation of the spirit of Manicheism.

Huxley died from cancer on the same day that President Kennedy was slain. The assassination and the insane pattern of political behavior since then have given new meaning to the question that Will Farnaby raises in *Island*: "which is better—to be born stupid into an intelligent society or intelligent into an insane one?" (p. 216).[12] Huxley in this last novel of his seems to feel, though with some reservations, that Pavlovian conditioning of individuals to a sane society is preferable to letting society play Russian roulette by allowing each person relative freedom in developing his individuality. And yet the eroding question persists: hasn't Huxley really embraced the very nightmare he was caustically rejecting in 1932 when he wrote his *Brave New World*? Hasn't he sacrificed the soul's freedom for a feckless fraternity and bartered individual man created in the image of God for a faceless citizen created in the public image? Much as I admire Huxley's attempts to help bring sanity into a world veering into madness, I am not yet ready to accept Dostoevsky's Grand Inquisitor's panacea for the world's problems. What is missing from *Island* is the Savage from *Brave New World*.

But one flawed island need not fatally impair the value of Huxley's other landmarks. As one glances back at his distinguished diversity, one can find obvious flaws; certainly his projected reforms for society can draw rebuttals from people of many different political persuasions. His seeming inconsistencies, his almost complete about-face from *Brave New World* to *Island*, can excite the scorn of logicians. And yet, as a prophet (his *Brave New World*, like Orwell's *1984*, still threatens to become fact, perhaps is already fact), as a Jeremiah (note his lamentations that we are destroying ourselves through overpopulation and through exploitation of the world's natural resources), as essentially a humanist who chastises man only to humanize him, as a man whose encyclopedic knowledge makes pseudo-Brobdingnagians feel like Lilliputians, Huxley stands almost alone in his majestic eclecticism.

Whatever else Aldous Huxley may have been, he was not a romantic, at least not a dedicated one. The romantic preoccupation with love and Nature is manifestly absent from his writings. In his attacks on romantic love, he sometimes displays the virulence of a Swiftian perversity; in his analysis of Nature as a source of value, he is somewhat more benign but still comfortably far from Wordsworthian proselyting.

Love

Unlike his friend D. H. Lawrence, whose "only god is the god of the sexual mystery,"[1] Huxley has seldom found sexual love to be either worthy of divine worship or mysterious. From his earliest novel, *Crome Yellow*, to his last, *Island* (in spite of his attempts there to preach the yoga of love), sexual relationships are never considered a source of value. His comments about love in his nonfiction works likewise treat physical love disparagingly. With the exception of several artificially delineated happy marriages in *Island*, there is not a single love affair in all of Huxley's novels that is successfully and satisfyingly consummated; the marital and extramarital relationships all lead to pain or frustration. Let us look at his works more analytically to substantiate this observation and to probe the reasons for this antierotic attitude.

There is first of all the kind of love affair in which the male character yearns for physical consummation and suffers painful frustration either because the woman he is in love with is oblivious of his intentions or because he himself suffers feelings of shame over his carnal desires. For example, in *Crome Yellow*, Huxley's earliest novel, Denis is passionately enamored of Anne; despite all his attempts to make known his feelings toward her, he is completely unsuccessful. He writes a poem to her, expecting her to divine from the poem his love, but she fails to plumb his intentions from the poem; finally, when he does try to make love to her, she gently chides him as might an older sister her brother who is caught attempting to purloin some cookies. Similarly, in *Brave New World*, both Bernard Marx and the Savage yearn to have an affair with Lenina; although she is only too willing to yield to them, both men are haunted with feelings of guilt over the prospect of succumbing to carnal impulses. Again, in *After Many a Summer Dies the Swan*, the young, idealistic scientist Pete thinks that he is in love with Virginia, but he does not want "those huggings after the third or fourth cocktail, those gropings by the roadside in a parked car" (p. 199). In *The Genius and the Goddess*, John Rivers, also a scientist, is conscience-stricken as he realizes that he is falling in love with the wife of his employer, the brilliant "genius," Henry Maartens. In his last novel, *Island*, Will Farnaby, the central character, suffers guilt feelings because he believes that his termination of his affair with Molly has led to her fatal car crash. He still recollects, with feelings of both nostalgia and guilt, his previous visits to his mistress, Babs. Although the utopian island of Pala impresses Will with the "happy" love-making of its people, what dominates the reader's impression is not the luminous yoga of love taught Will by Susila but the fact that the female insect destroys the male after the act of copulation at the end of the novel.

Another kind of love affair causing affliction to the male character is the one in which physical consummation is followed by the male's jealousy and by the female's cruelty. Walter Bidlake, in *Point Counter Point*, is subjected to humiliation and torture by

Lucy Tantamount, his mistress, as she writes to him about the other love affairs she is having on her trip to Paris. When we last glimpse Walter, he buries his head in a pillow as he reads the letter from Lucy. Similarly, Casimir Lypiatt, in *Antic Hay*, suffers unbearably because the woman he loves, Mrs. Viveash, refuses to get emotionally involved with him:

> "Poor Casimir!" she said. Why was it that people always got involved in one's life? If only one could manage things on the principle of the railways! Parallel tracks—that was the thing. For a few miles you'd be running at the same speed. There'd be delightful conversation out of the windows; you'd exchange the omelette in your restaurant car for the vol-au-vent in theirs. And when you'd said all there was to say, you'd put on a little more steam, wave your hand, blow a kiss and away you'd go, forging ahead along the smooth polished rails. But instead of that, there were these dreadful accidents; the points were wrongly set, the trains came crashing together; or people jumped on as you were passing through the stations and made a nuisance of themselves and wouldn't allow themselves to be turned off. Poor Casimir! But he irritated her, he was a horrible bore. She ought to have stopped seeing him. (P. 111)

Sometimes, the male is not even aware of the female's duplicity. Lord Edward Tantamount, in *Point Counter Point*, busies himself with his scientific experiments while his wife is having an affair with another man; similarly, Henry Maartens, in *The Genius and the Goddess*, is grateful for the presence of his wife because without her, he is completely incapacitated; he does not realize, however, that while she is ministering to his needs, she is also committing adultery with his assistant. The list of marital dupes in Huxley's novels is a long one.

In cases where the male does seem to enjoy his indulgence in carnal lust, his satisfaction is short-lived. Thus, while Anthony and Helen are making love on the roof of Anthony's house, their love-making is interrupted by a low swooping airplane spattering the bloody body of a dead dog on the roof. Similarly, in *Point Counter Point*, John Bidlake, the amorously successful painter, realizes the evanescence of carnal triumphs as he sees his body being wasted by cancer. Huxley seems to be implying that those who look to physical love for meaningful satisfaction are inevitably faced with disappointment or moral degeneracy or physical decrepitude.

In Huxley's attacks on physical love as a basis for satisfactory personal relationships, it would seem that the females suffer the greater onus for the debilitating results. Most of his female characters seem to personify what David Daiches calls "the bitch motif so common in Huxley."[2] Females such as Mary (*Crome Yellow*), Mary Thriplow (*Those Barren Leaves*), Mrs. Viveash (*Antic Hay*), Lucy Tantamount (*Point Counter Point*), Lenina Crowne (*Brave New World*), Virginia (*After Many a Summer Dies the Swan*), Veronica Thwale (*Time Must Have a Stop*), and Katy (*The Genius and the Goddess*) are dissected by Huxley. They seem to be completely insensitive to the more delicate nuances of love or the cravings in their lovers for emotional as well as physical satiety. Lenina Crowne (in *Brave New World*) symbolizes this preoccupation with the physical side of love when she cannot understand why the Savage and Bernard Marx are so hesitant in making love to her, especially in view of the many testimonials of other men to her "pneumatic" quality. Similarly, to Virginia, love is a potpourri of romanticized twaddle:

> Real romance, like in the pictures, with moonlight, and swing music, or perhaps a torch singer (because it was nice to feel sad when you were happy), and a boy saying lovely things to you, and a lot of kissing, and at the end of it, almost without your knowing it, almost as if it weren't happening to you, so that you never felt there was anything wrong, anything that Our Lady would really mind . . . . (*After Many A Summer Dies the Swan*, pp. 203–204)

Not that all these women are completely without justification for their adulterous conduct. Lady Tantamount is married to a scientist who is manifestly boring to her; consequently, she tries to find relief by having affairs with other men. In view of the values of the world in which Virginia was raised, it is inevitable that she would succumb to Jo Stoyte and become his mistress, for he is the egotistical millionaire who owns half of California: "it was axiomatic that a man who could make a million dollars must be wonderful. Parents, friends, teachers, newspapers, radio, advertisements—explicitly or by implication, all were unanimous in proclaiming his wonderfulness" (*ibid.*, p. 52). There is also some justification for Lucy Tantamount's physical debasement; at least there is to her: "I came out of the chrysalis during the war, when the bottom had been knocked out of everything. I don't see how our grandchildren could possibly knock it out any more thoroughly than it was knocked then" (*Point Counter Point*, p. 133). And yet despite her declaration that "One ought to have had all the experiences," somehow her attempts at self-justification do not fall upon sympathetic ears. To Huxley, as to the reader, the implication is quite strong that transcending the limitations of one's environment is more admirable than yielding to them.

One would think that inasmuch as Huxley attacks the female sensualist in our world, he would be inclined to treat more sympathetically those female characters in his novels who fear physical manifestations of love. Not so, however. Such characters as Marjorie Carling and Beatrice (*Point Counter Point*) and Emily (*Antic Hay*) do manage to attract the reader's sympathy but hardly his admiration. It is true that these female characters fear the manifestations of the carnal passion; their fear may stem from inherent timidity or from some traumatic experience; they seek to find emotional attachments or platonic relationships with their male friends; however, they experience discomfort when these relationships eventually turn to physical consummation. Marjorie Carling realizes too late that her maternal attachment for Walter Bidlake has become converted into a rather sordid relationship; similarly, Beatrice discovers that the spiritual oozings of Burlap have led but to a physical relationship after all. It is not the sensual longing which Huxley is deprecating in these women; it is their emotional immaturity and lack of perception.

The male lovers in Huxley's novels are by no means exculpated. These male lovers fall into three categories: the timid male who either allows the female to dominate him or else permits his pursuit of sensual longings to be bogged down by guilt feelings and excessively romanticized idealizations of women; the sensual hypocrite who mouths spiritual platitudes while having affairs with courtesans or else seducing gullible maidens; the cynical lover who is completely successful in his conquests and uses these to confirm his belief that there are no significant values in life. Among the timid lovers are such men as Walter Bidlake (*Point Counter Point*), Pete (*After Many a Summer Dies the Swan*), Brian Foxe (*Eyeless in Gaza*), and John Rivers (*The Genius and the Goddess*). They all tend to idealize woman as a kind of goddess immune to carnal desires. They are baffled and pained when they see that these "goddesses" too have mortal longings. Some of the sensual hypocrites are Sidney Quarles and Burlap (*Point Counter Point*), Jeremy Pordage (*After Many a Summer Dies the Swan*), and Eustace Barnack (*Time Must Have a Stop*). The third type of male lover, the cynic, includes such characters as Spandrell (*Point Counter Point*) and Dr. Obispo (*After Many a Summer Dies the Swan*). Spandrell's cynicism is perhaps due to his disappointment when his mother remarried; he then lost his faith in all his ideals, and the remainder of his days is devoted to both a masochistic and sadistic demonstration of what he feels are the world's illusions. He is no longer capable of loving, only of destroying. Thus, when an old courtesan is tenderly admiring the beauty of flowers, he diabolically destroys them:

> "Oh, the foxgloves!" cried Connie, who hadn't even been listening. She ran toward them, grotesquely unsteady on her high heels. Spandrell followed her.
> "Pleasingly phallic," he said, fingering one of the spikes of unopened buds. And he went on to develop the conceit, profusely.
> "Oh, be quiet, be quiet," cried Connie. "How can you say such things?" She was outraged, wounded. "How can you—here?"
> "In God's country," he mocked. "How can I?" And raising his stick he suddenly began to lay about him right and left, slash, slash, breaking one of the tall proud plants at every stroke. The ground was strewn with murdered flowers. (Pp. 343–44)

What makes Huxley's attitude toward love even more bleak is that it is not only the extramarital relationships that end in pain and futility. With the exception of several marriages in *Island* (to be discussed later), there is not one marriage in Huxley's novels that is meaningfully happy or complete. In some instances, the husband is completely unaware of his wife's duplicity. For example, Lord Edward Tantamount, Shearwater, and Henry Maartens are so engrossed in their work (as it happens, all three are scientists) that they do not realize that their wives are having affairs with the other men; De Vries (in *Time Must Have a Stop*) is thinking grandiosely of improving international amity while his wife is committing adultery. Other marriages are tainted not by adultery, but by the lack of compatibility between husband and wife. Mrs. Fred Poulshot (in *Time Must Have a Stop*) is married to a gloomy hypochondriac and tries to cover up her marital inadequacies with attempts at jests. Similarly, the wife of Philip Quarles becomes increasingly frustrated because her husband is more interested in making philosophical generalizations than he is in declaring intimately his affection for her. She even thinks of having an affair with another man just to provoke some emotional reaction on her husband's part. The list of unhappy marriages in Huxley's novels can be extended further.

The love-making scenes in his novels are always suffused with sardonic revulsion. I have already mentioned the scene in *Eyeless in Gaza* when the love-making of Anthony and Helen is interrupted by the dropping of the blood-spattered body of a dog. In *Ape and Essence*, the women of the country wear patches with the word "No" covering the sexually functional parts of the body. There is also a scene in the book in which there is an orgiastic public mating accompanied by the strains from Wagner's *Parsifal*. Love-making is either repulsive or else leads to physical decay. In *Eyeless in Gaza*, Huxley describes what happens to a woman who relies on her sexual attraction to keep alive her love. Mary Amberley, the former mistress of Anthony Beavis, retreats into the stupor of alcohol as she realizes that her physical beauty is no longer sufficiently attractive to keep Anthony as her lover. Similarly, in *Time Must Have a Stop*, there is a pathetic scene between Eustace Barnack and Laurina; she is talking to him on the telephone, trying to revive his former passion by reading to him a tender letter he had written to her years ago in which he had declared, "You have the power of arousing desires that are infinite . . ." (p. 98). But Eustace is anxious to get away from the now arthritic Laurina and to return to the "merely finite" body of Mimi, the courtesan in his room. Perhaps what Huxley is portraying is the fleeting satisfaction of merely

physical love, but there seems to be also an almost Swiftian hatred
of the physical act of love-making as well.

In the essay "Fashions in Love" (included in *Do What You Will*),
Huxley condemns both the nineteenth-century conception of love
and the modern attitudes toward love. The former, which he says
was the result of the combined influences of Christianity and romanticism, was too exclusive, too unrealistic, and too intellectual-
ized; the latter he condemns because love which is too easily
obtained and too unrestrained soon spends itself. In this essay, he
seems to prefer D. H. Lawrence's prescription for love: "Mr. D.
Lawrence's new mythology of nature (new in its expression, but
reassuringly old in substance) is a doctrine that seems to me fruitful in possibilities" (p. 139). He endorses Lawrence's prescription
of love because it is a "natural love" that is free from the artificial
restraints of the Platonic, Christian, and romantic notions. He believes that this freedom from artificiality will eliminate many of the
evils caused by an unrealistic conception of love:

> If men had always tried to deal with the problem of love in terms of
> known human rather than of grotesquely imagined divine interests,
> there would have been less "making of eunuchs for the kingdom of
> heaven's sake," less persecution of "sinners," less burning and im-
> prisoning of the heretics of "unnatural" love, less Grundyism, less
> Comstockery, and, at the same time, less dirty Don-Juanism, less
> of that curiously malignant and vengeful love-making so character-
> istic of the debauchee under a Christian dispensation. Reacting
> against the absurdities of the old mythology, the young have run into
> absurdities no less inordinate at the other end of the scale. A sordid
> and ignoble realism offers no resistance to the sexual impulse, which
> now spends itself purposelessly, without producing love, or even, in
> the long-run, amusement, without enhancing vitality or quickening
> and deepening the rhythms of living. (Pp. 141–42)

This endorsement of Lawrence's conception of love is not without reservations, however; love, to Huxley, is a much more complicated phenomenon than simply a yielding to one's natural instincts.
What frequently happens, according to Huxley, is that most lovers
tend to idealize the object of their love and consequently love an
imaginary person. "They are in love with somebody else—their

own invention. And sometimes there is a secret reality; and sometimes reality and appearance are the same. The discovery, in either
case, is likely to cause a shock" (*Antic Hay*, p. 180). Calamy, in
Those Barren Leaves, similarly speaks of the dilemma the lover
faces: either the lover is carried away by the image his imagination
has created, or else, if he is not in love, then love becomes "a mere
experiment in applied physiology, with a few psychological inves-
tigations thrown in to make it a little more interesting" (p. 69).
Love then is reduced to a choice between the enslavement with a
passion largely imagined and the debauchery and self-abasement
which are the consequences of a passionless love. Where the lover
tends to idealize his love, then the matter becomes further complicated by the lover's penchant for writing letters:

> Absence makes for idealization—particularly when there is an ex-
> change of letters. The writers of love letters are compelled to express
> and explain their feelings to an extent unknown to lovers who enjoy
> one another's physical presence . . . . The constant repetition of these
> generally exaggerated verbal affirmations acts as an auto-suggestion;
> absent, but letter-writing, lovers tend, therefore, to work themselves
> up into frenzies of love for an unrecognizably idealized object. If
> this process goes too far, meeting and consummation can hardly fail
> to be a horrible disappointment. One admires the wisdom of Dante
> who platonically loved a memory, while living with a perfectly solid
> and actual wife. (*Texts and Pretexts*, p. 144)

In searching for a way out of this apparent dilemma, Huxley is
beset with many difficulties. He seems to be repulsed by the animality of physical love-making, and yet he writes in *The Olive Tree*
that the "distinction between sacred and profane, spiritual and
fleshly love is an arbitrary, gratuitous and metaphysical distinction"
(p. 144). He wants to embrace Lawrence's mystical (and sometimes mystifying) credo that love must be natural and passionate,
not conscious or cerebrated, and yet he cannot get so passionately
involved about love as did Lawrence and calls it "that most perfect
of time-killers" (p. 143). He wants to believe that love can be a
source of value and meaning, and yet, as this example from *Time
Must Have a Stop* illustrates, he is always repulsed by the apparent
carnality of it:

They had reached the head of the steps, and she halted to look down, between the cypresses, at the roofs of Florence. Shamelessness at the core; but on the surface Brunelleschi and Michelangelo, good manners and Lanvin clothes, art and science and religion. And the charm of life consisted precisely in the inconsistency between essence and appearance, and the art of living in a delicate acrobacy of *sauts périlleux* from one world to the other, in a prestidigitation that could always discover the obscenity of rabbits at the bottom of even the glossiest high hat and, conversely, the elegant decency of a hat to conceal even the most pregnant and lascivious of rodents. (Pp. 186–87)

Up to the time that he embraced mysticism as a way of life, Huxley had been grappling with the problem of sex and love and had come up with no satisfying solution. In 1923, he had written in *Antic Hay* that "Somewhere there must be love like music. Love harmonious and ordered: two spirits, two bodies moving contrapuntally together. Somewhere the stupid brutish act must be made to make sense, must be enriched, must be made significant" (p. 245). He had searched for years and never found that "somewhere." Consequently, when he ponders the question of the normality of love after he has given up searching for ideal love, he finds in *After Many a Summer Dies the Swan* that there is no answer. "What sort of sexual behaviour was normal in that sense of the word? And Mr. Propter had answered: None" (p. 260). He has come to realize that those who look to love as a source of enduring value are inevitably frustrated. Freud, perhaps, was wrong in assigning to sex the importance he did: "Were Freud right and sex supreme, we should live almost in Eden. Alas, only half right" (*Eyeless in Gaza*, p. 111).

The closest that Huxley has come to a resolution of the problem of sexual love in our society is his endorsing Dr. J. D. Unwin's theories on the subject. Huxley wrote an introduction to Unwin's *Hopousia—or the Sexual and Economic Foundations of a New Society*, and also has commented on Unwin's *Sex and Culture* in his essay "Ethics," published in *Ends and Means*. Unwin writes that the world is faced with two choices: continence and energy; or sexual indulgence and loss of mental and social energy. Unfortunately, the energy released by sexual restraints is frequently used for evil purposes; note, for example, the ruthlessness displayed by the Puritans. Hence, there is great need for a third choice which has never been tried before:

> We can retain prenuptial chastity and absolute monogamy, at any rate for the ruling classes of our societies; but instead of associating these practices with the subjection of women, we can make women the legal equals of man. In this way, as Dr. Unwin suggests, and in this way only will it be possible to avoid that revolt against chastity which, in the past, has resulted in the decline of once energetic societies. (P. 368)

To Unwin, the greatest contributions to civilization have been made by those people who imposed restraints on their sexual impulses. Huxley agrees with this contention but urges that the energies thus released by sexual restraints be diverted along "ethically reputable channels." Otherwise, the resulting energy will but lead to the excesses of puritanism and warlike aggressiveness. When sexual love and hunger become an addiction, the mental health of a person is endangered. When sexual energy is sublimated into drives for power or social distinction, the results are also undesirable. It is clear that Huxley advocates sexual restraint; what is vague is his advocacy of a sexual behavior which somehow could facilitate both a union with other people and a life in which one's attention would be redirected from oneself to the divine essence. Unfortunately, Huxley never actually clarifies what exactly he means by this ideal sexual behavior; consequently, he is, to say the least, ambivalent, if not ambiguous. As he himself had written in *After Many a Summer Dies the Swan*, normality in love differs with the type of individual and the type of society. Consequently, the choice he expresses in the following excerpt from *Devils of Loudun* is more descriptive than definitive: "Sex can be used either for self-affirmation or for self-transcendence—either to intensify the ego and consolidate the social persona by some kind of conspicuous 'embarkation' and heroic conquest, or else to annihilate the persona and transcend the ego in an obscure rapture of sensuality, a frenzy of romantic passion or, more creditably, in the mutual charity of the perfect marriage" (p. 28).[3]

In his last novel, *Island*, Huxley attempts to incorporate love-making into the general framework of the utopia he has artificially created on the island of Pala. The enlightened Palanese seek to combine the best of Western science and Eastern Buddhism. In their society, love is no longer looked upon with shame or lust. It is one of the paths which can lead to beatific enlightenment and union with the Godhead. Children are taught the proper techniques of love-making, and so there are no guilt-ridden escapes into extramarital promiscuity. What is significant to note about the three "happy" marriages, however, is that in one of them (that of Dr. and Mrs. Mac Phail) the wife is dying of cancer; in the second, Susila is the widow of a husband killed in a mountain-climbing accident; and in the third (that of the Vijayas), the happiness is merely stated, not dramatized or developed in any way. Furthermore, it is difficult to take the last marriage seriously inasmuch as their child is the result of AI (Artificial Insemination), and the scene of domestic bliss is presented as an example of the Pavlovian conditioning which Will Farnaby, the central character in the book, finds so congenial—almost. What happens to Will reveals Huxley's final statement on the paradoxes of love. Will is exposed to this "luminous bliss" when Susila teaches him the yoga of love. What precisely this entails, however, is left unexplained and undramatized. Furthermore, the appearance of the copulating insects at the end of the book indicates that the search for an ideal love remained abortive.

It is tempting, though difficult, to speculate upon the reasons for Huxley's animadversions on physical love. One could, of course, state that the 1920's and 1930's were periods of debunking and that therefore love came in for its share of satire. The novels of Evelyn Waugh, for example, deride love-making in a fashion comparable to Huxley's; and yet one wonders whether Huxley's mocking is really not an attempt to shield his disappointment at seeing love degenerate into sex in modern society; it may also be a facade behind which to hide his grief over his mother's death. Julian Huxley, in recalling the funeral of his mother, writes:

> At the funeral my brother Trev and I were on the verge of tears, but Aldous, then at the critical age of fourteen, stood in stony misery. We know now, from several of his early novels, what sense of irreparable

bereavement occupied his mind and soul; I am sure that this meaningless catastrophe was the main cause of his protective cynical skin
in which he clothed himself (and his books) in the twenties.[4]

In a letter to Jelly d'Aranyi, written October, 1915, Huxley affectionately recalls his mother and tells Miss d'Aranyi, "You never
knew my mother—I wish you had because she was a very wonderful woman."[5] In expressing his disappointment to his father at the
latter's dislike of *Antic Hay*, Huxley was particularly sensitive in
denying the allegation that he had offended his mother:

> I can't say that I expected you would enjoy the book. But on the other
> hand I expected that my contemporaries would; and so far as I know
> by what people have written to me, they have.
>   And there, I think, I had better leave it, only pausing long enough
> to express my surprise that you should accuse me, when I speak of a
> young man's tender recollections of his dead mother, of botanizing
> on my mother's grave.[6]

One also recalls the idealized portrait of the mother that Julian
Huxley gives in his autobiographic reminiscences, in which he says
that he can best describe her by quoting from Wordsworth's "Perfect Woman":

> A perfect woman, nobly plann'd
> To warn, to comfort, and command;
> And yet a spirit still, and bright
> With something of angelic light.[7]

Julian also points out how embarrassed Aldous was once when
he discovered photographs of a young married couple taken in the
nude. When one also recalls the similarity of Huxley to Philip
Quarles, the cerebrotonic in *Point Counter Point*, one can then perhaps see why to Huxley love-making can never be quite completely
divorced from the vision of copulating apes and hideous insects. A
tough, cynical debunking can sometimes be a solace to a sensitive
and somewhat puritanical conscience.[8]

Toward the end of his life, Huxley became interested in bridging
what seemed to him a painful and unnecessary hostility between
opposing camps—science and literature. Western civilization and
Eastern quietism, the products of technology and the insights of

religion, physical passion and the yoga of love. He tried seriously
to construct these bridges—especially in his last two books, *Island*
and *Literature and Science*—but the constructions turn out to be
precariously flimsy. Perhaps he tried to do intellectually something
he found emotionally impossible. No wonder poor Will Farnaby
takes mushroom-derived drugs to help him achieve an otherwise
unattainable euphoria.

What can then be said in summarizing Huxley's attitudes toward
love as a source of value? First, the act of love-making is to him personally revolting. Second, sexual love should be restrained because
love is a thirst which can never be adequately quenched and because it destroys the energies needed for more civilized activities.
Third, those who tend to look to their love as a source of permanent
satisfaction are doomed to eventual disappointment. Fourth, although there is no marriage in any of Huxley's novels which serves
as a source of permanent bliss to either husband or wife (with the
exception of the marriages in *Island,* but these are presented more
with tongue in cheek than with heartfelt conviction), those who
seek satisfaction by extramarital affairs are also faced with ultimate
frustration. At best, sexual love is to be looked upon as a kind of
inevitable evil, an evil best combated either by continence and
sublimation, or by careful restraints of the sexual impulse.

In *Grey Eminence*, Huxley cites the following excerpt from Matthew Arnold's "The Buried Life":

> Only—but this is rare—
> When a beloved hand is laid in ours . . . ,
> A bolt is shot back in our breast; . . .
> A man becomes aware of his life's flow
> And hears its winding murmur . . . ,
> And then he thinks he knows
> The hills where his life rose
> And the sea where it goes. (P. 75)

Huxley likes the clause "he thinks he knows" because Arnold thereby admitted realistically that perhaps he did not know. Browning,
Huxley tells us, would have been more optimistically definite and
would have asserted that he did know that in love is found the
meaning in life. Huxley concludes: "Those who enjoy the natural

ecstasies of passion and affection do not know; they merely think they know" (p. 76). His preference of Arnold's skepticism to Browning's optimism reveals Huxley's view of love as being no longer a meaningful source of value for the modern world. His *Island* in no way affects the continent of Eros that he had earlier constructed.

Nature

Nature plays a comparatively unimportant role in Huxley's works. The sea, which plays so symbolic a role in Virginia Woolf's novels, never appears in his works; the contrast between the unspoiled beauties of the country and the corrupting influences of the city sometimes serves as background in some of the novels of D. H. Lawrence and E. M. Forster. In Huxley's novels, Nature is almost completely absent; to this extent, he might be called an urban novelist. He is primarily concerned with the life in the cities, the sophisticated conversations held in drawing rooms. Nearly all his characters are members of the upper classes and of the genteel professions. There are no laborers or rustics in his works; his dialogue never has the Hardy earthiness; his characters speak aphoristically. The forces of Nature play no significant role either in the setting or the characterization of his novels. And yet, in a sense, Huxley does analyze Nature as a source of value: he first attacks that romantic conception of Nature which seeks to find in Nature the source of wisdom and beneficence; he also warns us that if we are to continue the callous exploitation of Nature's resources, then we are faced with a far graver crisis than the political struggle of opposing ideologies.

Huxley's antipathy toward the romantic conception of Nature dates back to the 1920's. In *Jesting Pilate*, he observes: "If Wordsworth had been compelled to spend a few years in Borneo, would he have loved nature as much as he loved her on the banks of Rydal Water?" He answers this question by stating that if *The Excursion* had "equatorial Africa" as a background instead of Westmoreland, "old William's mild pantheism would have been, I suspect, a little modified" (p. 259).

In his essay "Francis and Grigory," published in *Do What You Will* in 1929, Huxley castigates those who are dedicated to "Nature-worship." He praises the Greeks who "were not Wordsworthians or Meredithians; they never went for walking tours nor wasted their energies unnecessarily climbing to the tops of mountains" (p. 157). But it should be noted that a few pages later he writes, without being aware of the apparent inconsistency: "A man misses something by not establishing a participative and living relationship with the non-human world of animals and plants, landscapes and stars and seasons" (pp. 165–66).

Perhaps the clearest expression of his objection to the Wordsworthian conception of Nature is found in his essay "Wordsworth in the Tropics," published in *Do What You Will*. In it, he berates Wordsworth for giving an essentially false, anthropomorphic interpretation of Nature. He writes that in his youth, Wordsworth did understand and follow the instinctive urges of Nature; after he was thirty years old, Wordsworth modified the mysteries and the strangeness of Nature to fit his metaphysical, Anglican system of philosophy. Instead of Nature being the teacher, Nature became a pupil, taking lessons from Wordsworth. "The Wordsworthian adoration of Nature" was defective for two reasons: first, it is possible only in countries where Nature's forces have been conquered by man; secondly, it can be possessed only by those who, like Wordsworth, "are prepared to falsify their immediate intuitions of Nature." To Huxley, the word *river* connotes *bridge;* the word *plain* connotes *farming and roads.* The same kind of verbal association is characteristic of other objects in Nature:

> The corollary of mountain is tunnel; of swamp, an embankment; of distance, a railway. At latitude zero, however, the obvious is not the same as with us. Rivers imply wading, swimming, alligators. Plains mean swamps, forests, fevers. Mountains are either dangerous or impassable. To travel is to hack one's way laboriously through a tangled, prickly, and venomous darkness. "God made the country," said Cowper, in his rather too blank verse. In New Guinea he would have had his doubts; he would have longed for the man-made town. (P. 116)

In *Texts and Pretexts,* Huxley again attacks this anthropomorphic deification of Nature. This adoration of Nature is possible, Huxley reminds us, in civilized and temperate countries, but not very likely in less temperate climates. Even in temperate countries, Nature occasionally erupts violently and "reveals herself as a being either marvellously and beautifully, or else, more often, terrifyingly alien from man" (p. 60). He attacks Wordsworth again for falsifying Nature but does praise Wordsworth's courage in one instance: he quotes a passage from Wordsworth's *The Prelude* (the one in which Wordsworth is rowing in a small boat and is troubled by "a huge peak, black and huge") and says that very few "nature-poets" would have been sufficiently courageous "to admit that their goddess lives with an unknown mode of being, that she sometimes reveals herself, unequivocally as the most terrifying and malignantly alien of deities" (p. 63). In *Beyond the Mexique Bay*, he makes a similar point about the potential hostility of Nature. People, he writes, enjoy mountain climbing only because they have the comforting realization that after they get through with their sport, they can return to their towns, their buses, and their civilized refinements. Where Nature has to be fought bitterly for man's survival, then the "sublimities of Nature . . . come to be regarded, not with adoration, but with rage, not as evidences of God's handiwork, but as booby-traps put in your way by some insufferably waggish devil" (p. 128).

Occasionally, however, Huxley betrays the same longing to find in Nature the symbolic meaning which he deprecates in Wordsworth. Thus, for example, as early as in 1925, we find in *Those Barren Leaves* the following description of Calamy as he is contemplating retiring to the mountains: "Perhaps he had been a fool, thought Calamy. But looking at that shining peak, he was somehow reassured" (p. 380). It is true that Huxley does not frequently allude to Nature in such terms. It is far more typical of Huxley to write: "Flowers are beautiful. But flowers, we discover, grow from dung" (*Texts and Pretexts*, p. 180). But that hidden Wordsworthian yearning to find reassurance in Nature does manifest itself, even if only very rarely: "as long as the desert lilies continue to make their appearance, as long as these denizens of the world of space remain capable of repeating their miracle, all is not lost even in our dismal universe of history. In the teeth of our most determined efforts at self-destruction, life may be trusted to save us from ourselves."[9]

It is not often that we find Huxley looking to Nature for solace. He is much more concerned with the exploitation by man of Nature's resources. In *Point Counter Point*, Lord Edward Tantamount, the biologist, warns Webley, the Fascist, that politicians would be wiser in paying less attention to political and technological progress and more attention to the conservation of natural resources: "You ought to take a few lessons in my subject. Physical biology. Progress, indeed! What do you propose to do about phosphorus, for example?" (p. 68). In his essay "The Double Crisis" (*Themes and Variations*), in *Science, Liberty and Peace*, and in sections of many of his other works, he constantly makes reference to the need for stopping the unscientific, greedy exploitation of natural resources. He is much concerned with the uncontrolled growth of population throughout the world and with the continued waste of our natural resources. He warns us that unless we start controlling both the growth of population and the waste of these natural resources, we are faced not only with eventual starvation but with the inevitability of continuous warfare. He resorts in "The Double Crisis" to historical analogies to impress upon us the necessity of treating Nature with wisdom and restraint:

> The Greeks, for example, knew very well that hubris against the essentially divine order of Nature would be followed by its appropriate nemesis. The Chinese taught that the Tao, or indwelling Logos, was present on every level from the physical and the biological up to the spiritual; and they knew that outrages against Tao, in Nature no less than in man, would lead to fatal results. We have to recapture some of this old lost wisdom. (P. 271)[10]

Of all the sources of value which Huxley writes about in his works, Nature is perhaps the most scantily treated. Like Charles Lamb, Huxley prefers the city to the country. When he does discuss Nature, he generally attacks the writers who have found in Nature the source of wisdom and beneficence; it should be noted, however, that Huxley does occasionally, in his more desolate moments, look to Nature for at least solace, if not philosophical guidance. He wants Nature to be treated with the kind of restraint and wisdom which would enable man to achieve the highest value—knowledge and love of God; he feels that Nature is no longer a source of value, but a valuable means to an end.

To Huxley, physical love and Nature no longer were satisfying sources of meaning. With the mystic's detachment, he turned to drink at other founts of inspiration. He became intoxicated with a Buddhist-like unitive love for God, but as is clear in his last writings, the seeming alienation from Eros and Pan ultimately was a temporary estrangement, not a final divorce. Huxley looked at love and Nature not as a typical romantic but rather as a man with a double vision—the eye of a mystic and the eye of an ecologist. It is debatable whether this optic marriage is either possible or compatible.

But even if I could be Shakespeare,
I think I should still choose to be
Faraday.

—ALDOUS HUXLEY, *Along the Road*

No one will deny the impact that science has had on the twentieth century. The effects of its technology are too demonstrably evident in all parts of the world to warrant any detailed substantiation. No such unanimity exists, however, when we try to assess the worth of this impact. While Bertrand Russell was claiming, in his earlier writings, that the methodology of science would solve many of mankind's problems if applied to all areas of human conduct, writers like D. H. Lawrence were denouncing science and the mechanization it has brought into our lives.[1] In between these extremes, others, like Julian Huxley, J. B. S. Haldane, and Dean Inge, have tried to reconcile the values of science with those of religion; they have maintained that although science can improve our material world, it remains for religion to evaluate human conduct and to enrich our spiritual awareness of existence.[2] In recent years, the debate over the impact of science on our world has become more intense. Bertrand Russell, losing some of his earlier enthusiasm for the ability of science to act as a panacea for many of the world's ills, contended that "the present state of the world and the fear of an atomic war show that scientific progress without a corresponding moral and political progress may only increase the magnitude of the disaster that misdirected skill may bring about."[3] The Snow-

Leavis "two cultures" controversy (which seems to be an inferior reenactment of the nineteenth-century debate between T. H. Huxley and Matthew Arnold over the relative merits of science and literature) shows that the examination of science as a source of value has continued unabated.[4]

Aldous Huxley has actually espoused several positions on science: he has defended it, he has attacked it, and he has also tried to arrive at a solution that would maintain the contributions of applied science while simultaneously eliminating the methodology of science from the spheres of philosophy and religion. Huxley's original love was science, not literature. Were it not for his very poor eyesight, he might well have followed in the footsteps of his famous paternal grandfather, T. H. Huxley, and his equally famous brother, Julian. Early in his work, in *Along the Road*, Huxley expresses disappointment at his failure to become a scientist:

> If I could be born again and choose what I should be in my next existence, I should desire to be a man of science—not accidentally but by nature, inevitably a man of science. Fate might offer other alternatives—to have power of wealth, be a king or a statesman. These glittering temptations I should have small difficulty in rejecting; for my objection to the irritating turmoil of practical life is even stronger than my love of money or power, and since these cannot be obtained without plunging into practical life, I can sacrifice them cheerfully. It is easy to make a virtue of psychological necessity. The only thing that might make me hesitate would be an offer by fate of artistic genius. But even if I could be Shakespeare, I think I should still choose to be Faraday. (P. 223)

Huxley preferred Faraday to Shakespeare because the artist deals primarily with human emotions, but the scientist works chiefly with nonhuman phenomena, and "I personally would rather be subdued to intellectual contemplation than to emotion, would rather use my soul professionally for knowing than for feeling" (p. 225).

Physical inability to become a scientist did not prevent him, however, from appraising science as a source of value to our civilization. His comments on science can be divided into three categories: first, his rejection of science as an adequate means of evaluating ethics, aesthetics, and the nature of reality; second, his attack on science for contributing significantly to the loss of creative individuality and liberty and to the intensification of standardization and mediocrity; third, his suggestions for utilizing science in helping to solve the world's ecological problems and in the attainment of man's ultimate end: a unitive knowledge and love of God.

Despite his declared love for science as a profession, Huxley has never veered from his belief that science is inadequate in explaining all of life's intricate problems. As early as 1926, in *Jesting Pilate*, he was already blaming science for the disappearance of values from our civilization:

> In Europe such attempts as have been made to alter the existing standard of values have generally taken the form of denials of the existence of values. Our belief that things possess value is due to an immediate sense of intuition; we feel, and feeling we know, that things have value. If men have doubted the real existence of values, that is because they have not trusted their own immediate and intuitive conviction. They have required an intellectual, a logical and "scientific" proof of their existence. Now such a proof is not easily found at the best of times. But when you start your argumentation from the premises laid down by scientific materialism, it simply cannot be discovered. Indeed, any argument starting from these premises must infallibly end in a denial of the real existence of values. (Pp. 306–307)

In his essay "One and Many," published in *Do What You Will*, he further elaborates on the inadequacy of science. He writes that "Science is no 'truer' than common-sense or lunacy, than art or religion" (p. 3). It enables us to perceive the world of the senses but tells us nothing about "the real nature of the world to which our experiences are supposed to refer." Science, furthermore, actually isolates us from the far more meaningful world of inner experience. To the extent that art does interpret the world of psychological experiences, it is far superior to science as a method of discovering the nature of reality. He makes the same observation in *Ends and Means* when he comments that human problems are too complex to be solved simply by measurable means; furthermore, science has excluded aesthetic and religious matters from its consideration. In "Writers and Readers," published in *The Olive Tree*, he again blames science for turning men from religion to preoccupation with materialism:

> By discrediting the Bible and providing a more obviously useful sub-stitute for the study of the dead languages, triumphant science has completed the work of spiritual disunion which was begun when it undermined belief in transcendental religion and so prepared the way for the positivistic superstitions of nationalism and dictator-worship. It remains to be seen whether it will discover a way to put this shattered Humpty-Dumpty together again. (P. 46)

When Huxley uses the term *science*, he does not make quite clear whether he would add psychology and social sciences to physics, chemistry, biology, and the other natural sciences. But he does not think very highly of twentieth-century psychology either. In *The Perennial Philosophy*, he writes: "One of the most extraordinary, because most gratuitous, pieces of twentieth-century vanity is the assumption that nobody knew anything about psychology before the days of Freud" (p. 114).[5] In Huxley's opinion, people like Bud-dha, St. Augustine, Pascal, La Rochefoucauld, and Machiavelli knew more about the hidden motivations of human conduct than twentieth-century psychologists. What he says in *The Perennial Philosophy* about modern psychologists could apply with equal validity to modern scientists:

> all these men, even La Rochefoucauld, even Machiavelli, were aware of certain facts which twentieth-century psychologists have chosen to ignore—the fact that human nature is tripartite, consisting of a spirit as well as of a mind and body; the fact that we live on the border-line between two worlds, the temporal and the eternal, the physical-vital-human and the divine; the fact that, though nothing in himself, man is "a nothing surrounded by God, indigent of God, capa-ble of God and filled with God, if he so desires." (P. 115)

In his nonfiction, Huxley attacks the inability of science to com-prehend the complexities of reality; in his novels, he satirizes the immaturity of the scientists: Shearwater (*Antic Hay*), Lord Ed-ward Tantamount (*Point Counter Point*), Pete (*After Many a Summer Dies the Swan*), Dr. Poole (*Ape and Essence*), Henry Maartens (*The Genius and the Goddess*), and a few others; they are all childish cuckolds. Thus, Shearwater, the physiologist, is so immersed in experimenting with the human kidneys that he is completely oblivious of his wife's infidelity. Similarly, Lord Edward Tantamount, the biologist, buries himself in his laboratory, incapable of coping with the world of human relationships outside the laboratory. Pete, the young scientist who is helping Dr. Obispo to find means to prolong human life, does not know how to pursue successfully his employer's mistress; the complete futility of his situation is symbolized by his death—he is shot by his employer, who mistakes him for someone else. Dr. Poole, the botanist in *Ape and Essence*, is characterized as an emotional fledgling who has relied too much on maternal direction. Henry Maartens is supposed to be one of the world's leading scientists, but he has to rely on his wife to run his life for him; she too proves unfaithful to him although he is not aware of her infidelity. Obviously, the inadequacy which characterizes all these scientists is also typical of most of Huxley's other characters; what Huxley is doing essentially is to expose the inadequacy not only of science as a way of life, but of other misdirected sources of value as well—hedonism, intellectualism, false spirituality, and sentimentalism. In a sense, most of Huxley's scientists could be classified as cerebrotonics. But they are cerebrotonics in a very special way; they might be classified as "scientific cerebrotonics" whereas people such as Philip Quarles, Walter Bidlake, Denis Stone might be called "artistic cerebrotonics." Huxley uses both his "artistic" and "scientific" cerebrotonics to demonstrate the inadequacy of the arts and sciences in enabling one to live a harmonious and satisfying life.

In his attitude toward applied science or technology, Huxley has not been very consistent. In 1926, in *Jesting Pilate*, he vigorously embraced the materialism to which science has contributed:

> It is for its "materialism" that our Western civilisation is generally blamed. Wrongly, I think. For materialism—if materialism means a preoccupation with the actual world in which we live—is something wholly admirable. If Western civilisation is unsatisfactory, that is not because we are interested in the actual world; it is because the majority of us are interested in such an absurdly small part of it. (P. 129)

In the same section from *Jesting Pilate*, he advocates "more materialism and not, as false prophets from the East assert, more 'spirituality'—more interest in this world, not in the other" (pp. 129–30). In view of his later rejection of materialism and his espousal of mysticism, it is puzzling to hear him advocating more interest in this world and less preoccupation with "The Other World—the world of metaphysics and religion." It is even more incongruous in view of the attack he had leveled against the "goddess of Applied Science" in his earliest novel, *Crome Yellow*, published in 1921:

> With the gramophone, the cinema, and the automatic pistol, the goddess of Applied Science has presented the world with another gift, more precious even than these—the means of dissociating love from propagation. . . . An impersonal generation will take the place of Nature's hideous system. In vast state incubators, rows upon rows of gravid bottles will supply the world with the population it requires. The family system will disappear; society, sapped at its very base, will have to find new foundations; and Eros, beautifully and irresponsibly free, will flit like a gay butterfly from flower to flower through a sunlit world. (Pp. 49–50)

Huxley's objections to the encroachment of applied science upon our lives are twofold: first, applied science, he argues, has intensified standardized mediocrity and the loss of attention to intellectual and spiritual values; second, the technology of the scientist has contributed to the destructiveness of war and to the diminishing of individual freedom.

Perhaps the most forceful exposition of the effects of technology is given in Huxley's *Brave New World*. In this technological utopia, it will be recalled, the methodology of science has been applied to every facet of human life. Babies are no longer delivered; the very word *mother* has become a term of opprobrium. Eugenics has triumphed to the point where babies are "decanted" in accordance with the needs of society: so many Alphas (the future elite of the society), so many Betas, and so on down to the lowly Epsilons. Each group, by a process of conditioning known as hypnopaedia, is taught to accept and like its lot in life. The entertainment these people get appeals only to the sensations and serves but to increase their happiness. Catharsis in the Aristotelian sense is never a func-

tion of the arts. If by some unfortunate and unforeseen miscalcula-
tion a person should wax morose, there is always the drug *soma* to
restore the individual to the peak of the technologically efficient
euphoria. Once a month everybody is given a "Violent Passion Surrogate," which is the "complete physiological equivalent of fear and
rage. All the tonic effects of murdering Desdemona and being mur-
dered by Othello, without any of the inconveniences" (p. 288).
Even death has lost some of its former awesomeness because now
everybody is gradually conditioned to accept death with the same
indifference as would be accorded to the decanting of babies; and,
after death, the corpse is removed to a laboratory so that the chemi-
cals of the body can be extracted for further experimental and
industrial use. It is true that in this utopia, such concepts as the family, monogamy, romance, art, and religion have become obsolete,
but no one in this society would exchange his happiness, comfort,
and stability for any of these outmoded sources of value. "Our
Ford" and his psychological vicar Freud have replaced God. The
symbol of the cross has yielded to the sign of the T (made, appro-
priately enough, on the stomach); the World Controller is spoken
of as "Our Fordship"; neuroses and psychoses have disappeared
from the world because "Ford's in his flivver . . . All's well with the
world" (p. 51). The triumph of applied science is complete.

This attack on technological science is reinforced in Huxley's
other writings. He observes in *Themes and Variations* that man is
not a machine; therefore, machine-like efficiency cannot be applied
to the regulation of his life and, if it is, all originality, all genuine
emotion, all questioning intellectuality disappear:

> the real horror of the situation in an industrial or administrative
> Panopticon is not that human beings are transformed into machines
> (if they could be so transformed, they would be perfectly happy in
> their prisons); no, the horror consists precisely in the fact that they
> are not machines, but freedom-loving animals, far-ranging minds and
> God-like spirits, who find themselves subordinated to machines and
> constrained to live within the issueless tunnel of an arbitrary and in-
> human system. (P. 207)

Besides making us (in the words of Mark Rampion) "barbarians
of the intellect," technological science is also causing unemploy-

ment. In his title essay "The Olive Tree," Huxley sadly notes how "Even the majestic stability of agriculture has been shaken by the progress of technology" (pp. 303–304). The silkworms which, in previous years, had made the farmers of the Rhône valley prosperous had yielded to the encroachment of "viscose." The instability of technology will continue. "A few years from now, no doubt, the Germans will be making synthetic peaches out of sawdust or coal tar. And then—what?" (p. 304).

The claim made by advocates of technological science that it has made life more exciting and interesting is also questioned by Huxley. He points out in *Themes and Variations* that the advances made by applied science do not change the individual basically because (1) physiologically, "man's organic life is intrinsically nonprogressive. It does not keep on going up and up, in the manner of the graphs representing literacy, or national income, or industrial production"; and (2) psychologically, man ceases to look upon a novelty as a novelty for any length of time; "the most amazing novelty becomes in a few months, even a few days, a familiar and, as it were, a self-evident part of the environment" (p. 69). The benefits of technological science, therefore, are merely illusory:

> Because technology advances, we fancy that we are making corresponding progress all along the line; because we have considerable power over inanimate nature, we are convinced that we are the self-sufficient masters of our fate and captains of our souls; and because cleverness has given us technology and power, we believe, in spite of all the evidence to the contrary, that we have only to go on being yet cleverer in a yet more systematic way to achieve social order, international peace and personal happiness. (*Perennial Philosophy*, p. 142)

Sometimes, Huxley finds, the effects of technological improvement are just the opposite of what was anticipated. Thus, if the eugenicists succeed in improving the caliber of human beings of the future, they may succeed only in destroying mankind, for, as Huxley asks, who will be left to do the necessary, although socially inferior, work of the farmers, clerks, laborers, and factory workers?[6] Furthermore, those who thought that the movies, the radio, television, drugs would lessen boredom have discovered that the masses, instead of being relieved of the tedium of living, crave additional and more stimulating diversions. The creation of new pleasures merely leads to a greater desire for more pleasures. With his characteristic sardonic irony, he comments in *Music at Night*:

> So far as I can see, the only possible new pleasure would be one derived from the invention of a new drug—of a more efficient and less harmful substitute for alcohol and cocaine. If I were a millionaire, I should endow a band of research workers to look for the ideal intoxicant. If we could sniff or swallow something that would, for five or six hours each day, abolish our solitude as individuals, atone us with our fellows in a glowing exaltation of affection and make life in all its aspects seem not only worth living, but divinely beautiful and significant, and if this heavenly, world-transfiguring drug were of such a kind that we could wake up next morning with a clear head and an undamaged constitution—then, it seems to me, all our problems (and not merely the one small problem of discovering a novel pleasure) would be wholly solved and earth would become paradise. (P. 227)

In addition to pointing out how many of the benefits of technological science are illusory and how applied science leads to the dangers of mechanized mediocrity and unemployment, Huxley also elaborates upon yet another disadvantage: science, he writes, has led to a loss of individual freedom and to the intensification of the threat of totalitarianism. In *Science, Liberty and Peace*, Huxley indicates how science has been one of the causes of the loss of personal liberty. First of all, by helping to create such weapons of war as tanks, atomic bombs, and chemical warfare, the scientists have given the political leaders of the world more effective means of holding the masses in constant fear and oppression. Second, the scientists, he alleges, have silently acquiesced in the barbarous uses to which their inventions were put; for example, the Nazi scientists did not object to the cruelties inflicted upon millions of people by their political leaders. Third, the political leaders have used the principle of science—that of reducing "diversity to identity"—in stamping out opposition and, in so doing, have stated that they were simply being "scientific." Thus, both the Fascists and Nazis (and later the Communists) have prided themselves on being scientifically efficient in administering their governments. Furthermore, science has brought about technological unemployment, and unemployed people, Huxley reminds us, will easily give up their liberty for security. Thus, by snuffing out unorthodoxy and spirituality and by stressing the importance of efficiency at the expense of every human criterion, the scientific spirit has facilitated the spreading of totalitarianism.

In *Ape and Essence*, he further elaborates upon the dangers which science and technology have brought into our lives:

> Love casts out fear; but conversely fear casts out love. And not only love. Fear also casts out intelligence, casts out goodness, casts out all thought of beauty and truth. . . . And fear, my good friends, fear is the very basis and foundation of modern life. Fear of the much touted technology which, while it raises our standard of living, increases the probability of our violently dying. Fear of the science which takes away with one hand even more than what it so profusely gives with the other. Fear of the demonstrably fatal institutions for which, in our suicidal loyalty, we are ready to kill and to die. Fear of the Great Men whom we have raised, by popular acclaim, to a power which they use, inevitably, to murder and enslave us. Fear of the War we don't want and yet do everything we can to bring about. (Pp. 51–52)[7]

And yet, scientists did not always submit so abasedly to their political leaders. Mustapha Mond, in *Brave New World*, relates how in his youth he was a promising scientist who could have used his talent to achieve a greater and more meaningful glory than that of technological efficiency; he was given the choice of either being exiled to an island or of conforming and being trained to take over the Controllership. He chose conformity. John Rivers, the physicist in *The Genius and the Goddess*, complains about the lack of freedom for scientists and nostalgically reminisces about the dreams he had when he was thinking of science as a career:

> Those were the days, remember, when you could be a physicist without feeling guilty; the days when it was still possible to believe that you were working for the greater glory of God. Now they won't even allow you the comfort of self-deception. You're paid by the Navy and trailed by the FBI. Not for one moment do they permit you to forget what you're up to. *Ad majorem Dei gloriam*? Don't be an idiot!

Ad maiorem hominis degradationem—that's the thing you're working for. But in 1921 infernal machines were safely in the future. (P. 49)[8]

Has science, then, no value for man? Huxley tries to work out a kind of conciliatory compromise which would maintain the contributions of science in helping to solve man's ecological problems while it would also tend to eliminate some of the evils that an uncontrolled technology would create. He wants scientists to be more actively responsible for the technological improvements they help to bring into existence; in other words, he wants them to be morally responsible for their actions or, as has been the case in the past, for their lack of active protests against producing more destructive weapons of mass annihilation. He also wants people to recognize the fact that the advantages of technology also bring with them disadvantages. "We believe that men and women will be happy when they are surrounded with the right kind of gadgets. Our forefathers believed that they would be happy if they achieved what one of the greatest of Christian saints called a 'holy indifference' to their material surroundings" ("Who Are You?" p. 424). The only justification that technological comfort has is to facilitate thought and time for contemplation. Unfortunately, Huxley finds, comfort in the modern world has become an end in itself. The old world did not have our comfort, but it did have beauty—beautiful palaces, beautiful churches, magnificent art: "The modern world seems to regard it [comfort] as an end in itself, an absolute good. One day, perhaps, the earth will have been turned into one vast featherbed, with man's body dozing on top of it and his mind underneath, like Desdemona, smothered" (*Proper Studies*, p. 299). If people wish to enjoy the comforts of technology they should not allow technology to dominate their lives: "The first step would be to make people live dualistically, in two compartments. In one compartment as industrialized workers, in the other as human beings. As idiots and machines for eight hours out of every twenty-four and real human beings for the rest" (*Point Counter Point*, p. 357).

This duality which Huxley speaks of in *Point Counter Point* has also another meaning for him. He asks the question, both in *Beyond the Mexique Bay* (pp. 231–32) and in *Ends and Means*

(p. 23), whether it is possible to combine the advantages of primitive living and technological comforts. He does not think that primitive societies such as that of the Pueblo Indians can adopt the benefits of a scientific industrialization without the accompanying evils of a technological life; he does feel, however, that the industrialized West, being more educated and therefore more adaptable, can assimilate the instinctive integration of the primitive way of life. The answer is not the abolition of science:

> Lawrence so much hated the misapplications of science, that he thought that science itself should be abolished. But the only thing that can prevent science from being misapplied is more science of a higher quality. If Miahuatlan were the only possible alternative to Middlesborough, then really one might as well commit suicide at once. But luckily it is not the only alternative. (*Beyond the Mexique Bay*, pp. 231–32)

This compromise between the insanity of a scientifically controlled world and the lunacy of primitivism is further developed in Huxley's 1950 introduction to a reprint of *Brave New World*. What he advocates here is a community of refugees from the "utopia"; the refugees' government and economics would be decentralized and cooperative. "Science and technology would be used as though, like the Sabbath, they had been made for man, not (as at present and still more so in the Brave New World) as though man were to be adapted and enslaved to them" (p. xxii). Everything would be subordinated to man's final end: "the unitive knowledge of the immanent Tao or Logos, the transcendent Godhead or Brahman" (*ibid.*).

Huxley never loses sight of the fact that science and technology, despite their disadvantages, still help to feed the millions of people on earth. If they were to be abolished, mankind would starve. But he is equally anxious to stress the point that material well-being by itself is not enough: "enlightened self-interest must somehow be made as thrilling as unenlightened animal impulse. To discover how this may be done is incomparably more important than to discover new varieties of the banana" (*Beyond the Mexique Bay*, pp. 16–17).

In the last ten years of his life, Huxley found another use for science. To help him expand his sense of awareness, he first experimented with the drug mescalin and recorded these experiences in *The Doors of Perception*, published in 1954. In it, he describes how mescalin brought him in touch with eternity, infinity, and the absolute. Mescalin made him forget for the moment "the world of selves, of time, of moral judgments and utilitarian considerations, the world (and it was this aspect of human life which I wished, above else, to forget) of self-assertion, of cocksureness, of overvalued words and idolatrously worshiped notions."[9]

In *Island* (1962) and *Literature and Science* (1963), Huxley's return to his first love, science, is almost complete, but not quite. In *Island* the utopian society makes full use of science to achieve terrestrial beatitude; unfortunately, the military forces of Colonel Dipa are too strong to allow this utopia to continue; science and technology apparently will no longer serve Buddhist goals—not that they ever did completely anyway; they will be subservient to the political-military tyranny of Colonel Dipa. Similarly, in *Literature and Science*, he tries to achieve a compromise in the Leavis-Snow controversy: literature and science can both be useful in helping to achieve a sane society. The objective truths of science are to be made more meaningful by the effective language in which literature presents the findings of science: "Man cannot live by contemplative receptivity and artistic creation alone. As well as every word proceeding from the mouth of God, he needs science and technology" (p. 39).

In his evaluation of science as a source of value, Huxley assigns to science the same function he did to the arts: facilitating the apprehension of the nature of ultimate reality. Science, like the arts, should never become an end in itself; both science and the arts should not be worshiped as ultimately divine entities. Science and technology, unless carefully controlled, can cause many evils: increased mediocrity, rising unemployment, and the barbarisms of warfare and totalitarianism; science and technology can, however, help man wisely use the earth's natural resources and can even aid him in achieving "the end and ultimate purpose of human life: Enlightenment, the Beatific Vision" (*Doors of Perception*, p. 73).

Given the nature of spiders, webs
are inevitable. And given the nature
of human beings, so are religions.
Spiders can't help making flytraps,
and men can't help making symbols.
That's what the human brain is
there for—to turn the chaos of given
experience into a set of fairly
manageable symbols. Sometimes
the symbols correspond fairly closely
to some of the aspects of the external reality behind our experience;
then you have science and common
sense. Sometimes, on the contrary,
the symbols have almost no
connection with external reality;
then you have paranoia and de-
lirium. More often there's a mixture,
part realistic and part fantastic;
that's religion. Good religion or bad
religion—it depends on the blending
of the cocktail.

— ALDOUS HUXLEY, *Island*

Huxley's ideas have been subjected to much criticism. Those which have been most criticized deal with religion; they have been attacked not only by the critics who have been disturbed by their religious and philosophical implications, but by those who have been bored by Huxley's occasionally excessive didacticism. D. Marshall, writing in the 1930's, attacks the "neo-pagans of what might be called the Lawrentian party—D. H. Lawrence himself, Aldous Huxley, Richard Aldington."[1] C. E. M. Joad objects to Huxley's mysticism because it is at variance with Joad's personal interpretations of Christianity. Both William York Tindall[2] and Richard V. Chase[3] decry Huxley's association with Gerald Heard, the British anthropologist who has preached the mystical spiritualism of the East in preference to the materialism of the West; Chase writes: "The secluded spirit may find peace or the fleeting vision of Utopia in the ecumenical church of the mind, but looking from the gray shadows and intervening in the sunlit world, the spirit pays the price of its isolation, by losing all its elegance and becoming pompous and crude. The mystic mutation of the spirit is austere megalomania, but megalomania is not the way of nature . . . ."[4]

Although Huxley's comments on religion can be criticized, they can hardly be ignored. He saw the potential value of the arts, education, government, love, nature, and science as ways to a better life, but he criticized those who regarded these means as ends in themselves. His search for ultimate answers led him, in his examination of religion, into all kinds of paradoxical complexities which were not resolved very clearly in his works and into all kinds of generalizations which have little meaning when subjected to detailed scrutiny. For example, he will sometimes speak of Christianity or Judaism as if they were monolithic entities. Furthermore, when he talks of Buddhism, Confucianism, Hinduism, or Mohammedanism, he does not consider the evolutionary changes that have been incorporated into these beliefs so that when he makes criticisms about them, one is not sure, for example, whether he is castigating the Mohammedanism of the late Middle Ages or the Mohammedanism of today.[5] Similarly, when he talks about Judaism, he does not take into account the four branches in existence today: Orthodox, Conservative, Reconstructionist, and Reform. One wishes at times that he would follow his own advice that he gave to the reader regarding governments, that one should not think of all-inclusive terms such as *state, party,* or *country*; one should think in terms of individuals. It makes a difference when one is talking about "Christianity," for example, whether one is discussing Henry the Eighth or Martin Luther.

There are other difficulties besides trying to find specific meaning in the welter of generalizations one finds in Huxley's comments on religion. There is the difficulty in trying to grasp Huxley's attempts to reconcile religion with philosophy, aesthetics, ethics, and government. There is also the problem of endeavoring to find a relationship between religion considered as a metaphysical concept and religion considered as ritual and as a practical guide to mundane problems. Huxley himself indicates in *The Perennial Philosophy* the manifold facets of the problem when he writes: "In studying the Perennial Philosophy we can begin either at the bottom, with practice and morality; or at the top, with a consideration of metaphysical truths; or, finally, in the middle, at the focal point where mind and matter, action and thought have their meeting place in human psychology" (p. 1). What makes it difficult is that Huxley, at times, seems to be going in all three directions simultaneously.

Huxley's first comments on religion indicate that he began as a sardonic skeptic. In one of his earliest novels, *Antic Hay*, for example, we find one of the characters commenting on God: "I am that I am . . . . But I have with me . . . a physiologue, a pedagogue and a priapagogue; for I leave out of account mere artists and journalists whose titles do not end with the magic syllable. And finally . . . plain Dog, which being interpreted kabalistically backwards signifies God. All at your service" (p. 79). In *Jesting Pilate*, published in 1926, he writes that it may be true that "religion is a device employed by the Life Force for the promotion of its evolutionary designs. . . . [However, one might] be justified in adding that religion is also a device employed by the Devil for the dissemination of idiocy, intolerance, and servile abjection" (p. 58). In his essay "One and Many" (*Do What You Will*, published in 1929), he declares himself "officially an agnostic." He develops the theory that God is simply a projection of the human personality and that "men make Gods in their own likeness. To talk about religion except in terms of human psychology is an irrelevance" (p. 1). He ridicules the anthropomorphic conception of God because it reflects the weaknesses and aspirations of the society in which its particular God is worshiped. Using himself as an example, he writes that when he is enjoying good health and when the weather is propitious, then he can well believe that "God's in his heaven and all's right with the world." On other occasions, "skies and destiny being inclement, I am no less immediately certain of the malignant impersonality of an uncaring universe" (p. 2). In a poem he wrote in 1925 called "Philosophy," he says that it is difficult to hear what God is saying because "God stutters." He would prefer to believe in the sanctity of what he calls the "Human Personality" than in the "myth" of God. "We do at least know something of Human Personality, whereas of God we know nothing and, knowing nothing, are at liberty to invent as freely as we like" (*Do What You Will*, p. 141). The reason that people believe in this "theological game" is that they find it much more psychologically satisfying to conform to habit than to be subjected to the discomfort of rebellious skepticism.

The vacuum created by Huxley's rejection of an anthropomorphic religion was filled in the 1920's by his espousal of the Lawrentian doctrine of the instinctive life. Man should not favor what was felt to be a false spirituality but should live passionately and instinctively. In *Point Counter Point*, Mark Rampion (who is supposed to represent D. H. Lawrence) speaks of the three diseases plaguing mankind: "Jesus's and Newton's and Henry Ford's disease." All three diseases could be eliminated, both Lawrence and Huxley felt, by the rejection of science, technology, and traditional Christianity. In *Do What You Will*, published the same year as *Point Counter Point*, Huxley makes the same points. He writes that the world is faced with three dangers: (1) monotheism and the menace of the "super-humanist" ideal; (2) the "worship of success and efficiency"; (3) "the machine." Monotheism and the super-humanist ideal constitute a danger because they are not based on any foundation in reality and thus do not allow the living of the fully instinctive life. "The worship of success and efficiency constitutes another menace to our world. What our ancestors sacrificed on the altars of Spirituality, we sacrificed on those of the Bitch Goddess and Taylorism" (p. 83).[6] The machine is a menace because it robs man of his creativity and makes him merely a passively efficient robot. These three menaces have killed people's instinctive love of the fully integrated life, and the "result is that they lose their sense of values, their taste and judgment become corrupted, and they have an irresistible tendency to love the lowest when they see it" (p. 88).

When we analyze Huxley's comments on Judaism and Jews and on Christianity and Christians, we can readily appreciate why the Nazi propagandists used some of his statements in their attacks on Western democracies.[7] In 1929, in *Do What You Will*, for example, he made the following attack on the Jews: "Their mission, in a word, was to infect the rest of humanity with a belief which . . . prevented them from having any art, any philosophy, any political life, any breadth or diversity of vision, any progress. We may be pardoned for wishing that the Jews had remained, not forty, but four thousand years in their repulsive wilderness" (p. 18).[8] He blames the monotheistic religion of the Jews for the emphasis given by other peoples to wealth and materialism and for the sentimentality current in music.[9] It should be pointed out, however, that this blatant anti-Semitism disappeared after the advent of Hitler. In his later books, Huxley deprecates the savagery of the Nazis; in one of his novels, *After Many a Summer Dies the Swan*, one of the minor characters is a sympathetic Jew who falls a victim to the ruthless business cunning of Jo Stoyte, a non-Jew.

The kind of misfired generalization which characterizes his attack on the Jews also characterizes his castigation of what, at different times, he calls "Christianity," "Puritanism," "Calvinism," and "organized religion." His objections to Christianity are several: first of all, he attacks the cruel persecutions of the more fanatical Christians. In the following excerpt from *Do What You Will*, he is singling out the puritans, but it resembles his attacks on other Christian groups in many other works:

> The puritan was free to range the world, blighting and persecuting as he went, free to make life poisonous, not only for himself, but for all who came near him. The puritan was and is a social danger, a public and private nuisance of the most odious kind. Baudelaire was a puritan inside out. Instead of asceticism and respectability he practiced debauchery. The means he used were the opposite of those employed by the puritans; but his motives and theirs, the ends that he and they achieved, were the same. He hated life as much as they did, and was as successful in destroying it. (Pp. 192–93)

The cruelty which Huxley found so distasteful in the puritans is also the cruelty he discovers, in *The Devils of Loudun*, among the Catholics in the centuries during the Inquisition. "In medieval and early modern Christendom the situation of sorcerers and their clients was almost precisely analogous to that of Jews under Hitler, capitalists under Stalin, Communists and fellow travelers in the United States . . ." (p. 122). He describes the brutality of the Catholic hierarchy toward one of their own priests who refused to admit that he was inhabited by a devil. Their cruelty did not stem from their alleged hatred of heresy alone; it arose, according to Huxley, because their entire religion was motivated by hatred:

"Ecclesiastical history exhibits a hierarchy of hatreds, descending by orderly degrees from the Church's official and ecumenical hatred of heretics and infidels and the particular hatreds of Order for Order, school for school, province for province and theologian for theologian" (pp. 19–20).

Huxley also blames both the puritans and Catholics for making people believe that this world was but a gloomy journey to a posthumous celestial euphoria. "Christianity has always found a certain difficulty in fitting the unfatigued, healthy and energetic person into its philosophical scheme" (*Texts and Pretexts*, p. 287). If perchance Christianity does come upon a person who says that he is quite happy for the moment, then it reminds him that this state of well-being is but illusory and certainly temporary; every silver lining is hiding an imminent cloudburst. The Greeks, Huxley avers, were far wiser in being realistically pessimistic and in using this pessimism to justify their epicurean and instinctive way of life. Huxley here seems to ignore the fact that the same society which gave rise to the Epicureans also produced the Stoics.

Huxley attacks other features in Christianity. He seems to take unusual delight in pointing out that often the priests themselves did not practice the austerity they so unctuously preached. Thus, in *The Devils of Loudun*, he points out that essentially there were two Urban Grandiers: Grandier the sensualist and Grandier the sermonizing priest. He describes how between Grandier's weekly debaucheries he was preparing sermons filled with "What eloquence, what choice and profound learning, what subtle, but eminently sound theology!" (pp. 26–27). When Grandier hears the discomforting news from one of his female parishioners that he is the father of her unborn child, Huxley describes his hypocritical reaction:

> Shifting his hand from the bosom to the bowed head and changing his tone, without any transition, from the bawdy to the clerical, the parson told her that she must learn to bear her cross with Christian resignation. Then, remembering the visit he had promised to pay to poor Mme. de Brou, who had a cancer of the womb and needed all the spiritual consolation he could give her, he took his leave. (P. 35)

In his essay "Variations of a Philosopher," published in *Themes and Variations*, Huxley analyzes the term *shepherd* to demonstrate how, like sheep, people never stop to consider that "a shepherd is 'not in business for his health,' still less for the health of his sheep." If a shepherd takes good care of his flock it is only to fatten them for the eventual slaughter. People should consider the meaning of *shepherd* before speaking sentimentally about their pastors:

> Applied to most of the States and Churches of the last two or three thousand years, this pastoral metaphor is seen to be exceedingly apt —so apt, indeed, that one wonders why the civil and ecclesiastical herders of men should ever have allowed it to gain currency. From the point of view of the individual lambs, rams and ewes there is, of course, no such thing as a *good* shepherd; their problem is to find means whereby they may enjoy the benefits of a well-ordered social life without being exposed to the shearings, milkings, geldings and butcheries which have always been associated with the pastoral office. (P. 57)

There are still other serious faults that Huxley has found with "most of the States and Churches of the last two or three thousand years." He complains that "Compared with that of the Taoists and Far Eastern Buddhists, the Christian attitude towards Nature has been curiously insensitive and often downright domineering and violent" (*Perennial Philosophy*, p. 77). Encouraged by "an unfortunate remark in Genesis," Christians have treated animals as things to be exploited for their own benefit. Furthermore, Huxley is very bitter because the church has not offered any kind of opposition to the waging of wars. In *Ape and Essence*, where his bitterness has perhaps reached its most intense pitch, he writes:

> The brass bands give place to the most glutinous of Wurlitzers, "Land of Hope and Glory" to "Onward, Christian Soldiers." Followed by his very Reverend Dean and Chapter, the Right Reverend, the Baboon-Bishop of the Bronx advances majestic, his crozier in his jeweled paw, to pronounce benediction upon the two Field Marshalissimos and their patronage proceedings. (Pp. 45–46)

If we look at the ministers in Huxley's novels, we find that they are all satirically drawn. In *Crome Yellow*, we have the Reverend

Bodinham, who is much disturbed because his prediction of the coming of the Lord ("He'll sneak around like a thief") has not been realized. In *Antic Hay*, we have the Reverend Pelvey, whose ineffectiveness as a preacher is satirically demonstrated: while the Reverend Pelvey is preaching, one of the audience to whom his religious message is directed is thinking of "trousers with pneumatic seats." In *Eyeless in Gaza*, Mr. Thursley, a minister, is successful in his sermons and in the publication of his articles in the *Guardian*, but he becomes uncontrollably angry when his wife fails to fill up his inkwell. In *Time Must Have a Stop*, Huxley pictures the minister father of Mrs. Thwale as a completely futile man; while the minister is trying to reform the world, he does not realize that his daughter is becoming bitterly opposed to religion; ironically enough, it is the minister's daughter who worships material comfort and commits adultery.[10]

Of all the Christian faiths, he seems to have the greatest respect for Catholicism and the greatest admiration for Quakerism and those early Christians in whom he found mystic strains. The Quakers he admires for their opposition to war and for their contributions in alleviating some of the world's social and economic sufferings. As for his attitude towards Catholicism, in *Proper Studies* he writes:

> Catholicism is probably the most realistic of all Western religions. Its practice is based on a profound knowledge of human nature in all its varieties and gradations. From the fetish-worshipper to the metaphysician, from the tired business man to the mystic, from the sentimentalist and the sensualist to the intellectual, every type of human being can find in Catholicism the spiritual nourishment which he or she requires. For the sociable, unspiritual man Catholicism is duly sociable and unspiritual. For the solitary and the spiritual it provides a hermitage and the most exquisite, the profoundest models of religious meditation; it gives the silence of monasteries and the bareness of the Carthusian church, it offers the devotional introspection of À Kempis and St. Theresa, the subtleties of Pascal and Newman, the poetry of Crashaw and St. John of the Cross and a hundred others. The only people for whom it does not cater are those possessed by that rare, dangerous, and uneasy passion, the passion for liberty. (Pp. 186–87)

Presumably it is Huxley's "passion for liberty" which constitutes one of the reasons for his objection to Catholicism. But there are other reasons. I have already spoken of his attacks on Christianity because of its failure to oppose wars and its encouragement of materialistic success even to the extent of treating animals as mere property; Huxley does not exculpate Catholicism from his generalized attack on Christianity. He also objects to Catholicism (at least to Catholicism as it is practiced in England) because it stresses the ritual at the expense of the more meaningful "mental prayer." In *Eyeless in Gaza*, we note the following extract from the diary of Anthony Beavis: "For English Catholics, sacraments are the psychological equivalents of tractors in Russia" (p. 386).

His objection to ritual is not confined to Catholicism alone; he seems to find little value in the ritual of any religion. In *Eyeless in Gaza*, he describes a funeral in which he satirizes the significance of the accompanying ritual. After describing the playing of the organ, the "little procession of surplices," the flowers, the singing and the intoning of the funeral prayer, he points out the ineffectiveness of all this ritual on Anthony Beavis: "But Anthony hardly heard, because he could think of nothing except those germs that were still there in spite of the smell of the flowers, and of the spittle that kept flowing into his mouth . . ." (p. 25). Similarly, in *Ape and Essence*, he describes the procession in honor of Belial and refers to "the collective imbecility which are the products of ceremonial religion" (p. 108).

In his essay "Religious Practices," published in *Ends and Means*, he notes that ritual is but one of the four practices which he has observed in religion; he writes that ritual should not excuse people from "moral effort and intelligence" and should not lead to "neglect of God." The second religious practice, asceticism, may increase the individual's power of perception, but it is generally undesirable because it can become too rigorous on the body and because it tends to flatter the ego by becoming an end in itself. Belief in a personal deity, the third religious practice, may improve one's character but is also undesirable because it leads to oppression, injustice, and hatred; the people believing in an anthropomorphic conception of God tend to project upon God their own personal shortcomings.[11] The fourth religious practice, meditation, can be valuable only if it is self-transcendent and entertains thoughts of the essence of the divine Godhead.

There is one other feature of traditional Christianity, the value of which Huxley has questioned: the belief in a future life of punishment or reward. In his essay "Squeak and Gibber," published in his *Music at Night,* he dismisses the concept of Heaven and Hell. He prefers to agree with the "Scientific Psychical Researchers," whose views on the future life

> seem to be almost indistinguishable from those held by Homer and the author of Ecclesiastes. For all that survives, according to these researchers (and the existing evidence, it seems to me, does not justify one in going any further) is what Professor Broad calls a "psychic factor"—something which, in conjunction with a material brain, creates a personality but which, in isolation, is no more personal than matter. (Pp. 91–92)

This disbelief in a future life should not be discouraging, however, for it was Jesus, Huxley reminds the reader, who stated that the Kingdom of Heaven lies within us during our earthly life.

Huxley's few references to Mohammedanism indicate a dislike for that religion also. In the essay "In a Tunisian Oasis," published in *The Olive Tree,* he writes that "Too much insistence on the fatalism inherent in their [Arabs'] religion has reduced them to the condition of static lethargy and supine incuriousness in which they now find themselves" (p. 281). He blames the Arabs' religion for the fact that "half their babies die, and that, politically, they are not their own masters" (p. 290). This "static lethargy and supine incuriousness" which he attributes to the Mohammedan religion sounds rather incongruous when juxtaposed with the comment he made about Mohammedanism some eight years later in *The Perennial Philosophy*:

> Primitive Buddhism is no less predominantly cerebrotonic than primitive Christianity, and so is Vedanta, the metaphysical discipline which lies at the heart of Hinduism. Confucianism, on the contrary, is a mainly viscerotonic system—familial, ceremonious and thoroughly this-worldly. And in Mohammedanism we find a system which in-

corporates strongly somatotonic elements. Hence Islam's black record of holy wars and persecutions—a record comparable to that of later Christianity, after that religion had so far compromised with unregenerate somatotonia as to call its ecclesiastical organization "the Church Militant." (P. 158)

These then, briefly summarized, are Huxley's attitudes toward religion up to the time he embraced mysticism: despite his declaration that he was "officially an agnostic," his comments indicate more skepticism than agnosticism. He found little to admire in the religions of Judaism, Christianity, and Islam. He blamed Judaism for narrowness of vision and excessive preoccupation with material success; he castigated Christianity for its cruel oppression of heresy, its occasional hypocrisy, its failure to object to the existence of wars; he criticized Islam for its pessimism and fatalism. It should be remembered, however, that what he was specifically rejecting in these three religions was the nonmystical element; wherever he found elements of mysticism, as he did in the Book of Ecclesiastes; in the writings of such mystic Christians as St. Augustine, St. Bernard of Clairvaux, Meister Eckhart, Walter Hilton, William Law, St. François de Sales, Thomas Traherne, and others; in the Sufi books of Islam, he accepted their teachings of contemplation, renunciation of worldly preoccupation, and the practice of love. It is, therefore, not so much religion itself that he was rejecting but what he felt was the perversion of the religious essence. During the 1920's, he was not yet philosophically prepared to embrace actively the practice of mysticism; consequently, he tentatively endorsed the instinctive philosophy of D. H. Lawrence and the hedonistic teachings of the Epicureans. But despite his rejection of nearly all the traditional concepts of God, he almost intuitively felt that there was a way to God which existed despite the "incorrect" notions about God that have been held for the last several thousand years. As early as 1926, in *Jesting Pilate*, we find him writing: "The fact that men have had stupid and obviously incorrect ideas about God does not justify us in trying to eliminate God from out of the universe. Men have had stupid and incorrect ideas on almost every subject that can be thought about" (p. 219).

The substitutes that people have created for religion were also rejected by Huxley. In his essay "The Substitutes for Religion," in *Proper Studies*, he analyzes these substitutes and disapproves of all of them as sources of enduring value. The first substitute, nationalism, is rejected because it breeds wars. The second substitute, egalitarian democracy, is inadequate because it is impractical and because it lacks the pageantry of nationalism and does not attract as many people as does nationalism. The third substitute, the practice of ritual, is objectionable because it becomes an end in itself and may lead to such excesses as the Ku Klux Klan. Art, the fourth substitute, was formerly a handmaiden of religion but now has become an object of idolatrous worship:

> That it is an extremely inadequate substitute must be apparent to any one who has observed the habits of those who lead the pure, aesthetic life. Where beauty is worshipped for beauty's sake as a goddess, independent of and superior to morality and philosophy, the most horrible putrefaction is apt to set in. The lives of aesthetes are the far from edifying commentary on the religion of beauty. (P. 218)

The fifth substitute, the religion of sex, is equally undesirable because those who practice it become victims of their own self-abasement, and those who object to its immorality become merely self-righteous "smut-hounds" (a term Huxley borrows from H. L. Mencken). The sixth substitute, business, leads to the deification of money and "offers no coherent explanation of any universe outside of that whose centre is the stock exchange" (p. 221). The seventh substitute is found in "crank" beliefs such as homeopathy and antivivisection, obviously inadequate as a source of value. The eighth substitute, a belief in superstitions which manifests itself in such forms as belief in luck charms and fear of microbes, is again unworthy of consideration as a guide to intelligent living. The final substitute is the deification of artists, doctors (especially nerve doctors and psychiatrists), and lawyers. Huxley is against this substitute because to put faith in human beings is to put faith in fallible and corruptible individuals. In summary, Huxley states that there are no adequate substitutes for religion. The dilemma for Huxley during the period from the end of World War I to about 1935 was that he could not accept the substitutes for religion and was not yet ready to embrace the mysticism he later did adopt. His dilemma is evident in the sardonic tone of the following passage from *Texts and Pretexts*:

> There are escapes into drink, into sensuality, into play, into day-dreaming. None of these, however, provides the perfect refuge. Lust exhausts itself; there are nights of self-questioning insomnia after the day-dreams, mornings of sick repentance after the alcohol; as for play, only an imbecile could bear to play away his existence. No; of all the death-surrogates incomparably the best is what is called—rightly, after all—the higher life. Religious meditation, scientific experiment, the acquisition of knowledge, metaphysical thinking and artistic creation—all these activities enhance the subjective sense of life, but at the same time deliver their practitioners from the sordid preoccupations of common living. They live, abundantly; and they are, in the language of religion, "dead to the world." What could be more satisfactory? (Pp. 296–97)

Having rejected the nonmystic aspects of Judaism, Christianity, and Islam, having rejected the substitutes of religion which have infiltrated society, Huxley was ready to embrace what he felt would be a more satisfying source of value—mysticism.[12] Mysticism is not an easy concept to define. As Huxley himself wrote, there are elements of mysticism common to nearly all religions. Inasmuch as he embraces not the mysticism of any particular religion (although he leans more toward Buddhism than to any other) but rather mysticism itself as a kind of philosophical concept, perhaps the definition given by Evelyn Underhill, two of whose books he lists in his *Perennial Philosophy*, best clarifies Huxley's approach to mysticism: "I understand it to be the expression of the innate tendency of the human spirit towards complete harmony with the transcendental order; whatever be the theological formula under which that order is understood."[13] It is significant that the one book of Huxley's entirely devoted to a critical survey of mystical writings in all religions and in all ages is called *The Perennial Philosophy*, not *The Perennial Religion*. It is also important to note his admission of incompetence in this subject and his unwillingness to discuss "the doctrinal differences between Buddhism and Hinduism" (p. 9). In examining the development of mysticism in Huxley's thought, therefore, I shall not delve into the doctrinal differences among the various religions in which mysticism is found.[14]

Huxley's first comments on mysticism were hostile. In 1928, for example, he was writing in *Do What You Will*: "the mystics are never tired of affirming that their direct perceptions of unity are intenser, of finer quality and intrinsically more convincing, more self-evident, than their direct perceptions of diversity. But they can only speak for themselves. Other people's direct intuitions of diverse 'appearances' may be just as intensely self-evident as *their* intuition of unique 'reality'" (p. 38).[15] But in another essay in the same book, he admits that "It is also true that, in certain circumstances, we can actually *feel*, as a direct intuition, the existence of the all-comprehending unity, can intimately realize in a single flash of insight the illusoriness of the quotidian world of distinctions and relations" (p. 63). Even in his earlier novels, we detect some elements of mysticism—the urge for a contemplative life, the distrust of the life of action. Thus, in *Those Barren Leaves*, Calamy (who at the end of the book retires to the hills to start a life of pure contemplation) says: "The mind must be open, unperturbed, empty of irrelevant things, quiet. There's no room for thoughts in a half-shut, cluttered mind" (p. 347). Later in the book, he comes out even more strongly for the contemplative life:

> No, it's not fools who turn mystics. It takes a certain amount of intelligence and imagination to realize the extraordinary queerness and mysteriousness of the world in which we live. The fools, the innumerable fools, take it all for granted, skate about cheerfully on the surface and never think of inquiring what's underneath. They're content with appearances, such as your Harrow Road or Café de la Rotonde, call them realities and proceed to abuse any one who takes an interest in what lies underneath these superficial symbols, as a romantic imbecile. (P. 370)

It should not be concluded from excerpts like these that Huxley completely believed in mysticism back in the 1920's; but even when he denies the mystic's claim of achieving unity with God, he qualifies this denial by writing that "that does not in any way detract from the value of mysticism as a way to perfect health" (*Jesting*

Pilate, pp. 217–18). Similarly, in *Brave New World*, published in 1932, he is more against the tendency of the world to drift into a technological "utopia" than he is for mysticism; but in this book, also, we detect unmistakable signs of his eventual conversion to mysticism; as Mustapha Mond is signing the papers banning a work on "A New Theory of Biology," we learn that one of the reasons for his proscription of the book is that people might begin to think that "the goal was somewhere beyond, somewhere outside the present human sphere; that the purpose of life was not the maintenance of well-being, but some intensification and refining of consciousness, some enlargement of knowledge" (p. 211).

Eyeless in Gaza, published in 1936, contains Huxley's first complete endorsement of mysticism. Through his central character, Anthony Beavis, he outlines the details of his mysticism which he was to elaborate in later works. It is in this book that he first advocates the achievement of a union with God. Evil is that which separates man from his fellow man; manifestations of evils such as hatred, greed, and lust should be avoided. Good is that which unites; love, compassion, and understanding are manifestations of unity. Huxley admits that this unity is difficult to achieve, but man should at least try to achieve this unity through meditation and inner peace. Through the attainment of this inner calm, he will be better able to withstand the external evil which is the condition of the world. Anthony Beavis' notebook expresses Huxley's mysticism:

Empirical facts:
One. We are all capable of love for other human beings.
Two. We impose limitations on that love.
Three. We can transcend all these limitations—*if we choose to.* (It is a matter of observation that anyone who so desires can overcome personal dislike, class feeling, national hatred, colour prejudice. Not easy; but it can be done, if we have the will and know how to carry out our good intentions.)
Four. Love expressing itself in good treatment breeds love. Hate expressing itself in bad treatment breeds hate.
In the light of these facts, it's obvious what inter-personal, inter-class and inter-national policies should be. But, again, knowledge cuts little ice. We all know; we almost all fail to do. It is a question,

as usual, of the best methods of implementing intentions. Among other things, peace propaganda must be a set of instructions in the art of modifying character. (P. 156)[16]

In *Ends and Means*, he repeats some of the thoughts concerning mysticism he expressed in *Eyeless in Gaza*, but he also adds some new features. He again writes that "Meditation . . . is the technique of mysticism" (p. 332). But he emphasizes in this book the necessity of intuition in attaining detachment from the world of animality. He again stresses the importance of will power in achieving the intuitive experience that will bring about the mystical state: "What we perceive and understand depends upon what we are; and what we are depends partly on circumstances, partly, and more profoundly, on the nature of the efforts we have made to realize our ideal and the nature of the ideal we have tried to realize" (p. 333). Huxley particularly urges the reader to remember Irving Babbitt's statement that meditation produces a "super-rational concentration of will." He concedes that all of us have animal instincts which cannot be ignored, but he does not want us to devote our entire attention to the satisfaction of these instincts. "Goodness is the method by which we divert our attention from this singularly wearisome topic of our animality and our individual separateness" (p. 346). This loss of preoccupation with bodily needs may cause some temporary physical suffering, but it is more than adequately compensated by the knowledge and inner serenity which accompany the mystical experience. The nonattachment of mysticism is infinitely preferable to the attachment of the individual to the pursuit of the life of meaningless action.

In his next novel, *After Many a Summer Dies the Swan*, Huxley further elaborates his theories of mysticism. When Pete asks Mr. Propter, the mystic in the novel, what good is and where it is to be found, Mr. Propter replies:

> On the level below the human and on the level above. On the animal level and on the level . . . well, you can take your choice of names: the level of eternity; the level, if you don't object, of God; the level of the spirit—only that happens to be about the most ambiguous word in the language. On the lower level, good exists as the proper functioning of the organism in accordance with the laws of its own

being. On the higher level, it exists in the form of a knowledge of the world without desire or aversion; it exists as the experience of eternity, as the transcendence of personality, the extension of consciousness beyond the limits imposed by the ego. Strictly human activities are the activities that prevent the manifestations of good on the other two levels . . . . Directly or indirectly, most of our physical ailments and disabilities are due to worry and craving. We worry and crave ourselves into high blood pressure, heart disease, tuberculosis, peptic ulcer, low resistance to infection, neurasthenia, sexual aberrations, insanity, suicide. Not to mention all the rest. (Pp. 99–100)

In addition to liberation from the fetters of the ego, Mr. Propter also wants liberation from time, which he describes as "a pretty bothersome thing." Furthermore, the cultivation of virtues is not sufficient; it must be the cultivation of the right virtues—specifically, understanding and compassion. The possession of the other virtues is no guarantee of virtuous conduct: "Indeed, you can't be really bad unless you *do* have most of the virtues. Look at Milton's Satan for example. Brave, strong, generous, loyal, prudent, temperate, self-sacrificing" (p. 95). But because Milton's Satan lacked the qualities of understanding and compassion, he could not be a virtuous leader.

In *Grey Eminence*, published in 1941, Huxley gives two additional suggestions to those who would embrace mysticism: first, the good achieved by a practice of mysticism "is a product of the ethical and spiritual artistry of individuals; it cannot be mass-produced" (p. 303). Second, people should beware of "only false, ersatz mysticisms—the nature-mysticism of Wordsworth; the sublimated sexual mysticism of Whitman; the nationality-mysticisms of all the patriotic poets and philosophers of every race and culture, from Fichte at the beginning of the period [the nineteenth century] to Kipling and Barrès at the end" (p. 77). The only valid manifestation of mysticism is that based on an intuitive knowledge and love of God.

In the introduction to *The Perennial Philosophy*, Huxley writes: "This book . . . is an anthology of the Perennial Philosophy; but, though an anthology, it contans [sic] but few extracts from the writings of professional men of letters and, though illustrating a

philosophy, hardly anything from the professional philosophers"
(p. viii). Only those who have made themselves "loving, pure in
heart, and poor in spirit" are capable of apprehending the nature
of this perennial philosophy, which, he says "is primarily concerned
with the one, divine Reality substantial to the manifold world of
things and lives and minds" (p. viii). The book is divided into
twenty-seven chapters dealing with various aspects of human and
divine experience. The importance of the book, however, lies not
in the selection of excerpts from the writings of others (excellent
as they may be) but rather in the ample comments Huxley makes
on these excerpts.

Every phase of human activity, he says, must be judged in terms
of its hindering or facilitating the achievement of the ultimate purpose of life: "In all the historic formulations of the Perennial Philosophy it is axiomatic that the end of human life is contemplation,
or the direct and intuitive awareness of God" (p. 294). That society is good which emphasizes not technological advances but
makes possible and desirable the pursuit of contemplation. The
love released by the exercise of this intuitive contemplation will
cure many of the evils plaguing mankind. This love will lead man
to treat Nature kindly; the earth's resources will no longer be rav-
aged by people motivated only by self-interest. Similarly, this love
will restore man's creativity in work so that he will no longer be a
slave to the machine. This love will also eliminate political oppression of people because presumably even their leaders will be guided
by a sense of love instead of a desire for power. Above all, it will
release the individual from bondage to selfhood and the fetters of
time and sensual demands. The liberation from these fetters will
even rid us of the ailments of "most of the degenerative diseases":
our heart, kidneys, pancreas, intestines, and arteries are now subject to deterioration because we do not live in harmony with "the
divine Nature of Things." Self-denial will not only bring us into
union with the essence of the divine Godhead, but will, in so doing,
relieve us ultimately of our physical pain.

Man should not be troubled by such problems as the origin of
this Divine Ground or the seeming injustice of seeing evil people
prosperous and good people impoverished. God *is* because He *is*:

"Only when the individual also 'simply is,' by reason of his union through love-knowledge with the Ground, can there be any question of complete and eternal liberation" (p. 238).[17] As for the seeming injustice of the bad man enjoying prosperity and the good man afflicted with poverty, Huxley offers the following explanation: "The bad man in prosperity may, all unknown to himself, be darkened and corroded with inward rust, while the good man under afflictions may be in the rewarding process of spiritual growth" (p. 239).

Until the "Perennial Philosophy" is adopted and recognized as "the highest factor common to all the world religions," until the worshipers of every religion renounce their egocentric, time-based, and false idolatries, then "no amount of political planning, no economic blue-prints however ingeniously drawn, can prevent the recrudescence of war and revolution" (p. 200). What is the way to achieve this ideal state? To answer this question, Huxley recommends Buddha's "Eightfold Path":

> Complete deliverance is conditional on the following: first, Right Belief in the all too obvious truth that the cause of pain and evil is craving for separative, egocentred existence, with its corollary that there can be no deliverance from evil, whether personal or collective, except by getting rid of such craving and the obsession of "I," "me," "mine"; second, Right Will, the will to deliver oneself and others; third, Right Speech, directed by compassion and charity towards all sentient beings; fourth, Right Action, with the aim of creating and maintaining peace and good will; fifth, Right Means of Livelihood, or the choice only of such professions as are not harmful, in their exercise, to any human being or, if possible, any living creature; sixth, Right Effort towards Self-control; seventh, Right Attention or Recollectedness, to be practised in all the circumstances of life, so that we may never do evil by mere thoughtlessness, because "we know not what we do"; and, eighth, Right Contemplation, the unitive knowledge of the Ground, to which recollectedness and the ethical self-naughting prescribed in the first six branches of the Path give access. Such then are the means which it is within the power of the human being to employ in order to achieve man's final end and be "saved." (Pp. 202–203)

Huxley is not excessively optimistic that these prescriptions will be followed by most people; "But then no saint or founder of a religion, no exponent of the Perennial Philosophy, has ever been optimistic" (p. 211).

One would think that Huxley's search for the ideal religion would end where so many of our religions began—in the East. His teleological and axiological quest, however, did not end there. Huxley's soul was always the battleground between the challenging barks of "Darwin's bulldog" (his paternal grandfather's sobriquet) and the melancholy promptings for withdrawal of his maternal granduncle, Matthew Arnold. The urgings for self-transcendence occasionally gave way to scientific probing. And so in his essay "The Double Crisis," published in *Themes and Variations* in 1950, Huxley again calls upon science to help solve the world's problems. It is somewhat difficult to reconcile the advocacy of self-mortification found in *The Perennial Philosophy* with this advice:

> Man cannot live by bread alone; but still less can he live exclusively by idealism. To talk about the Rights of Man and the Four Freedoms in connection, for example, with India is merely a cruel joke. In a country where two thirds of the people succumb to the consequences of malnutrition before they reach the age of thirty, but where, nonetheless, the population increases by fifty millions every decade, most men possess neither rights nor any kind of freedom. The "giant misery of the world" is only aggravated by mass violence and cannot be mitigated by inspirational twaddle. Misery will yield only to an intelligent attack upon the causes of misery. (P. 257)

In the last ten years of his life, he continued to turn to science both to help solve the problems of feeding the world's excessive population and solving its economic dilemmas and to provide the means to increase his own aesthetic and religious perceptions. All the books published in the last decade of his life—*The Doors of Perception, Heaven and Hell, Tomorrow and Tomorrow and Tomorrow, Brave New World Revisited, Island,* and, finally, *Literature and Science*—indicate Huxley's return to his first love, science. He himself has experimented with several drugs—mescalin, LSD, and others—to help him increase his aesthetic and spiritual awareness. Huxley's intention was to utilize science to facilitate the achievement of a beatific union with the Godhead, but one wonders whether in his metaphysical edifice, the temple has not become the waiting room to the laboratory.

In his last published novel, *Island*, Huxley no longer offers man the choice he offered him in *Brave New World*, published thirty years earlier: the meaningless diversions of a mechanized utopia and the almost equally narrow existence of the primitive. In his last utopia, Huxley attempts to make the best of both worlds. He had always realized, his attacks on the Judeo-Christian tradition notwithstanding, that "The ethical doctrines taught in the Tao Te Ching, by Gotama Buddha and his followers of the Lesser and above all the Greater Vehicle, in the Sermon on the Mount and by the best of the Christian saints, are not dissimilar" (*Ends and Means*, p. 327). What Huxley actually wanted was a kind of fusion of the mystical contributions of the East with the technological improvements of the West. What had happened, unfortunately, was that the East and West had borrowed not the best, but the worst features of each other's cultures; in *Ape and Essence*, he comments on how Belial "persuaded each side to take only the worst the other had to offer. So the East takes Western nationalism, Western armaments, Western movies and Western Marxism; the West takes Eastern despotism, Eastern superstitions and Eastern indifference to individual life. In a word, He [Belial] saw to it that mankind should make the worst of both worlds" (p. 184). In *Island*, Huxley found the perfect solution: "Our recipe is rather different: Take twenty sexually satisfied couples and their offspring; add science, intuition and humor in equal quantities; steep in Tantrik Buddhism and simmer indefinitely in an open pan in the open air over a brisk flame of affection" (p. 103). The marriage of science and religion does not seem to work very well in his fictional island of Pala, for at the end of the book the greedy and the vulgar are about to smash the *moksha*-induced beatitudes of the fortunate ones. The insects at the end of the book are still vulgarly copulating—to the background music of Bach's Fourth Brandenburg Concerto—and the female insect still devours the male after the sexual consummation. It is quite true that Will Farnaby, the novel's central character, has learned *Karuma* (Compassion) and has achieved an inner strength to help him withstand the inevitable onrush of idiocy, materialism, and war. But one wonders whether this inner light is the result of wisdom and free will or of the *moksha*-medicine, "the reality revealer, the truth-and-beauty pill." Curiously enough, *moksha*, as the Indian scholar S. Nagarajan relates,[18] means "freedom for evermore." A freedom induced by a drug extracted from mushrooms seems hardly different from the euphoria induced by *soma* in *Brave New World*.

Essentially, then, Huxley's religious quest has been paradoxical and tortuous. He began by mocking and rejecting the Judeo-Christian tradition (though accepting its occasional manifestations of mysticism), flirted temporarily with the Lawrentian doctrine of instinctive living and "blood consciousness," changed to contemplative investigation, turned to the East for further illumination, and died in the West trying to balance, in an uneasy syncretism, the Caliban of Western science with the Ariel of Buddhist mysticism. One is saddened to observe that the religious syncretism turned out to be a synthetic product, that his metaphysical quest ended with a pharmacological solution.

This book has sought to answer the question Huxley asked in *Ends and Means*: "Does the world as a whole possess the value and meaning that we constantly attribute to certain parts of it (such as human beings and their works); and, if so, what is the nature of that value and meaning?" (p. 312). During his lifetime, Huxley evolved many answers.

Those types of characters, corresponding to Dr. William Sheldon's cerebrotonics, viscerotonics, and somatotonics, Huxley found inadequate: the cerebrotonic because his excessive reliance on mental activities tends to exclude the emotional life; the viscerotonic because his hedonistic preoccupations render him incapable of attaining spiritual and aesthetic fulfillment; the somatotonic because his drive for power generates a hatred which destroys both society and himself. To replace these types, Huxley evolved two kinds of the ideal character: the first one espoused D. H. Lawrence's theory of the instinctive life-worshiper; the second one was the mystic whose attempts at self-transcendence did not prevent him from coping with mankind's mundane problems—ranging from incorrect diet to wars.

Despite Huxley's admission that people seldom exist in pure Sheldonian states and despite the inevitable distortion and lack of profundity in Huxley's character types, nevertheless, these do contribute to our understanding of certain temperaments found throughout literature—in Homer, Chaucer, Shakespeare, and such twentieth-century writers as James Joyce, D. H. Lawrence, Virginia Woolf, and E. M. Forster. These authors may have used different techniques in their delineation of character, but cerebrotonic, viscerotonic, somatotonic traits and the search for the ideal character have had a seemingly indestructible durability. In making use of these types, Huxley helped to illuminate the directions of human behavior.

His survey of the traditional sources of value was also axiological. Literature, music, and painting can be valuable if created by talented artists only and if they help one to apprehend the nature of the Godhead. He preferred the classicists and realists such as Homer, Chaucer, Mozart, and Goya to romanticists and ultramodernists; in the arts, at least, he advocated tradition over radical experimentation. Our judgment of his comments on the purposes of the arts, like our reaction to his preference of artists and the techniques they employ, will depend more on our own aesthetic tastes than on any objective criteria.

If education guides a person in attaining a knowledge and love of God, then Huxley would find it meaningful. Education should be adapted to the student's qualifications and needs, should avoid excessive discipline and permissiveness, should stress both theoretical knowledge and practical training, and, above all, should help to insure that the code of ethics outside the school parallels the moral training received in school. In education, as in the arts, Huxley tended to be a traditionalist.[1] It would seem that very few educators would disagree with Huxley's goals; the argument would arise over the means best suited to achieve these aims.

Government, to Huxley, can be a source of value if it is decentralized, does not seek power through conquest, and chooses leaders who are both educationally and psychologically suited for their positions. Although he had reservations about democracy, he preferred it to any other kind of government. A similar lack of enthusiasm characterizes his endorsement of a world government. Even the best kind of government, however, should not be worshiped idolatrously; that government is best which most successfully helps to create the conditions for the attainment of the life of self-transcendence.

Despite his own two happy marriages, Huxley's writings display repugnance toward love and marriage and disappointment at seeing love and marriage degenerate into self-abasement and concealed adultery; in his fiction and nonfiction, physical love (except the somewhat fuzzy affair in *Island* between Will Farnaby and Susila) and marital relationship no longer serve as sources of enduring worth. One thinks of the relationship between Leopold and Molly Bloom in Joyce's *Ulysses*; of the disastrous marriage between Rickie and Agnes in Forster's *The Longest Journey*; of the uncomfortable incompatibility of the Dalloways in Virginia Woolf's *Mrs. Dalloway*, and one can see that Huxley's estimate of love between the sexes is typical of many twentieth-century British novelists.

The apotheosis of Nature which so often characterized the romantics is almost completely absent from Huxley; I say "almost" because, occasionally, one can find gleams of solace in his lyrical descriptions of mountains or flowers. Generally, however, Nature for him does not serve as a substitute for a life of transcendent nonattachment. In all his works, there is the note of warning that man should treat Nature kindly; otherwise, man will deplete the earth of natural resources and hasten thereby his own extinction.

Although Huxley never embraced science as a satisfactory way to gauge the nature of ultimate reality, he always favored the methodology of science in the attainment of a knowledge and mastery of the material universe. He criticized D. H. Lawrence because Lawrence never "looked through a microscope." He also blamed science for its contribution to the standardized inanity prevalent in the world and for the silent acquiescence of scientists in the destructive use to which many of their inventions were put by political leaders. His experiments with hallucinogenic drugs in the latter years of his life and his restored faith in science (as shown in his last published book, *Literature and Science*) demonstrate why he would have preferred to have been Faraday rather than Shakespeare.

Religion, however, was the frame of reference through which he scrutinized all the other sources of value. Beginning as a skeptical agnostic, he ended trying to make the best of both worlds by combining Western faith in science with his own modified version of Eastern Buddhism. In his search for a satisfactory religious and philosophical system he attacked the nonmystical parts of Judaism, Christianity, and Islam. He was particularly critical of what he felt to be the failure of these religions to attack materialism and the waging of wars. Although he showed a preference for the mysticism of Buddhism, he acknowledged that the "Perennial Philosophy" which preaches a life of nonattachment to selfhood and a love and knowledge of an immanent and transcendent God has been characteristic of nearly all the world's religions.

Several observations can be made in summarizing Huxley's quest for values. First, his writings encompass so much diversified material that one is led to question his competence as an authority in all fields. What exactly were his qualifications to speak on the arts, education, government, history, semantics, philosophy, religion, sociology? Surely, although we are not likely to deny the brilliance of his mind and the keenness of his perception, we are somewhat mystified by his encyclopedic range. He was attracted to so many facets of human experience that we wonder whether he was more interested in knowledge itself or in the significance of the knowledge. When, in *Antic Hay*, Gumbril Junior tells his father that he is interested in everything, his father's sagacious observation is: "Which comes to the same thing . . . as being interested in nothing" (p. 27).[2]

Second, Huxley's quest for values led him into all kinds of inconsistencies. Thus, for example, he will attack the tendency of some writers to use abstractions instead of concrete language; he claimed that such words as *good, bad, spirit, beauty* are comparatively meaningless, but these abstract terms are exactly what he himself uses, particularly in his descriptions of the "Perennial Philosophy." Similarly, he will advocate the creation of "bridges" to help eliminate the misunderstandings existing among nations; and yet he laughs at the attempts of one of his characters (De Vries in *Time Must Have a Stop*) to create such "bridges." He will write that the creation of meaningful arts is dependent upon the existence of conflict and obstacles, but he deprecates the existence of strife and other hindrances to the attainment of a life of nonattachment. He disparages the technological advances made in Western society, but it is technological improvement which he deems imperative in helping to solve the economic problems of Eastern nations. The list of inconsistencies can be extended almost indefinitely. Perhaps this abundance of inconsistencies is the result of his being influenced by so many different writers. He gave an excellent description of his "amoeboid" tendencies when he wrote of his autobiographical character that

> There was something amoeboid about Philip Quarles's mind. It was like a sea of spiritual protoplasm, capable of flowing in all directions, of engulfing every object in its path, of trickling into every crevice, of filling every mould, and, having engulfed, having filled, of flowing on toward other obstacles, other receptacles, leaving the first empty and dry. At different times in his life and even at the same moment he had filled the most various moulds. He had been a cynic and also a mystic, a humanitarian and also a contemptuous misanthrope; he had tried to live the life of detached and stoical reason and another time he had aspired to the unreasonableness of natural and uncivilized existence. The choice of moulds depended at any given moment on the books he was reading, the people he was associated with. (*Point Counter Point*, p. 230)

Third, his limitless curiosity led him into making some spurious generalizations. He will make attacks on Judaism, Christianity, Islam, democracy, modern music which lack any kind of specific substantiation. One wishes, at times, that he would heed his own advice which he gave in his essay "Historical Generalizations" to the effect that it is extremely difficult to generalize: "You can no more indict an age than you can a nation" (*Olive Tree*, p. 135). Furthermore, he sometimes seems to be more guided by the aphoristic brilliance of a phrase than by its accuracy. Undoubtedly, his two biographies, *Grey Eminence* and *The Devils of Loudun*, were the result of much research, but occasionally they seem to be better fiction than his *Brave New World*.

Fourth, the philosophical system he finally evolved is difficult to accept for several reasons. He wrote in the 1920's that it is chiefly by intuition that the mystical experience can be attained; yet in 1933 in *Texts and Pretexts* he wrote: "I still prefer reason and experiment to plain-pathed experience and its wish-fulfilments, to even the most high-class instinct, the most appealingly feminine intuition" (p. 173). Granted that this was written before his complete conversion to mysticism; yet this belief in intuition seems somewhat paradoxical when placed with his subsequent experiments with hallucinogenic drugs. He stated that the attainment of a unitive knowledge and love of God is primarily a matter of free will, but he also commented in *Eyeless in Gaza,* the first novel to include a mystic character: "Humiliating to find that one's supposed good qualities are mainly due to circumstances and the bad habit of indifference" (p. 266). He urged individuals to create conditions of humility, self-mortification, and purity so as to be able to achieve the mystical union with God, and yet we find the following in *Texts and Pretexts*: "Man might be happier if the conditional clauses of the mystics were fulfilled—happier, but less interesting and, at bottom, ignobler" (p. 18). Are we to reject the advice given in 1933 simply because three years later he was to change his mind? It would seem to me that beliefs should replace each other logically, not chronologically. Furthermore, despite his plea that man should abandon the fetters of this world and concern himself only with the spiritual needs of a life of nonattachment, he consistently returned to the problems of this world. One speculates whether mysticism, for Huxley, became a way of life or an escape from life. Furthermore, when one considers that toward the end of his life, he tried to facilitate the attainment of mystical beatitude by taking hallucinogenic drugs, the speculation borders on consternation.

In spite of the inadequacies, Huxley has contributed significantly to the intellectual currents of twentieth-century life. The very qualities sometimes making his investigation logically defective make his style attractive. His predilection for aphoristic generalizations gives his writing a vivacity and verve frequently missing from more erudite and ponderous works. Perhaps there are more accurate accounts of Father Joseph and Cardinal Richelieu, but certainly few of them read as vividly as Huxley's *Grey Eminence.*

This lucidity is found in his novels, too. There is none of the obfuscation which makes Joyce's *Ulysses* and *Finnegans Wake* esoteric, and less of the emotional excess which occasionally mars D. H. Lawrence's work.

Second, Huxley brought to all his writing a perceptive intelligence and a mind steeped in readings in science, sociology, religion, history, psychology, and the belles lettres. One may disagree with some of his conclusions and observations, but one has to respect the breadth of his learning and the scope of his vision. His writings are not confined to any particular epoch or country. Thus, *Brave New World* is a projection into the twenty-sixth century; *Grey Eminence* and *The Devils of Loudun* discuss conditions in seventeenth-century France; *The Perennial Philosophy* anthologizes and interprets religious writers of previous centuries from many parts of the world. Similarly, *Texts and Pretexts* does not limit its poetry selections to one country. His essays comment on a multitude of subjects, from the low state of modern music to the sermon which can be learned by observing the habits of cats. In his search for values, there are few areas that he has overlooked.

Third, despite his occasional facade of sophisticated irony, there is a current of sincerity in his writings which stamps upon his observations a moral earnestness the more welcome for its freedom from painful solemnity. He can be serious without taking himself seriously; he can be wrathfully prophetic without being pretentiously condescending. Like John Donne, he can talk about God because he knows so well the temptations of the flesh.

Fourth, there is a tone of moderation in much of his writings which seeks not only to analyze but also to synthesize. Although he may be dismayed by the encroachment of standardization and mechanization into the civilization of Western countries, he is sufficiently realistic to acknowledge that it is technology which may save Eastern lands from economic disintegration. Similarly, although he appreciates the mysticism and quietism preached by the Hindu and Buddhist religions, he deprecates Eastern despotism and technological incompetence. What he essentially was trying to do was to fuse the best features of both worlds into a mutually acceptable syncretism. This spirit of conciliation also characterizes his examination of education, science, literature, and the other areas of human experience. He appreciates the value of an academic education but he notes the importance of practical experience; and while he values the "analytical" approach of D. H. Lawrence and other modern writers, he will advocate a compromise between the "analytical" methods of modern writers with the "synthetic" methods of more traditional writers.

Fifth, although his solutions for the evils of the world varied from time to time, his diagnosis of the troubles plaguing our civilization remained fairly consistent. From the very beginning of his career, he was against war; soulless mechanization; sensual debauchery; exploitation of natural resources; the development of one of the three parts composing the human personality (body, mind, and soul) at the expense of the other two; mediocrity at any level, whether it be in education, the arts, or the modern forms of entertainment; false idolatries, whether it be the idolatry of material success or the idolatry of aestheticism; narrowness of vision, whether found in aggressive nationalism or religious self-righteousness. Against these eight "cardinal sins" he always inveighed; there is thus a consistency in his diagnosis of the ills besetting the world that adds a coherence to his quest for values, a consistency which is not negated by the inconsistencies found in his changing prognosis. As Philo Buck states: "Nor need we accept his solution unqualifiedly, for one gains in understanding by a question well stated even when one rejects the answer."[3]

Sixth, in evolving from a sophisticated skeptic to a God-intoxicated mystic, Huxley represents a generation of writers who began the century by searching and frequently discarding the traditional beliefs and later returned to the more orthodox values. The first three decades of this century saw writers like Joyce, E. M. Forster, and D. H. Lawrence trying to escape the "nets" of orthodox religion, nationalism, romantic love, family life; since then, some writers like T. S. Eliot and Evelyn Waugh returned to religious orthodoxy. In this shifting search for values, Huxley has been an articulate symbol.

The answer, therefore, to the question postulated at the beginning of this book is: yes, the world as a whole does possess value and meaning, but not the value and meaning that we often attribute to it. For Huxley, it had the kind of value and meaning which for the last twenty-five years of his life he found in a unitive knowledge and love of God. His quest led him to embrace different forms of "perfection"; but like Plato's aim for perfection, perhaps the goal of discovering the ultimate meaning and value is always to be strived for but never to be attained on this earth.

Finally, since man lives in many compartments, Huxley also compartmentalized himself. His spiritual self sought value and meaning by turning ultimately to a unitive knowledge and love of God; his societal self realized that man does not live by spirit alone, and thus he wrote frequently about society's need to adopt rational and scientific approaches for its many problems such as an inadequate supply of food, overpopulation, and the threat of man's extinction by war. The inner search and external quest thus formed the two foci of his elliptical journey through life. It was a journey well taken.

NOTES

1. For a listing of these, see under "Plays and Scripts," _Letters of Aldous Huxley,_ ed. Grover Smith (New York and Evanston: Harper & Row, 1969), p. 976; there are twenty-two such adaptations.

2. "Beliefs," _Ends and Means: An Inquiry into the Nature of Ideals and into the Methods Employed for Their Realization_ (New York: Harper & Bros., 1937.), p. 312. All subsequent references to and quotations from this work, and each of the other works by Huxley, are to the edition cited in the first footnote reference and listed in the first section of the Bibliography. Each work is cited in full only once; thereafter, citation is by short title and page number only, inserted parenthetically in the text.

3. _English Literature between the Wars,_ 2nd ed. (London: Methuen & Co., 1949), p. 58.

I. Introduction

1. David Daiches, _The Novel and the Modern World_ (Chicago: University of Chicago Press, 1939), p. 197.

2. C. E. M. Joad, *Return to Philosophy: Being a Defense of Reason, an Affirmation of Values and a Plea for Philosophy* (New York: E. P. Dutton & Co., 1936), p. 35.

3. Fred B. Millett, John M. Manly, and Edith Rickert, *Contemporary British Literature: A Critical Survey and 232 Author-bibliographies,* 3rd ed. (New York: Harcourt, Brace and Co., 1950), p. 36.

4. Edwin Berry Burgum, "Aldous Huxley and His Dying Swan," *The Novel and the World's Dilemma* (New York: Oxford University Press, 1947), p. 142.

5. Morris R. Cohen, *The Faith of a Liberal: Selected Essays* (New York: Henry Holt and Co., 1946), p. 301.

6. Jocelyn Brooke, *Aldous Huxley.* The British Book Council Pamphlet in "Writers and Their Work: No. 55" (London: Longmans, Green & Co., 1954), p. 7.

7. *Those Barren Leaves* (London: Chatto & Windus, 1925), p. 53.

8. *Jesting Pilate: An Intellectual Holiday* (New York: George H. Doran Co., 1926), pp. 325–26.

9. "Sir Christopher Wren," *Essays New and Old* (New York: George H. Doran Co., 1927), pp. 185–86.

10. "Personality and Discontinuity of Mind," *Proper Studies* (London: Chatto & Windus, 1927), p. 247.

11. *Texts and Pretexts: An Anthology with Commentaries* (New York and London: Harper & Bros., 1933), p. 55.

12. "Modern Fetishism," *The Olive Tree* (New York and London: Harper & Bros., 1937), p. 109. Incidentally, he does not feel that the purchase would encourage these manifestations.

13. *Letters of Aldous Huxley,* ed. Smith, p. 538. In a letter to E. S. P. Haynes, Huxley also admits, "I remain sadly aware that I am not a born novelist" (*ibid.,* p. 495).

14. She calls *Point Counter Point* "a roman-à-clef [*sic*] par excellence, where Aldous, in the persons of Philip Quarles and Walter Bidlake, reveals some facets of his own character." Julian Huxley, ed., *Aldous Huxley, 1894–1963: A Memorial Volume* (New York: Harper & Row, 1965), p. 43.

15. *Point Counter Point,* Modern Library Edition (New York: Random House, 1928), p. 350.

16. Most critics (for example, Lewis Gannett, Edward Wagenknecht, Joseph Warren Beach, David Daiches, Alexander Henderson, Charles Rolo, and John Atkins) minimize Huxley's skill as a novelist and assert that Huxley uses the novel as a springboard for his ideas. Only Peter Bowering and Jerome Meckier attempt to show that Huxley's techniques of fiction warrant serious consideration. Perhaps the best comment about Huxley as a novelist is one that he himself made in regard to Anatole France: "He does not understand characters in the sense that, say, Tolstoy understands them; he cannot, by the power of imagination, get inside them . . ." (*Essays New and Old,* p. 266). Huxley's inability to get inside his characters may be an intentional protective device, for as one of Huxley's characters in *Crome Yellow* (New York: George H. Doran Co., 1922) says: "if one had an imagination vivid enough and a sympathy sufficiently sensitive really to comprehend, and to feel the sufferings of other people, one would never have a moment's peace of mind" (p. 160).

17. *After Many a Summer Dies the Swan* (New York: Avon Publications, 1954), pp. 200–201. Similarly, he has one of the characters in *Eyeless in Gaza* (New York: Bantam Books, 1954), Mark Staithes, comment on how the traditional sources of value have become vulgarized: "It's [i.e., death] the only thing we haven't succeeded in completely vulgarizing. Not from any lack of the desire to do so, of course. We're like dogs on an acropolis. Trotting round with inexhaustible bladders and only too anxious to lift a leg against every statue. And mostly we succeed. Art, religion, heroism, love—we've left our visiting-card on all of them. But death—death remains out of reach. We haven't been able to defile *that* statue. Not yet, at any rate" (p. 280). In his next novel, *After Many a Summer Dies the Swan,* Huxley describes how even death is no longer immune to vulgarization.

18. *Women in Love,* Modern Library Edition (New York: Random House, 1922), p. 144.

19. Clifton Fadiman, ed., *I Believe: The Personal Philosophies*

of Certain Eminent Men and Women of Our Time (New York: Simon and Schuster, 1939), p. 79.

II. *Huxley's Heritage and Environment*

1. *Themes and Variations* (New York: Harper & Bros., 1950), p. 77.
2. *Music at Night and Other Essays* (New York: Doubleday Doran & Co., 1931), p. 215.
3. Sir Julian Huxley, "The Huxleys," *Sunday* (London) *Times Weekly Review*, April 12 ,1970, p. 25.
4. *Ibid.*
5. Cited by Ronald W. Clark, *The Huxleys* (New York and Toronto: McGraw-Hill Book Co., 1968), p. 183.
6. *Ibid.*, p. 151.
7. *Beyond the Mexique Bay* (New York and London: Harper & Bros., 1934), p. 115. Huxley is generally critical of what he calls the "Victorian tradition." Consider, for example, the following excerpt taken from his "Reflections on Progress," *Vedanta for Modern Man*, ed. Christopher Isherwood (New York: Harper & Bros., 1951), p. 37: "Those of us who are old enough to have been brought up in the Victorian tradition can recall (with a mixture of amusement and melancholy) the basic and unquestioned assumptions of that consoling *Weltanschauung*. Comte and Spencer and Buckle expressed the matter in respectably abstract language; but the gist of their creed was simply this: that people who wore top hats and traveled in railway trains were incapable of doing the sort of things that the Turks were doing to the Armenians or that our European ancestors had done to one another in the bad old days before steam engines."
8. Clark, *The Huxleys*, p. 130.
9. *Ibid.*, p. 154. Quoted by Clark from a letter Huxley had written to his cousin Gervas. In *The Art of Seeing* (New York and London: Harper & Bros., 1942), Huxley writes in the Preface: "At sixteen, I had a violent attack of *keratitis punctata*, which left me (after eighteen months of near-blindness, during which I had to

depend on Braille for my reading and a guide for my walking)
with one eye just capable of light perception, and the other with
enough vision to permit my detecting the two-hundred foot letter
on the Snellen chart at ten feet" (p. vii).

It was also about this time that his older brother Trev committed
suicide. Although it was apparently nervous exhaustion which led
to Trev's suicide, Huxley wrote to his cousin Gervas that it was
"the highest and best in Trev—his ideals—which have driven him
to his death . . ." (Clark, *The Huxleys*, p. 164). Huxley's other older
brother, Julian, is the famous biologist; one of his half-brothers,
Andrew, won the Nobel Prize in physiology in 1963; the other half-
brother, David Bruce, became attorney-general of Bermuda.

10. *Along the Road: Notes & Essays of a Tourist* (London:
Chatto & Windus, 1925), p. 253.

11. *The Burning Wheel*, "Adventurers All" Series No. 7 (Oxford: G. H. Blackwell, 1916), p. 26.

12. "The Bookshop," *Limbo* (New York: George H. Doran Co.,
1920), p. 268. The quotation includes an excerpt from Fulke-
Greville's poem, which he later used as the epigraph for *Point
Counter Point*.

13. Huxley in his later works criticized Lawrence for neglecting
the importance of scientific objectivity. To feel, as Lawrence did,
that the truth lies in the "stomach" was not sufficient for Huxley.
The trouble with Lawrence was, according to one of Huxley's
characters in *Eyeless in Gaza* (p. 246), that he "never looked
through a microscope."

14. Besides his *After Many a Summer Dies the Swan*, a sarcastic
satire on the materialism in the United States, see also "America,"
the final section of *Jesting Pilate*, pp. 291–326.

15. *This Timeless Moment: A Personal View of Aldous Huxley*
(New York: Farrar, Straus & Giroux, 1968), p. 119.

16. *Ibid.*, p. 117.

17. "In Chancery," *The Forsyte Saga* (New York: Charles Scribner's Sons, 1922), pp. 413–14. Huxley did not have a high opinion
of Galsworthy. He wrote to Miss Jelly d'Aranyi, in 1915: "After
this war I dont [*sic*] think it will be the fashion to write depressing
books any more—Ibsen and Galsworthy and all that nonsense will

be quite démodé [*sic*]" (*Letters of Aldous Huxley*, p. 68). In another letter, written in 1937 to his brother Julian, he again disparages Galsworthy: "The best they cd [*sic*] in Hollywood was to ask me to adapt *The Forsyte Saga* for the screen; but even the lure of enormous lucre cd [*sic*] not reconcile me to remaining closeted for months with the ghost of the late poor John Galsworthy. I couldn't face it!" (*ibid.*, p. 428).

18. *The Condition of Man* (New York: Harcourt, Brace and Co., 1944), p. 413.

19. Quoted by Basil Willey, *The Seventeenth Century Background: Studies in the Thought of the Age in Relation to Poetry and Religion* (New York: Doubleday Anchor Books, 1953), p. 18. That the seventeenth and twentieth centuries have much in common is a notion not to be discarded. Consider, for example, how the following quotation from Donne's *Anatomy of the World* could apply with much force to the first half of the twentieth century:

> And new Philosophy calls all in doubt,
> The Element of fire is quite put out;
> The Sun is lost, and th' earth, and no mans wit
> Can well direct him where to looke for it.
> And freely men confesse that this world's spent,
> When in the Planets, and the Firmament
> They seeke so many new; they see that this
> Is crumbled out againe to his Atomies.
> 'Tis all in peeces, all cohaerence gone;
> All just supply, and all Relation.

20. Alfred North Whitehead, *Science and the Modern World* (New York: New American Library, 1949), p. 3.

21. H. V. Routh, *English Literature and Ideas in the Twentieth Century: An Inquiry into Present Difficulties and Future Prospects*, 2nd ed. (London: Methuen & Co., 1948), p. 3.

22. Irwin Edman, *The Contemporary and His Soul* (New York: Jonathan Cape & Harrison Smith, 1931), p. 13.

23. Robert Graves and Alan Hodge, *The Long Week End: A Social History of Great Britain, 1918–1939* (New York: Macmillan Co., 1941), p. 5.

24. See Bertrand Russell in *Living Philosophies* [editor's name not listed] (New York: Simon and Schuster, 1931), pp. 9-20.

25. *Experiment in Autobiography: Discoveries and Conclusions of a Very Ordinary Brain* (*Since 1866*) (New York: Macmillan Co., 1934), p. 45.

26. See Graves and Hodge, *Long Week End*, pp. 4–5.

27. Routh, *English Literature and Ideas*, p. 4.

28. *Ibid.*

29. Millett, Manly, Rickert, *Contemporary British Literature*, p. 9.

30. *Ibid.*, p. 13.

31. Daiches, *The Novel and the Modern World*, p. 7.

32. *The Portable James Joyce*, ed. Harry Levin (New York: Viking Press, 1949), p. 468.

33. *Ibid.*, p. 525.

34. Modern Library Edition (New York: Random House, 1924), p. 117.

35. *Ibid.*, p. 322.

36. "Art for Art's Sake," *Harper's Magazine*, Aug. 1949, p. 34.

37. Bernard Blackstone, *Virginia Woolf: A Commentary* (New York: Harcourt, Brace and Co., 1949), p. 250. The following excerpt from this book seems applicable to all the writers of this period: "Essentially, Virginia Woolf's writing is a search for value. In what does value consist? she seems to ask. In beauty? in intellect? in understanding? Does it reside in the service of one's country, or of a cause? Is it a personal thing, bound up with the cultivation of personal life? Can we find it in love, or in art, or in work? Is it easiest to discover in a community like Cambridge; or shall we find it alone in an attic room in a London street?" (p. 206).

38. *The Letters of D. H. Lawrence*, ed. Aldous Huxley (New York: Viking Press, 1932), p. 96.

39. Alexander Henderson, *Aldous Huxley* (New York and London: Harper & Bros., 1936), observes that the most important influences on the English writers at the turn of the century were French: "Baudelaire, Rimbaud, Verlaine, Laforgue and Anatole France had between them said what was indubitably, the last word. This feeling persisted on beyond the turn of the century,

and Aldous Huxley assiduously read Anatole France and the French poets. The irony, the intellectual contempt of these writers for the gross practical world he found essentially congenial" (p. 13). In addition to the influence of these writers, the techniques of Thomas Love Peacock and André Gide are sometimes mentioned as having some effect on Huxley's style.

40. If the titles of Huxley's books are any index of his literary preferences, the only conclusion to be drawn is that he exercised a catholicity of taste: to Shakespeare, Huxley is indebted for five of his titles—*Brave New World, Mortal Coils, Time Must Have a Stop, Ape and Essence,* and *Tomorrow and Tomorrow and Tomorrow; After Many a Summer Dies the Swan* is from Tennyson; *Beyond the Mexique Bay* from Andrew Marvell; *The Doors of Perception* and *Do What You Will* from Blake; *Eyeless in Gaza* from Milton; *Jesting Pilate* from Bacon; *Proper Studies* from Pope; *Those Barren Leaves* from Wordsworth; *Heaven and Hell* from Swedenborg; *Antic Hay* from Christopher Marlowe.

41. Quoted by Sir Julian Huxley, *Sunday* (London) *Times Weekly Review,* April 12, 1970, p. 25.

42. *Letters of Aldous Huxley,* p. 935.

43. *Ibid.,* p. 373.

III.   The Nature of Reality

1. (New York: D. Appleton and Co., 1925), p. 52.

2. "Swift," *Do What You Will* (London: Chatto & Windus, 1929), p. 99. For a Freudian defense of Swift and a rebuttal of Huxley's analysis, see Norman O. Brown, *Life against Death: The Psychoanalytical Meaning of History* (New York: Vintage Books, Random House and Alfred A. Knopf, Inc., 1959), pp. 179–85. The conflicting interpretations of Swift by the Freudian-oriented Brown and the non-Freudian-oriented Huxley provide another instance in which the same corpus of evidence results in opposing analyses, depending on the predilections of the interpreter.

3. *Ends and Means,* p. 311. See also *Science, Liberty and Peace* (New York and London: Harper & Bros., 1946), pp. 36–38.

4. *Grey Eminence: A Study in Religion and Politics* (New York: Harper & Bros., 1941), p. 17.

5. In his last novel, *Island* (New York: Harper & Bros., 1962), he projected the possibility of controlling one's heredity as well. The more enlightened parents of Pala now produce children with the genetic qualities they desire. This genetic perfection is accomplished through AI (Artificial Insemination).

6. In *Island*, the Palanese children undergo careful conditioning to enable them to meet the emotional crises in life with Pavlovian consistency.

7. Huxley, however, believed that only a certain amount of wealth is necessary for well-being. In *Ends and Means*, he seemed to approve a judge's estimate that five thousand pounds a year is the right amount. If this sum is exceeded, "satisfaction seemed generally to decline" (p. 186).

8. *Antic Hay*, Modern Library Edition (New York: Random House, 1923), p. 207.

9. (New York and London: Harper & Bros., 1945), p. 179.

10. *Proper Studies*, p. 208. In *Ends and Means* (p. 26), Huxley seems to contradict himself. He writes that "we see that 'unchanging human nature' is not unchanging, but can be, and very frequently has been, profoundly changed."

11. See *Beyond the Mexique Bay*, pp. 164–65.

12. *Time Must Have a Stop* (New York and London: Harper & Bros., 1944), p. 297.

13. *Brave New World* (New York: Harper & Bros., 1950), p. 213.

14. This preoccupation with time is also found in *Island*. Note the following excerpt: " 'Time, time, time,' Will mocked. 'Time even in this place of timeless meditation. Time for dinner breaking incorrigibly into eternity.' He laughed. Never take yes for an answer. The nature of things is always no." But one of his spiritual advisers tells Will that the curse of time can be lifted. " 'But sometimes,' she said with a smile, 'it's eternity that miraculously breaks into time—even into dinnertime' " (p. 216).

15. See the last chapter of *The Devils of Loudun* (New York: Harper & Bros., 1952), pp. 313–27, and "Some Reflections on Time," *Vedanta for Modern Man*, ed. Isherwood, pp. 118–21.

16. In a letter to Reid Gardner in 1962, Huxley wrote: "In experiments with LSD and psilocybin subsequent to the mescalin

experience described in *Doors of Perception,* I have known that sense of affectionate solidarity with the people around me, and with the universe at large—also the sense of the world's fundamental All Rightness, in spite of pain, death and bereavement" (*Letters of Aldous Huxley,* pp. 938–39). It is also significant that of all the subjects indexed by Grover Smith, there are more entries under "Psychedelic drugs" than under any other subject.

17. See opening quotation of this chapter.

IV.   Huxley's Character Types

1. Charles J. Rolo, *The World of Aldous Huxley: An Omnibus of His Fiction and Non-Fiction over Three Decades* (New York and London: Harper & Bros., 1947), Introduction, p. xiv.

2. For a discussion of the first three types, see Huxley's article, "Who Are You?" *Harper's Magazine,* CLXXXIX (Nov. 1944). Huxley also discusses these types in *The Perennial Philosophy,* pp. 147–52; here he goes even a step further: he applies the Sheldonian designations not only to individuals but also to religions. See above, pp. 162–63.

3. In his last published work, *Literature and Science* (New York: Harper & Row, 1963), Huxley no longer expressed quite the same vibrant optimism in man's potential for change through the exercise of free will. He writes: "Predestined by their heredity, human beings are postdestined by their environment. A mildly bad predestination may be offset by a more than averagely good postdestination; but even the best of postdestinations has never as yet shown itself capable of nullifying the effects of a very bad predestination" (p. 85). One of the charms—and frustrations—in reading Huxley is that his catholicity of inconsistencies is made to suit almost every kind of palate.

4. *The Defeat of Youth and Other Poems* (Oxford: B. H. Blackwell, 1918), p. 37.

5. These ways of how the mystic can help the world to achieve salvation were obtained from *Grey Eminence,* pp. 317–21.

6. In *Island* (p. 39), the Buddhist panaceas are found chiefly in a little book left by the Old Raja, *Notes on What's What and on*

What It Might be Reasonable to Do about What's What. It's rather significant that the development of the ideal character in this last novel of Huxley's is now a matter for eugenics to determine; free will seems to have lost its potency.

V. *Huxley Among the Muses*

1. In his last published book, *Literature and Science,* Huxley also reminds us that science too is capable of helping us attain metaphysical enlightenment: "That so few contemporary poets should go in for scientific reference on a large scale or in detail is not surprising. What is surprising is that there are not more of them to whom, as to Tennyson, for example, and Laforgue, science is a personal-metaphysical concern, as well as a concern on the political and cultural levels of public experience" (p. 62).

2. In his last few years, Huxley, tending to assign to science a more functional role than earlier in his career, endorsed the taking of drugs to enlarge aesthetic and religious awareness. In his last published novel, *Island,* he feels that artists could be the result of inherited genius. One of the minor characters says: "my baby might grow up to be a painter—that is, if that kind of talent is inherited. And even if it isn't he'll be a lot more endomorphic and viscerotonic than his brothers or either of his parents" (p. 219). Will Farnaby, the central character of the novel, is more accurate, however, when he realizes that although the island of Pala may offer freedom from pain and guilt, it offers no breeding ground for artists. Art, in order to flourish, requires the conflict of paradoxes and dualities.

3. He makes a similar comment in "Reflections on Progress," *Vedanta for Modern Man,* ed. Isherwood, p. 39: "It is obvious that in a society where all the necessary goods are produced by machines in highly organized factories, the arts and crafts will not flourish."

4. He makes the same point in many of the passages in Philip Quarles's notebooks in *Point Counter Point*; note also the following excerpt from *After Many a Summer Dies the Swan*: "Art can be a lot of things, but in actual practice, most of it is merely the mental equivalent of alcohol and cantharides" (p. 132).

5. Although it may be misleading, of course, to assume that an author's character necessarily reflects the author's attitude, what Mark Staithes has said here does reflect Huxley's opinion on the occasional irrelevance of the arts—as well as of the other "symptoms of progress." In a letter to Julian Huxley (Oct. 27, 1946), Huxley notes: "The unchanging essence of existence consists . . . in 'picking one's nose and looking at the sunset.' Most of the social, political, artistic and scientific developments, which are ordinarily classified as symptoms of progress, have little influence on the physiological and lower mental processes, which, for the vast majority, constitute the real substance of life. . . . People like ourselves, who are interested in other things besides a strictly private life, have always been in a minority. . . . The truth is, I believe, that people have enormously exaggerated the role of art, philosophy, pure science, and the other indices of progress, as expressions of the general life of their period" (*Letters of Aldous Huxley*, pp. 552–53).

6. See Huxley's Introduction to his edition of *The Letters of D. H. Lawrence*, pp. ix–xxxiv.

7. In his last novel, *Island,* the same incongruity can be seen. As Will Farnaby is enjoying the magnificence of Bach's Fourth Brandenburg Concerto, he opens his eyes and sees a lizard. Then the ugliness replaces the intensity of the beatific vision he had seen before: "Everything still pulsed with life, but with the life of an infinitely sinister bargain basement. And that, the music now affirmed, that was what Omnipotence was perpetually creating—a cosmic Woolworth stocked with mass-produced horrors. Horrors of vulgarity and horrors of pain, of cruelty and tastelessness, of imbecility and deliberate malice" (p. 319).

8. (New York: Harper & Bros., 1955), p. 9.

9. In his posthumously published article, "Shakespeare and Religion," completed the day before his death, Huxley again reaffirms his admiration of Shakespeare's basic honesty. In trying to answer the question of what were Shakespeare's religious beliefs, Huxley writes: "The question is not an easy one to answer; for in the first place Shakespeare was a dramatist who made his characters express opinions which were appropriate to them, but which may not have been those of the poet. And anyhow did he himself have the

same beliefs, without alteration or change or emphasis, throughout his life?" "Shakespeare and Religion," *Aldous Huxley, 1894–1963: A Memorial Volume,* ed. Julian Huxley, p. 168.

10. In *Themes and Variations* he writes: "Wordsworth (in his youth) was a great poet, capable of creating, within the splendid tradition of English poetry, a new medium of expression as nearly adequate to ineffable experience as any expression can be. . ." (p. 80). Huxley was later to abandon his advocacy of the Dr. Jekyll–Mr. Hyde life.

11. In *Literature and Science,* Huxley reiterates the need of the poet to include the findings of science in the poet's vision of man and Nature.

12. "Seen through the eyes of the philosophic historian, the Puritan reveals himself as the most abnormal sexual pervert of whom we have record, while Grundyism stands out as the supremely unnatural vice." From "To the Puritans All Things Are Impure," *Music at Night,* p. 157.

13. Huxley's opinion of modern literature is not very high. In *Point Counter Point,* Walter Bidlake, a book reviewer, contemplates the books he has to review and thinks sadly thus: "It was the day of Shorter Notices. Between them, on the table, stood the stacks of Tripe. They helped themselves. It was a Literary Feast—a feast of offal. Bad novels and worthless verses, imbecile systems of philosophy and platitudinous moralizings, insignificant biographies and boring books of travel, pietism so nauseating and children's books so vulgar and so silly that to read them was to feel ashamed of the whole human race—the pile was high and every week it grew higher" (p. 193).

Huxley similarly deprecates the modern status of drama. Whereas for the Greeks, "dramatic festivals were 'solemn and rare,' " drama for the moderns has degenerated to the point where "it is merely a form of emotional masturbation" (*Ends and Means,* p. 237).

14. As mentioned in the first section of this chapter, the greater purity and effectiveness of the language of literature are also discussed in Huxley's last published work, *Literature and Science.*

15. He makes a similar point in *Along the Road*: "we are con-

stantly giving the same name to more than one thing, and more than one name to the same thing. The results, when we come to argue, are deplorable" (p. 133).

16. See Huxley's essay "Words and Behaviour" in *The Olive Tree*, pp. 84–103, for his discussion of the effects of words on people's conduct.

17. In *Island*, the central character, Will Farnaby, learns that the islanders also distrust words: "Words about sibling rivalry and hell and the personality of Jesus are no substitutes for biochemistry" (p. 176).

18. "Art is not the discovery of Reality—whatever Reality may be, and no human being can possibly know" (*Jesting Pilate*, pp. 108–109).

19. *Aldous Huxley, 1894–1963: A Memorial Volume*, ed. Julian Huxley, p. 129.

20. In addition to criticizing the popular arts such as the movies, radio, newspapers, he also reproaches the tendency of women to make themselves only physically beautiful. In his essay "The Beauty Industry," found in *Music at Night*, he reminds us that it is more important to have a beautiful soul than a beautiful skin. In spite of the millions of dollars that women spend on cosmetics, lotions, and other products of the beauty industry, many of them, he observes, still look bored and callous.

21. In a letter to his son, Matthew, Huxley observed: "You sound just too busy—and so am I. It is a curse and an addiction, this being busy overmuch and one shd [*sic*] do something about it —a course on Antabuse-iness [anti-busyness?], and membership in Busy-bodies Anonymous" (*Letters of Aldous Huxley*, p. 941).

22. Life-worshiping involves many interests: ". . . since life is diverse, the new relation will have to have many Gods" ("One and Many," *Do What You Will*, p. 51).

VI. Education

1. "Education," *Proper Studies*, p. 91. For the essay which discusses his views on education most comprehensively, see his "Education," *Ends and Means*, pp. 204–59.

2. Huxley advocates also the Dalton system of education, whereby each student is allowed to work according to his own rate of speed and interests.

3. Huxley did intend his ideas in *Island* to be taken seriously rather than ironically. Note his comment in his letter to H. H. Maharaja Dr. Karan Singh (*Letters of Aldous Huxley*, p. 944): "*Island* is a kind of pragmatic dream—a fantasy with detailed and (consciously) practical instructions for making the imagined and desirable harmonization of European and Indian insights become a fact." His brother, Julian, also observed that Aldous regarded *Island* "as one of his major contributions to serious thought, and he was saddened and upset by the incomprehension of so many of its reviewers, who treated it as a not very successful work of fiction, and science fiction at that" (*Aldous Huxley, 1894–1963: A Memorial Volume*, p. 24).

VII. The Societal Self

1. Irving Howe (*Politics and the Novel* [Greenwich, Conn.: Fawcett Publications, 1957, 1967], p. 19) defines a political novel as one "in which political ideas play a dominant role in which the political milieu is the dominant setting."

2. See his essay, "On the Charms of History and the Future of the Past," *Music at Night*, pp. 119–36.

3. For a comparison of this novel with George Orwell's *1984*, see Gaylord Le Roy, "A.F. 632 to 1984," *College English*, XII (Dec. 1950), 135–38.

4. As for the military "type," so frequently an adjunct of the totalitarian government, he has only satiric contempt. Spandrell's summary of his stepfather's military career could well symbolize Huxley's opinion of the military prototype: "Superannuated from Harrow . . . passed out from Sandhurst at the bottom of the list, he had a most distinguished career in the Army, rising during the war to a high post in the Military Intelligence Department . . . . If you look up 'Intelligence' in the new volumes of the Encyclopaedia Britannica . . . you'll find it classified under the following three heads: Intelligence, Human; Intelligence, Animal; Intelligence,

Military. My stepfather's a present specimen of Intelligence Military" (*Point Counter Point*, p. 99).

5. See E. M. Forster's discussion of the weaknesses as well as the strengths of democracy in his *Two Cheers for Democracy* (New York: Harcourt, Brace and Co., 1951), pp. 69–76.

6. *Ape and Essence* (New York: Harper & Bros., 1948), p. 42.

7. In the index to Huxley's edition of *The Letters of D. H. Lawrence,* we find under "Hatreds": "the public, the people, society, democracy, aristocracy." Knud Merrild, in his *A Poet and Two Painters* (New York: Viking Press, 1939), pp. 239–40, tells us that Lawrence sometimes felt the urge to kill not innocent animals, but "some of the beastly disdainful bankers, industrialists, lawyers, war makers and schemers of all kinds."

8. These three principles are found in his *Ends and Means*, pp. 53–55.

9. He admits, somewhat sadly on the next page, that "Society can never be greatly improved until such time as most of its members choose to become theocentric saints." The likelihood of most people's becoming "theocentric saints" does not leave much room for optimism.

10. It is true that Huxley, with his usual inconsistency, occasionally laughs at these "bridge-builders." For example, notice how he satirizes the "bridge-building" of De Vries in *Time Must Have a Stop*.

11. See also his essay, "Indian Philosophy of Peace," *Vedanta for Modern Man*, ed. Isherwood, pp. 294–96.

12. Many of the ameliorative schemes that Huxley develops in *Island* he had already outlined in his Foreword to a reprinting of *Brave New World*. To the two horns of the dilemma he had analyzed in *Brave New World* (either a mindless, materialistic society or the withdrawal of the primitives into their Reservation), Huxley adds a preferable alternative: "In this community economics would be decentralist and Henry-Georgian, politics Kropotkinesque and co-operative. Science and technology would be used as though, like the Sabbath, they had been made for man, not (as at present and still more so in the Brave New World) as though man were to be adapted and enslaved to them. Religion would be the

conscious and intelligent pursuit of man's Final End, the unitive knowledge of the immanent Tao or Logos, the transcendent God-head or Brahman. And the prevailing philosophy of life would be a kind of Higher Utilitarianism, in which the Greatest Happiness principle would be secondary to the Final End principle—the first question to be asked and answered in every contingency of life being: "How will this thought or action contribute to, or interfere with, the achievement, by me and the greatest possible number of other individuals of man's Final End?' " (*Brave New World*, Foreword, p. xxii)

VIII.   Love and Nature

1. *The Portable D. H. Lawrence,* ed. Diana Trilling (New York: Viking Press, 1954), p. 8.

2. *The Novel and the Modern World,* p. 195.

3. See also his advocacy of "Male Continence" in his *Tomorrow and Tomorrow and Tomorrow and Other Essays* (New York: Harper & Bros., 1956), pp. 289–301.

4. *Sunday* (London) *Times Weekly Review,* April 12, 1970, p. 25.

5. *Letters of Aldous Huxley,* p. 83.

6. *Ibid.,* p. 224.

7. *Sunday* (London) *Times Weekly Review,* April 12, 1970, p. 25.

8. There is nothing in Huxley's private life which would indicate marital incompatibility as the source of his animadversions upon love and marriage. His first marriage to Maria Huxley was a long and felicitous one. Gerald Heard, a close personal friend of Huxley, tells us ("The Poignant Prophet," *The Kenyon Review,* Winter 1965, pp. 66–67): "Few husbands have had such a partner: house-keeper, cook, constant reader in the long evenings when his eyes could no longer feed his avid mind; amanuensis when the constant stream of manuscript poured out all day; secretary to guide his hours of work and ration his hours of audience; companion and guide on walks; chauffeur and 'dragoman' on their extensive travels —and, as the man-written medieval manual on the right wife sums

it up, 'ever shall she be buxom at board and bed.' " Maria Huxley died in 1955. Subsequently, Huxley married again—and Laura Archera Huxley proved equally a loving and understanding wife.

9. "Consider the Lilies," *The Los Angeles Times*, Magazine Section (Jan. 2, 1954), p. 29. For other expressions of lyricism over Nature, see "In a Tunisian Oasis," *The Olive Tree*, p. 287, and "Variations on El Greco," *Themes and Variations*, pp. 196–97.

10. The scientist's role in solving this "ecological" problem will be discussed in my next chapter.

IX.   Science and Technology

1. See especially Lawrence's poems "The Triumph of the Machine" and "What Is Man to Do," in *The Ship of Death and Other Poems* (London: Martin Secker, 1933).

2. See *Science and Religion: A Symposium*, with a Foreword by Michael Pupin (New York: Charles Scribner's Sons, 1931).

3. "Ideas That Have Helped Mankind," *Unpopular Essays* (New York: Simon and Schuster, 1950), p. 134.

4. For relevant books on the Snow-Leavis controversy, see *Cultures in Conflict: Perspectives on the Snow-Leavis Controversy*, ed. David K. Cornelius and Edwin St. Vincent (Chicago: Scott, Foresman & Co., 1964); Martin Green, *Science and the Shabby Curate of Poetry* (London: Longmans, Green & Co., 1964); F. R. Leavis, *Two Cultures? The Significance of C. P. Snow* (and "An Essay on Sir Charles Snow's Rede Lecture," an appendix by Michael Yudkin) (New York: Pantheon Books, 1963); C. P. Snow, *Recent Thoughts on the Two Cultures* (London: J. W. Ruddock & Sons, 1963); and Snow's *The Two Cultures: And a Second Look* (London and New York: Cambridge University Press, 1959, 1963). In a letter to his son, Matthew, Huxley writes: "All the essays on the subject [of his last published book, *Literature and Science*]— from T. H. Huxley's and Matthew Arnold's in the 1880's (still the best in the field) to [Sir Charles] Snow's, [F. R.] Leavis's, [Lionel] Trilling's and [J. R.] Oppenheimer's—are too abstract and generalized. I am trying to approach the subject in more concrete terms, thinking about what might be done by men of letters in our age of

science and reflecting on what in fact has been done by earlier men of letters in relation to the science of their day" (*Letters of Aldous Huxley*, pp. 941–42).

5. Freud has always been criticized by Huxley. Huxley felt that Freud did not take into account the influence of one's somatic and chemical structure on one's temperament. In *Literature and Science* (pp. 88–89), he also attacks Freud for overemphasizing Ate, "the state of mind-body that leads to disaster," and not even considering Menos, "the state of mind-body that leads to success."

6. See Huxley, "A Note on Eugenics," *Proper Studies*, pp. 272–82.

7. In "Who Are You?" Huxley states that the "Somatotonic Revolution [by which is meant the acceleration of extraverted activity leading to a lust for physical power] has been greatly accelerated by technological advances."

8. See also his essay, "Origins and Consequences of Some Contemporary Thought Patterns," *Vedanta for Modern Man*, ed. Isherwood, pp. 327–31.

9. *The Doors of Perception* (New York: Harper & Bros., 1954), p. 36. *Heaven and Hell* (New York: Harper & Bros., 1956) similarly deals with Huxley's experimentation with hallucinogenic drugs. These books were written after the hallucinogenic effects had worn off. If the reader wishes to find out how Huxley (and his second wife) reacted during a psychedelic session, he may read the written version of a tape recording of such a session; it is found in Mrs. Huxley's *This Timeless Moment: A Personal View of Aldous Huxley* in the chapter "Love and Work," pp. 163–86.

X. Religion

1. D. Marshall, "The War of the Machines, The Enemies of the Modern World, 3. Aldous Huxley," *The Catholic World*, CXLV (May 1937), 184.

2. "The Trouble with Aldous Huxley," *The American Scholar*, XI (Oct. 1942), 452–64. In his *Forces in Modern British Literature* (New York: Alfred A. Knopf, 1947), Tindall also berates Huxley's espousal of mysticism. He writes, for example: "the pity is that

good cynics are uncommon in English literature and preachers are a dime a dozen" (p. 211).

3. "The Huxley-Heard Paradise," *Partisan Review*, X (March–April 1943), 153–58.

4. *Ibid.*, p. 158.

5. In addition to the two anthologies by Christopher Isherwood (*Vedanta for Modern Man* and *Vedanta for the Western World*), the reader is also urged to read the following books to enable him to read Huxley's comments on the Eastern religions and mysticism with at least a minimum of critical comprehension: Jack Finegan, *The Archeology of World Religions: The Background of Primitivism, Zoroastrianism, Hinduism, Jainism, Buddhism, Confucianism, Taoism, Shinto, Islam, and Sikhism* (Princeton: Princeton University Press, 1952); Albert Schweitzer, *Indian Thought and Its Development* (Boston: The Beacon Press, 1954), trans. from the 1935 ed. by Mrs. C. E. B. Russell; Evelyn Underhill, *Mysticism: A Study in the Nature and Development of Man's Spiritual Consciousness* (New York: E. P. Dutton & Co., 1911).

6. Frederick Winslow Taylor (1856–1915) was an American efficiency engineer who wrote many articles on efficiency for *The Proceedings of the American Society of Mechanical Engineers.* "Taylorism" would therefore be excessive preoccupation with efficiency.

7. Wilhelm Poschmann, "Das Kritische Weltbild bei Aldous Huxley. Eine Untersuchung über Bedeutung, Grenzen und Mittel seiner Kritik" (Diss., Bonn, 1937). See especially "Der Jude als Feind menschlicher Kultur," pp. 39–40; "Huxleys Kritik am Demokratismus, Marxismus und Bolshevismus," pp. 42–48; "Ablehnung des Amerikanismus und des jüdischer Einflusses," pp. 60–63.

8. That Huxley's knowledge of Judaism was superficial can be seen from a letter written to Camille R. Honig in 1952. "My silence in regard to Jewish mysticism has a painfully simple explanation— ignorance. [G. G.] Scholem's *Major Trends in Jewish Mysticism* has only recently come into my hands—too recently for me to have had time (since I am compelled by a visual handicap to ration my reading) to read it. Before that I had looked at the *Kabbalah* and quailed before its bulk and complexity. I am not a scholar and can

lay no claim to exhaustiveness or accuracy, thinking it best to write of what I happen to know a little about [rather] than to wait until I had made my knowledge a little more (but always how little more!) adequate to the all but infinite subject" (*Letters of Aldous Huxley*, pp. 659–60).

9. Huxley's attitude toward the Jews is a curious blend of latent antipathy and some sympathy for the sufferings they often endured. In *Along the Road*, he sympathizes with those who have to work "eight hours a day in an office for the greater enrichment of the Jews" (p. 79). In *Antic Hay*, a stranger whom Gumbril meets on the train complains: "Hideous red cities pullulating with Jews, sir. Pullulating with prosperous Jews. Am I right in being indignant, sir?" (p. 263). That this character reflects Huxley's attitude is seen in a comment that Huxley made to his brother Julian in 1943: "Other curious and rather ominous consequences of war are the increased anti-Semitism which one meets with in all classes, particularly the common people, and the strong recrudescence of anti-negro passions in the South. The first is due to the age-old dislike of a *monied, influential and pushing minority* [italics added], coupled with a special grudge against the Jews as being chiefly instrumental, in popular opinion, in getting America into the war" (*Letters of Aldous Huxley*, p. 486). And yet Leonard Woolf recalls how both Aldous and Julian Huxley helped some of the Jewish victims of the Nazis prior to 1939. (See p. 35 of *Aldous Huxley, 1894–1936: A Memorial Volume*.) His refusal of Jacob I. Zeitlin's request to write a public statement about the atrocities committed by the Nazis on the Jews (see p. 439 of *Letters of Aldous Huxley*) indicates that it was not the first time that Huxley was pulled in opposing directions.

10. The satire on ministers is not confined to the novels. In his books of essays, he also minimizes the effectiveness of churchmen when they attempt to practice their "Christian" ideals: "In the lounge, waiting for the coffee, we got into conversation with the clergyman. Or rather, he got into conversation with us. He felt it his duty, I suppose, as a Christian, as a temporary chaplain in the Anglican diocese of Southern Europe, to welcome the newcomers, to put them at their ease. 'Beautiful evening,' he said, in his too

richly cultured voice. (But I loved him for his trousers.) 'Beautiful,' we agreed, and that the place was charming. 'Staying long?' he
asked. We looked at one another, then round the crowded hall,
then again at one another. I shook my head. 'Tomorrow,' I said, 'we
have to make a very early start' " ("Paradise," *Do What You Will*,
pp. 111–12).

11. Note also the following: "Belief in a personal God has released a vast amount of energy directed towards good ends; but it
has probably released an almost equal amount of energy directed
towards ends which were evil. This consideration, taken in con-
junction with the philosophical improbability of the dogma, should
make us extremely chary of accepting belief in a personal deity"
("Justifications," *The Olive Tree*, p. 202).

12. After he had embraced mysticism, Huxley no longer regarded religion as a "death-surrogate." Thus, when Sebastian Barnack, in *Time Must Have a Stop*, thinks of the substitutes used by
people to fill the vacuum left by the disappearance of religion—the
substitutes of nation, class and party, culture and art—he writes
in his diary: "But regard them dispassionately, *sub specie aeterni-
tatis*. How unutterably odd, silly and satanic!" (p. 291). Religion,
to Huxley, was no longer the best of the "death-surrogates," but a
way of life.

13. Underhill, *Mysticism*, p. x. Isherwood, who espouses the
Vedanta type of mysticism, writes: "Vedanta also teaches the practice of mysticism; it claims, that is to say, that man may directly
know and be united with his eternal Nature, the Atman, through
meditation and spiritual discipline, without the aid of any church
or delegated minister" (*Vedanta for Modern Man*, pp. xii–xiii). To
Huxley, mysticism is one of the two branches of spirituality: "Spirituality is the art of achieving union with God, and consists of two
branches—asceticism and mysticism, the mortification of the self
and that contemplation by means of which the soul makes contact
with ultimate Reality" ("Readings in Mysticism," *Vedanta for the
Western World*, p. 377). It should be noted, however, that Huxley
elsewhere speaks out against "the mortification of the self."

14. William Y. Tindall and Richard Chase have exaggerated the
influence of Gerald Heard on Huxley's mysticism. Huxley met

Heard in England in 1935; both belonged to a group of Hollywood writers espousing a Vedanta brand of mysticism. Both were pacifists and contributed to the two anthologies edited by Christopher Isherwood (*Vedanta for Modern Man* and *Vedanta for the Western World*); Huxley, however, showed mystical leanings in his work long before he presumably was influenced by the Heard and Isherwood groups in California.

15. For Huxley's conception of "ultimate reality," see ch. III, above.

16. Dr. Miller and the other mystic characters in his novels have already been discussed in ch. IV, above.

17. See also his two essays, "Seven Meditations" and "Reflections on the Lord's Prayer," *Vedanta for the Western World*, ed. Isherwood.

18. See Nagarajan's article, "Religion in Three Recent Novels of Aldous Huxley," *Modern Fiction Studies*, V, no. 2 (Summer 1959), 153–65.

XI. Conclusions

1. Eugene P. Chase, in his article "Does Research Need Revival?" (*American Association of University Professors Bulletin*, Autumn 1955, pp. 531–46), notes that Huxley once remarked to him somewhat sadly, "Yes . . . you and I received the last of the Renaissance education" (p. 533).

2. As is shown in my next paragraph, Huxley frequently changed his position. In *Island* he says just the opposite: "Patriotism is not enough. But neither is anything else. Science is not enough, religion is not enough, art is not enough, politics and economics are not enough, nor is love, nor is duty, nor is action however disinterested, nor, however sublime, is contemplation. Nothing short of everything will really do" (p. 152). Little wonder that *Island* is a utopian novel; the word *utopia*, as we all know, means "nowhere" in Greek.

3. Philo M. Buck, Jr., *Directions in Contemporary Literature* (New York: Oxford University Press, 1942), p. 170.

BIBLIOGRAPHY

The best bibliographical book on Huxley is the one by Claire John
Eschelbach and Joyce Lee Shober, *Aldous Huxley: A Bibliography
1916–1959*, with a Foreword by Aldous Huxley (Berkeley and Los
Angeles: University of California Press, 1961). Obviously, it does
not include the works of Huxley from 1959 until his death in 1963;
nor does it include the books and articles about Huxley published
since 1959, but it does contain 1,281 separate items, including all
of Huxley's books (and the different editions of these books),
pamphlets, articles and essays, short stories, poems, plays, reviews,
newspaper contributions, forewords, introductions, prefaces, trans-
lations, adaptations, scenarios, etc.—up to 1959; and an exhaustive
listing of books, articles, and dissertations about Huxley. The
reader who wishes to bring this bibliography up to date may
consult Thomas D. Clareson and Carolyn S. Andrews, "Aldous Huxley: A Bibliography, 1960–1964," *Extrapolation*, VI, 2–21 (Department of English, College of Wooster, Wooster, Ohio); and the
listings found in the Annual Bibliography editions of *The Publications of the Modern Language Association.*

The best and most inclusive editions of Huxley's books are those
published by Chatto & Windus (London) and by Harper & Brothers (now Harper & Row, New York). I occasionally have used

popular reprints in my citations, but I checked these with the editions of Chatto & Windus and those of Harper & Brothers, and the differences are solely ones of minor punctuation.

Books and Articles by Aldous Huxley (Selective List)

Adonis and the Alphabet, and Other Essays. London: Chatto & Windus, 1956. (This book was published by Harper & Bros. in 1956 as *Tomorrow and Tomorrow and Tomorrow, and Other Essays.*)

After Many a Summer Dies the Swan. New York: Avon Publications, 1954 (copyright, 1939).

Along the Road: Notes & Essays of a Tourist. London: Chatto & Windus, 1925.

Antic Hay. Modern Library Edition. Introduction by Lewis Gannett. New York: Random House, 1923.

Ape and Essence. New York: Harper & Bros., 1948.

The Art of Seeing. New York and London: Harper & Bros., 1942.

Beyond the Mexique Bay. New York and London: Harper & Bros., 1934.

Brave New World. New York: Harper & Bros., 1950 (copyright, 1932).

Brave New World Revisited. New York: Harper & Bros., 1958.

The Burning Wheel. "Adventurers All" Series No. 7. Oxford: B. H. Blackwell, 1916.

Collected Essays. New York: Harper & Bros., 1959.

"Consider the Lilies," reprinted from the *Lincoln-Mercury Times* in the Magazine Section of the *Los Angeles Times*, Jan. 2, 1954, pp. 9–29.

Crome Yellow. New York: George H. Doran Co., 1922.

The Defeat of Youth and Other Poems. Oxford: B. H. Blackwell, 1918.

The Devils of Loudun. New York: Harper & Bros., 1952.

The Doors of Perception. New York: Harper & Bros., 1954.

Do What You Will: Essays. London: Chatto & Windus, 1929.

Ends and Means: An Inquiry into the Nature of Ideals and into the

Methods Employed for Their Realization. New York: Harper & Bros., 1937.

Essays New and Old. New York: George H. Doran Co., 1927 (copyright, 1925).

Eyeless in Gaza. New York: Bantam Books, 1954 (copyright, 1936).

The Genius and the Goddess. New York: Harper & Bros., 1955.

Grey Eminence: A Study in Religion and Politics. New York: Harper & Bros., 1941.

Heaven and Hell. New York: Harper & Bros., 1956.

Island. New York: Harper & Bros., 1962.

Jesting Pilate: An Intellectual Holiday. New York: George H. Doran Co., 1926.

Letters of Aldous Huxley, ed. Grover Smith. New York and Evanston: Harper & Row, 1969.

The Letters of D. H. Lawrence, ed. Aldous Huxley. New York: Viking Press, 1932.

Limbo. New York: George H. Doran Co., 1920.

Literature and Science. New York: Harper & Row, 1963.

Music at Night and Other Essays. New York: Doubleday Doran & Co., 1931.

The Olive Tree. New York and London: Harper & Bros., 1937.

The Perennial Philosophy. New York and London: Harper & Bros., 1945.

Point Counter Point. Modern Library Edition. New York: Random House, 1928.

Proper Studies. London: Chatto & Windus, 1927.

Science, Liberty and Peace. New York and London: Harper & Bros., 1946.

Selected Poems. New York: D. Appleton and Co., 1925.

Texts and Pretexts: An Anthology with Commentaries. New York and London: Harper & Bros., 1933.

Themes and Variations. New York: Harper & Bros., 1950.

Those Barren Leaves. London: Chatto & Windus, 1925.

Time Must Have a Stop. New York and London: Harper & Bros., 1944.

Tomorrow and Tomorrow and Tomorrow, and Other Essays. New

York, Harper & Bros., 1956. (Published in London by Chatto & Windus as *Adonis and the Alphabet, and Other Essays.*)

"Who Are You?" *Harper's Magazine,* CLXXXIX (Nov. 1944) 512–22.

For Huxley's contributions to two books edited by Christopher Isherwood, see the latter's Vedanta for Modern Man *and* Vedanta for the Western World, *listed on p. 215, below.*

Books and Articles about Huxley (Selective List)

Like everyone else, the writer is predestined to transience and mortality. But being fossilizable, he is also predestined to a fate seemingly incompatible with the common fate of mankind. Whole slices of his transience refuse to pass away. Transformed by time into the equivalents of ammonites or petrified saurians, they become museum pieces upon which the learned geologists of Criticism make their comments and erect their towering socio-aesthetic theories.

—ALDOUS HUXLEY, Foreword, *Aldous Huxley: A Bibliography 1916–1959,* by Eschelbach and Shober.

Alexander, Henry. "Lawrence and Huxley," *Queen's Quarterly,* Spring 1935, pp. 96–108.

Atkins, John. *Aldous Huxley: A Literary Study.* Rev. ed. New York: The Orion Press, 1967.

Bald, R. C. "Aldous Huxley as a Borrower," *College English, XI* (Jan. 1950), 183–87.

Beach, Joseph Warren. "Counterpoint: Aldous Huxley," *Twentieth Century Novel: Studies in Technique.* New York: Appleton-Century-Crofts, 1932. Pp. 458–69.

Beerman, Hans. "An Interview with Aldous Huxley," *Midwest Quarterly,* V (1964), 223–30.

Bentley, Joseph. "Huxley's Ambivalent Responses to the Ideas of D. H. Lawrence," *Twentieth Century Literature,* XIII, 139–53.

Bowering, Peter. *Aldous Huxley: A Study of the Major Novels.* New York: Oxford University Press, 1969.

Brooke, Jocelyn. *Aldous Huxley.* The British Book Council. Pamphlet in "Writers and Their Work: No. 55." London: Longmans, Green & Co., 1954.

Buck, Philo M., Jr. *Directions in Contemporary Literature.* New York: Oxford University Press, 1942. Pp. 169–91.

Burgum, Edwin Berry. "Aldous Huxley and His Dying Swan," *The Novel and the World's Dilemma*. New York: Oxford University Press, 1947. Pp. 140–56.

Chase, Richard V. "The Huxley-Heard Paradise," *Partisan Review*, X (March–April 1943), 143–58.

Clark, Ronald W. *The Huxleys*. New York and Toronto: McGraw-Hill Book Co., 1968.

Daiches, David. *The Novel and the Modern World*. Chicago: University of Chicago Press, 1939. Pp. 188–210.

Ghose, Sisirkumar. *Aldous Huxley: A Cynical Salvationist*. New York: Asia Publishing House, 1962.

Glicksberg, C. I. "Aldous Huxley's Intellectual Pilgrimage," *Dalhousie Review*, XIX (July 1939), 165–78.

Greenblatt, Stephen Jay. *Three Modern Satirists: Waugh, Orwell, and Huxley*. New Haven: Yale University Press, 1965.

Heard, Gerald. "The Poignant Prophet," *The Kenyon Review*, Winter, 1965, pp. 66–67.

Henderson, Alexander. *Aldous Huxley*. New York and London: Harper & Bros., 1936.

Hoffman, Frederick J. "Aldous Huxley and the Novel of Ideas," *Forms of Modern Fiction: Essays Collected in Honor of Joseph Warren Beach*, ed. William Van O'Connor. Minneapolis: University of Minnesota Press, 1948. Pp. 189–200.

Huxley, Julian, ed. *Aldous Huxley, 1894–1963: A Memorial Volume*. New York: Harper & Row, 1965.

Huxley, Laura Archera. *This Timeless Moment: A Personal View of Aldous Huxley*. New York: Farrar, Straus & Giroux, 1968.

Hyde, Lawrence. "Aldous Huxley: Life Worshipper," *The New Adelphi*, Dec. 1929–Feb. 1930, pp. 90–102.

Jouguelet, Pierre. *Aldous Huxley*. Éditions du Temps Présent. Paris: n.p., 1948.

Kennedy, Richard S., "Aldous Huxley: The Final Wisdom," *Southwest Review*, L (1965), 37–47.

Le Roy, Gaylord C. "A.F. 632 to 1984," *College English*, XII (Dec. 1950), 135–38.

Marshall, D. "The War of the Machines, The Enemies of the Modern World, 3. Aldous Huxley," *The Catholic World*, CXLV (May 1937), 184–86.

Maurois, André. *Prophets and Poets*, trans. Hamish Miles. New York and London: Harper & Bros., 1935. Pp. 287–312.

Meckier, Jerome. *Aldous Huxley: Satire and Structure*. New York: Barnes & Noble, 1969.

Nagarajan, S. "Religion in Three Recent Novels of Aldous Huxley," *Modern Fiction Studies*, V, No. 2 (Summer 1959), 153–65.

Pelham, Edgar. *The Art of the Novel from 1700 to the Present Time*. New York: Macmillan Co., 1933. Pp. 268–300.

Poschmann, Wilhelm. "Das Kritische Weltbild bei Aldous Huxley. Eine Untersuchung über Bedeutung, Grenzen und Mittel seiner Kritik." Friedrich-Wilhelms Universität, Diss., Bonn, 1937.

Quennell, Peter. "D. H. Lawrence and Aldous Huxley," *The English Novelists*, ed. Derek Verschoyle. London: Chatto & Windus, 1936.

Quinn, James H., Jr. "The Philosophical Phases of Aldous Huxley," *College English*, XXIII (May 1962), 636–41.

Rolo, Charles J. *The World of Aldous Huxley: An Omnibus of His Fiction and Non-Fiction over Three Decades*. New York and London: Harper & Bros., 1947. Introduction to the book first appeared in *The Atlantic* (Aug. 1947).

Savage, D. S. "Aldous Huxley and the Dissociation of Personality," *Critiques and Essays on Modern Fiction 1920–1951 Representing the Achievement of Modern American and British Critics*, ed. John W. Aldridge. New York: The Ronald Press Co., 1952. Pp. 340–61. (Reprint of an article in *The Sewanee Review*, 1947.)

Schmerl, Rudolf, "The Two Future Worlds of Aldous Huxley," *PMLA*, LXXVII, No. 3 (June 1962), 328–34.

Tindall, W. Y. "The Trouble with Aldous Huxley," *The American Scholar*, XI (Oct. 1942), 452–64.

Watts, Harold H. *Aldous Huxley*. New York: Twayne Publishers, 1969.

Yoder, Edwin M., Jr. "Aldous Huxley and His Mystics," *Virginia Quarterly Review*, XLII (1966), 290–94.

Books of Background Importance

Huxley, of course, derived some of his ideas from his omnivorous reading; furthermore, his opinions on many subjects are shared by too many reflective critics of society to be listed here. Those who wish to deepen their understanding of the background of twentieth-century intellectual life might consult The Modern Tradition: Backgrounds of Modern Literature, *ed. Richard Ellmann and Charles Feidelson, Jr. (New York: Oxford University Press, 1965).*

Blackstone, Bernard. *Virginia Woolf: A Commentary.* New York: Harcourt, Brace and Co., 1949.

Booth, Wayne C. *The Rhetoric of Fiction.* Chicago: University of Chicago Press, 1961.

Brewster, Dorothy, and Burrell, John Angus. *Modern World Fiction.* Ames, Iowa, 1951. (Originally published in New York: Columbia University Press, 1934. See especially "Aldous Huxley's *Point Counter Point* and André Gide's *The Counterfeiters*," pp. 248–72.)

Brown, Norman O. *Life against Death: The Psychoanalytical Meaning of History.* New York: Vintage Books, Random House and Alfred A. Knopf, 1959.

Bush, Douglas. *Science and English Poetry: A Historical Sketch, 1590–1950.* New York: Oxford University Press, 1950.

Carpenter, Edward. *Civilization: Its Causes and Cure—and Other Essays.* London: George Allen and Unwin, 1921.

Cohen, Morris R. *The Faith of a Liberal: Selected Essays.* New York: Henry Holt and Co., 1946.

Cultures in Conflict: Perspectives on the Snow-Leavis Controversy, ed. David K. Cornelius and Edwin St. Vincent. Chicago: Scott, Foresman & Co., 1964.

Cummings, B. F. (Barbellion). *The Journal of a Disappointed Man.* New York: George H. Doran Co., 1919.

Edman, Irwin. *The Contemporary and His Soul.* New York: Jonathan Cape & Harrison Smith, 1931.

Eliot, T. S. *Essays Ancient and Modern.* London: Faber and Faber, 1936.

————. *Notes towards the Definition of Culture.* New York: Harcourt, Brace and Co., 1949.

Evans, B. Ifor. *English Literature between the Wars.* 2nd ed. London: Methuen & Co., 1949.

Fadiman, Clifton, ed. *I Believe: The Personal Philosophies of Certain Eminent Men and Women of Our Time.* New York: Simon and Schuster, 1939.

Finegan, Jack. *The Archeology of World Religions: The Background of Primitivism, Zoroastrianism, Hinduism, Jainism, Buddhism, Confucianism, Taoism, Shinto, Islam, and Sikhism.* Princeton: Princeton University Press, 1952.

Forster, E. M. "Art for Art's Sake," *Harper's Magazine,* Aug. 1949, pp. 31–34.

————. *Aspects of the Novel.* New York: Harcourt, Brace and Co., 1947 (copyright, 1927).

————. *A Passage to India.* Modern Library Edition. New York: Random House, 1924.

————. *Two Cheers for Democracy.* New York: Harcourt, Brace and Co., 1951.

Galsworthy, John. *The Forsyte Saga,* with Introduction by Percy Hutchinson. New York: Charles Scribner's Sons, 1922.

Graves, Robert, and Hodge, Alan. *The Long Week End: A Social History of Great Britain, 1918–1939.* New York: Macmillan Co., 1941.

Green, Martin. *Science and the Shabby Curate of Poetry.* London: Longmans, Green & Co., 1964.

Haldane, J. B. S. *Science and Human Life.* New York and London: Harper & Bros., 1933.

Hoffman, Frederick J. *The Imagination's New Beginnings: Theology and Modern Literature.* South Bend, Ind.: University of Notre Dame Press, 1967.

Hopper, Stanley Romaine, ed. *Spiritual Problems in Contemporary Literature: A Series of Addresses and Discussions.* Religion and Civilization Series. New York: The Institute for Religious and Social Studies (distributed by Harper & Bros., New York and London), 1952.

Howe, Irving. *Politics and the Novel.* Greenwich, Conn.: Fawcett Publications, 1957, 1967.

Huxley, Sir Julian. *Memories.* London: Allen & Unwin, 1970. (Excerpts from the book appeared in *Sunday Times Weekly Review,* London, April 12, 1970, pp. 25–26; April 19, 1970, pp. 25–26; April 26, 1970, pp. 25–26.)

Isherwood, Christopher, ed. *Vedanta for Modern Man.* New York: Harper & Bros., 1951. (To this anthology, Huxley has contributed the following: "Reflections on Progress," pp. 34–45; "Further Reflections on Progress," pp. 46–48; "Art and Religion," pp. 56–59; "Some Reflections on Time," pp. 118–21; "William Law," pp. 168–74; "The Sixth Patriarch," pp. 185–88; "Indian Philosophy of Peace," pp. 294–96; " 'Give Us This Day Our Daily Bread,' " pp. 297–98; "Origins and Consequences of Some Contemporary Thought Patterns," pp. 327–31; "Notes on Zen," pp. 366–71.)

———. *Vedanta for the Western World.* Hollywood: The Marcel Rodd Co., 1945. (To this anthology, Huxley has contributed the following: "The Minimum Working Hypothesis," pp. 33–35; "Religion and Temperament," pp. 94–102; "Religion and Time," pp. 103–109; "The Magical and the Spiritual," pp. 112–15; "Distractions," pp. 125–35; "Seven Meditations," pp. 163–70; "From a Notebook," pp. 189–92; "On a Sentence from Shakespeare," pp. 209–211; "Man and Reality," pp. 273–77; "Words and Reality," pp. 278–82; "Reflections on the Lord's Prayer," pp. 298–312; "Action and Contemplation," pp. 366–70; "Readings in Mysticism," pp. 376–82; "Idolatry," pp. 427–31; "The Yellow Mustard" [poem], p. 447; "Lines" [poem], p. 452.)

Joad, C. E. M. *The Recovery of Belief: A Restatement of Christian Philosophy.* London: Faber and Faber, 1952.

———. *Return to Philosophy: Being a Defense of Reason, an Affirmation of Values and a Plea for Philosophy.* New York. E. P. Dutton & Co., 1936.

Lawrence, D. H. *The Ship of Death and Other Poems.* London: Martin Secker, 1933.

———. *Women in Love.* Modern Library Edition. New York: Random House, 1922 (copyright, 1920).

Leavis, F. R. *Two Cultures? The Significance of C. P. Snow* (and "An Essay on Sir Charles Snow's Rede Lecture," an appendix by Michael Yudkin). New York: Pantheon Books, 1963.

Living Philosophies (editor's name not listed). New York: Simon and Schuster, 1931.

Merrild, Knud. *A Poet and Two Painters.* New York: Viking Press, 1939.

Millett, Fred B.; Manly, John M.; and Rickert, Edith. *Contemporary British Literature: A Critical Survey and 232 Author-bibliographies.* 3rd ed. New York: Harcourt, Brace and Co., 1950.

Moore, Harry T., ed. *The Collected Letters of D. H. Lawrence.* New York: Viking Press, 1962.

Mumford, Lewis. *The Condition of Man.* New York: Harcourt, Brace and Co., 1944.

Northrop, F. S. C. *The Meeting of East and West.* New York: Macmillan Co., 1946.

Orwell, George. *1984.* New York: The New American Library of World Literature, 1951 (copyright, 1949).

Overstreet, H. A. *The Enduring Quest: A Search for a Philosophy of Life.* New York: W. W. Norton & Co., 1931.

Panichas, George A., ed. *Mansions of the Spirit: Essays in Religion and Literature.* With an Introductory Essay by Thomas Merton. New York: Hawthorn Books, 1967.

The Portable D. H. Lawrence, ed. Diana Trilling. New York: Viking Press, 1954.

The Portable James Joyce, ed. Harry Levin. New York: Viking Press, 1949.

Routh, H. V. *English Literature and Ideas in the Twentieth Century: An Inquiry into Present Difficulties and Future Prospects.* 2nd ed. London: Methuen & Co. 1948.

——. *Towards the Twentieth Century: Essays in the Spiritual History in the Nineteenth.* New York: Macmillan Co., 1937.

Russell, Bertrand. *The Impact of Science on Society.* New York: Simon and Schuster, 1951.

——. *Unpopular Essays.* New York: Simon and Schuster, 1950.

Schweitzer, Albert. *Indian Thought and Its Development*, trans. Mrs. C. E. B. Russell. Boston: The Beacon Press, 1954.

Science and Religion: A Symposium, with a Foreword by Michael Pupin. New York: Charles Scribner's Sons, 1931.

Shanks, Edward. "Friends of D. H. Lawrence," *London Mercury*, XXIX (Dec. 1933), 142–50.

Sheldon, William H., *et al. The Varieties of Human Physique*. New York: Harper & Bros., 1940.

Sheldon, William H., and Stevens, S. S. *The Varieties of Temperament*. New York: Harper & Bros., 1942.

Snow, C. P. *Recent Thoughts on the Two Cultures* (pamphlet). London: J. W. Ruddock & Sons, 1963.

————. *The Two Cultures: And a Second Look*. London and New York: Cambridge University Press, 1959, 1963.

Spender, Stephen. *The Creative Element: A Study of Vision, Despair and Orthodoxy among Some Modern Writers*. New York: British Book Center, 1954.

————. *The Destructive Element: A Study of Modern Writers and Beliefs*. Philadelphia: Albert Saifer, 1953 (copyright, 1935).

Tindall, W. Y. *Forces in Modern British Literature: 1885–1946*. New York: Alfred A. Knopf, 1947.

Underhill, Evelyn. *The Essentials of Mysticism and Other Essays*. New York: E. P. Dutton & Co., 1920.

————. *Mysticism: A Study in the Nature and Development of Man's Spiritual Consciousness*. New York: E. P. Dutton and Co., 1911.

Unwin, J. D. *Hopousia or the Sexual and Economic Foundation of a New Society*, with an Introduction by Aldous Huxley. London: George Allen and Unwin, 1940.

Wagenknecht, Edward. *Cavalcade of the English Novel from Elizabeth to George VI*. New York: Henry Holt and Co., 1943.

Wells, H. G. *Experiment in Autobiography: Discoveries and Conclusions of a Very Ordinary Brain (Since 1866)*. New York: Macmillan Co., 1934.

Wells, H. G.; Huxley, Julian B.; and Wells, G. P. *The Science of Life*. New York: The Literary Guild, 1934.

Whitehead, Alfred North. *The Aims of Education.* New York: The New American Library, 1951 (copyright, 1929).

————. *Science and the Modern World.* New York: The New American Library, 1949 (copyright, 1925).

Wickham, Harvey. *The Impuritans.* New York: The Dial Press, 1929.

Willey, Basil. *The Seventeenth Century Background: Studies in the Thought of the Age in Relation to Poetry and Religion.* New York: Doubleday Anchor Books, 1953 (copyright, 1934).

Aldous Huxley's Quest for Values was manually set on the Linotype in eleven point Caledonia with two-point line spacing. Torino Roman and Italic were selected for display. The book was designed by Jim Billingsley, composed and printed by Heritage Printers, Inc., Charlotte, North Carolina, and bound by Kingsport Press, Kingsport, Tennessee. The book is printed on paper designed for an effective life of at least three hundred years.

THE UNIVERSITY OF TENNESSEE PRESS
KNOXVILLE